Concrete g---thier

ug North...

J. Farnell Son...

KEBLE PAST AND PRESENT

KEBLE PAST AND PRESENT

EDITED BY AVERIL CAMERON AND IAN W. ARCHER

THIRD MILLENNIUM
PUBLISHING, LONDON

First published in 2008 by Third Millennium Publishing Limited,
a subsidiary of Third Millennium Information Limited.

2–5 Benjamin Street
London
United Kingdom
ECIM 5QL
www.tmiltd.com

ISBN: 978 1903942 71 0

British Library Cataloguing in Publication Data
A CIP catalogue record for this book is available from the
British Library.

Designed by Helen Swansbourne
Production by Bonnie Murray

Reprographics by Studio Fasoli, Italy
Printed by 1010 Printing International Ltd

ILLUSTRATIONS
Jacket front: The west end of the Chapel from the Arco roof
Frontispiece: A gargoyle on the Chapel
Endpapers: Butterfield's plans for the Hall, *front*, and the Library
bays, *back*

PICTURE CREDITS
Unless noted below, the illustrations in this volume have been provided by Keble
College. Every effort has been made to credit pictures correctly. Many of the non-
attributed photographs in recent years were taken by Nick Perry, Steve Kersley, and
members of the Development Office staff. Specialist photography for the book was
undertaken by Roy Fox.

All Saints, Little Bookham 41; All Saints, Thelwall 67; Ian Archer 143B, 144, 145T,
149, 168T, 169B, 172, 173B; David Bell 146T; Tom Brett 4, 90T, 91T, 95BR, 177;
Bridgeman Library 17B; Neil Burkey 37; W. Franklin G. Cardy 156; Guy Cheeseman
158B, 162TL; Martin Copus 139, 168B; Corbis 43CL, 135C; Bernard Crapper 66;
Hannah Davis 163R; Lucy Dickens 2, 51, 77, 101B, 103; Danny du Feu jacket front, 11,
180; English Heritage 16T, 84TL, 84TR, 84CL, 84CR; John Gedge 162TR, 165R, 175B;
Getty Images 52BR; Gillman and Soame 30L, 31R, 47TR, 49B, 68, 73, 104B, 122T,
132B, 173R, 174B; Dr Gareth Jones 142B; Jemimah Kuhfeld 57; Br Lawrence Lew, O.P.
8, 26, 27, 48B, 50T, 83, 88TL, 89L, 100T, 100B, 102T, 116, 158C; Claire Lewis 170;
Richard Lowkes 88B; Mary Evans Picture Library 153R; Rick Mather Architects, 97;
Normal McBeath 6, 28L, 76T, 79B, 86TL, 86CL, 86CR, 86BC, 92, 102B, 104T, 183; Peter
Moonlight 7, 86TR, 86C, 86BL, 86BR, 125, 138TR, 160T, 161T, 161B, 162B, 164T;
©NTPL/Steve Stephens 22B; ©NTPL/John Hammond 23T; Oxfordshire County
Council 84BL, 84BR, 117T, 117B, 118L; David Penwarden 154R; Geoffrey Rowell and
Gillman and Soame 164B; Noor Shabib 147T; St Barnabas, Oxford 40; Tessa Stanley-
Price 10T, 167T, 75, 85B, 124T, 151R, 176; Helen Swansbourne 101T, 105; Charles
Talbot 18T, 24B; Kalpen Trivedi 138TL; Tony Turner 152; David Warwick 14T; The
Dean and Chapter of Westminster 61T

CONTENTS

PREFACE

This book has taken shape as a result of a longstanding feeling that, with its very distinctive story, Keble deserved to have a published history. The brochure *Keble. The History*, of 1987, revised by Roger Boden in 1997, is an excellent introduction to the College and its past, but given its small size it could only hint at the richness of some of the available material. A talk given at the College by J. Mordaunt Crook in 1995, and an exhibition on William Butterfield, mounted by Marjory Szurko when she was the College Librarian and published in 2002 with additional material by Geoffrey Tyack as *William Butterfield and Keble College*, demonstrated the extent of public interest in the original architecture and history of the College. Geoffrey Rowell's chapter on Keble in the *History of the University of Oxford VII.2* (2000) is a valuable treatment of the foundation and early years. There are also a number of unpublished diaries to which we have had access, including the very lively diary kept by Lavinia Talbot during her husband's Wardenship and, for more recent years, the voluminous diaries of Douglas Price, which have provided both commentary and substance for many of the subjects covered in this book. Meanwhile, many old members of the College contributed their own anecdotes and personal material in the early 1990s in response to a request from Jean Robinson. Thus, when earlier attempts to prepare the material for publication, notably by Paul Hayes and Alec Campbell, sadly did not come to completion, we were left with a sense of unfinished business.

The appointment of Robert Petre as archivist in 2004 helped to make assembling further source material easier and more practicable, and after a lengthy exploration of possible ways forward we decided that the project was feasible with the help of Third Millennium, a specialist publisher who have recently produced volumes about Christ Church, St John's, several of the Cambridge colleges, and other institutions. Once the contract was signed in 2007, more material was invited from old members and others, and we were still receiving splendid contributions up to the eve of our deadline in early April, 2008. Sadly we have simply not been able to use all of it, and indeed at a late stage we found that we were 20,000 words over limit. Reductions and selections were unavoidable, but we are publishing some of the extra material on the College website.

Producing *Keble Past and Present* was a project which I dearly hoped to achieve while I was Warden. I knew I should enjoy writing and editing, but I also knew that I could not do it alone. Yet, since academics nowadays are under such pressure, and 2007 was the year when everyone had to produce the required number of high-quality research publications for the dreaded Research Assessment Exercise, I hardly dared hope to persuade a colleague or colleagues to share the work. Ian Archer was reluctant at first to be named as more than associate editor, but he had already taken on the task of dealing with Douglas Price's lengthy historical and personal

materials, including his massive diaries of his time at Keble, and as the work for *Keble Past and Present* progressed, he took on infinitely more than the title of associate editor might have implied. He and I have worked together throughout, and indeed, without his energy and commitment, it would have been impossible to produce the volume at all. He has also been a splendid ambassador for the book, giving talks, encouraging people to subscribe and intriguing fellows and students with well-chosen titbits. Through him we were also able to draw on the valuable help of a research assistant, Fleur Richards, and Isla Smith, Ruth Cowen, Steve Kersley and Robert Petre have also played crucial roles, not least in obtaining and identifying the many illustrations. We are especially grateful also to Lucy Dickens for generously allowing us to use her photographs of the College, and to Tom Brett, Brother Lawrence Lew, Peter Moonlight and Tessa Stanley-Price for their own.

Once we had settled on an overall structure for the book, Ian Archer and I divided up the chapters, so that I have been responsible for the first four, while he has been responsible for the chapters on academic and student life, which entailed drawing on the substantial mass of older and recent contributions from old members. However, the writing and research have not been as separate as this sounds, especially in the final stages when we have moved material about in the interests of balance and completeness, and of course it is not possible in practice to separate the personal and the institutional in the way the chapter headings might suggest. We decided together what features would be desirable; some of these have been solicited from others, whose names appear with their contribution, the rest have been written by ourselves. We could not have published this volume without Neil Burkey of Third Millennium as project manager, and our regular editorial meetings with Christopher Fagg and his colleagues have helped us to shape the book as well as to keep us to the timetable. Helen Swansbourne has done a wonderful job with the design and layouts.

We have, from the beginning, been supported by the enthusiasm and curiosity of colleagues and contributors, and we are immensely heartened by the large number of friends and old members who have subscribed to the volume ahead of its publication; their names are listed on pages 185–8, with our warm thanks.

We have been able to draw on a mass of material: archival, anecdotal, published and unpublished. Joy Crispin Wilson undertook at an earlier stage to visit and record the reminiscences of several significant Keble figures, and Trish Long unselfishly typed the resulting tapes. Basil Mitchell, Dennis Nineham and Dennis Shaw all allowed us to draw on their memoirs and memories, and Adrian Darby, James Griffin, Larry Siedentop, Sir Peter North, John Davies, Geoffrey Rowell and others have all been generous in answering questions and providing their own perspectives on the past. I am sure they will not mind if I add that, in the course of the project, I have learned that Thucydides was mistaken: oral history and personal participation in the events narrated are not automatically reliable. People remember things differently and, as Ian Archer points out in his chapter on academic life, there is more than one narrative of Keble's past.

However, this is not simply a volume for old members, and therefore insiders. The story of Keble College is in its way heroic. It is a story of triumph over difficult and uncertain beginnings, of faith maintained amid criticism and scorn, of persistence and determination. The College's founders took a leap of faith and they were not disappointed, nor were they let down by their successors. The College has adapted to drastically changed circumstances, and it can face the future knowing that few, indeed, of its present members are conscious of those early days of uncertainty, or of the criticisms which were launched against it. Nowadays we are, and yet we are not, just another college. Keble is, and has always been, different.

AVERIL CAMERON
April 2008

1 THE FOUNDATION

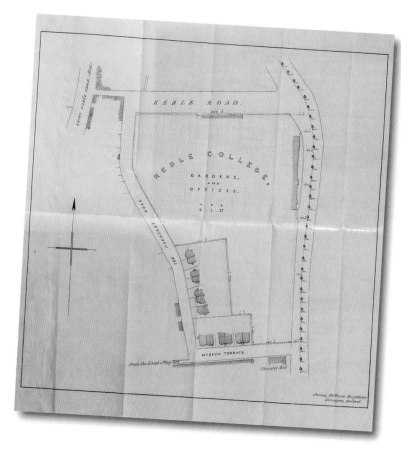

John Keble died on 29 March 1866 at Bournemouth, where he had moved during the previous winter because of his wife's ill-health. He had been ill himself for a week after what seems to have been a stroke, and he was buried at Hursley on 6 April. His wife Charlotte died less than two months later. Keble College, as it was to be known, took its origin from a decision taken by the group of friends who met at Sir William Heathcote's house on the day of the funeral and discussed the question of a suitable memorial to Keble. It was undoubtedly the association with Keble's name that made the raising of the money so comparatively easy, for his collection of poems, *The Christian Year,* had made him revered throughout England.

Among the group of Tractarians who decided to proceed with the establishment of a new college in Oxford (the first since Wadham in 1612 and Worcester in 1714) were H.P. Liddon and E.B. Pusey, both of whom were to be closely involved with the College in its early years. They were strongly supported by William Gladstone, who had been a 'proprietor' of King's College London, also founded on religious principles, since 1838 and who became a life governor in 1870. The idea of founding a new college in Oxford was not new. 'University extension' in Oxford had been debated since the 1840s; the question was how to achieve it. A committee had been set up in 1865 with the aim of drawing up plans, and this resulted in a report on the matter in the following year. A sub-committee of this group, chaired by W.E. Shirley and including Pusey, was already considering a plan for a college which would be designed on principles intended to cater for those who could not afford to attend the traditional colleges, and at the same time would serve to encourage the supply of High-Church ordinands. The students were however still to be 'gentlemen'. Shortly before his death, John Keble had seen and approved these plans. After his funeral, a meeting was arranged at Lambeth Palace on 12 May 1866, with the Archbishop of Canterbury presiding, and enquiries were made to St John's College about a site opposite the Parks, which the college had decided to develop.

Above: *Plan of the site of the College purchased from St John's*

Right: *The interior of the Chapel*

John Keble

Born in 1792 at Fairford in Gloucestershire, into a traditional High-Church clerical family, it was clear that John Keble was destined to be more than a conventional country parson. The countryside around his home kindled in him a deep love for the natural world, which quickly turned to an appreciation of the new romantic poets. His academic brilliance led to his becoming an undergraduate at Corpus Christi at the age of fourteen, gaining a double first and a fellowship at Oriel at the age of nineteen. Ordination followed in 1815, and he seemed to be set for a glittering career.

He deliberately turned his back on this path. To those who knew him, it was rather his humility and radiant holiness that impressed and awed them. In 1823 his father's infirmity led him to leave Oxford to serve in the humble role of curate, assisting in his father's parish. But his contact with undergraduates was not entirely severed as he continued to organize 'reading parties' during the Long Vacations for those preparing for ordination. For the young Richard Hurrell Froude, his time with Keble was nothing short of a revelation; in his person, Froude believed he had come as near as he ever would to encountering the sanctity that his romantic sensibilities so admired in the early church and the middle ages.

At a time when poets such as Shelley and Byron were associated with religious infidelity, as well as political subversion, Keble was instrumental in channelling the influence of Romanticism as a positive force on the side of Christianity. Keble's sense of natural beauty leading to the supernatural and the sacramental was first explored in his collection of poems *The Christian Year,* published in 1827. They were based around the liturgical calendar of the Church of England, and the book remained a best seller for over half a century, transforming him into a national figure. In 1831 he was elected to the Professorship of Poetry at Oxford, in which capacity he was to deliver some of the most influential lectures on poetic theory of the century.

However, between 1828 and 1833, the Church of England suffered what Keble and others perceived to be shattering blows. The status of Parliament as the lay synod of the Church and her appointed legislator was assailed when first Protestant dissenters and then Roman Catholics were admitted. The agitation surrounding the passing of the Reform Act in 1832 left many bishops beleagured, isolated and occasionally

Above: *Portrait of John Keble by George Richmond, 1876*

Left: *Portrait of John Keble by George Richmond, c. 1844, watercolour*

Right: *Study for John Keble's hand*

assaulted in the streets for opposing the measure. This culminated the following year with the suppression of ten bishoprics in Ireland at the behest of a seemingly hostile government. Keble spoke publicly of his fears. On 14 July 1833, he delivered what was to become one of the most famous sermons ever preached in the University Church. His subject was 'National Apostacy', and his theme the dangers of a people abandoning their God. The friendship between Keble, Newman and Froude, dating from the 1820s, formed the bedrock of the Oxford Movement, an attempt to revolutionize the nature of Anglicanism, shifting its focus from the Reformation to the early Church and giving renewed emphasis to the apostolic succession and the sacraments.

Yet they also aroused the ire of powerful forces fearful of this lurch towards 'Romanism'. In 1838 Keble and Newman were responsible for editing the posthumous works of Froude. The *Remains* revealed the latter's loathing of the Protestant reformers and glorification of medieval Catholicism, ideas abhorrent to most of his contemporaries. The greatest blow of all fell on Keble in 1845, when Newman converted to Roman Catholicism. They were not to meet again for 20 years. But the Movement that Keble had helped to nurture, the poetry he had written, and the benign personal influence he had exerted over so many were to continue.

George Herring (1974)

What though in poor and humble guise,
Thou here didst sojourn, cottage born?
Yet from Thy glory in the skies,
Our earthly gold Thou dost not scorn;
For love delights to bring her best,
And where love is, that offering evermore is blest.

Love on the Saviour's dying head,
Her spikenard drops embalm'd may pour,
May mount His cross, and wrap Him dead
In spices from the golden shore:
Risen, may embalm His sacred name,
With all a painter's art, and all a minstrel's flame.

Worthless and lost our offerings seem

PROPOSED

COLLEGE AT OXFORD,

In thankful Memory of

THE REV. JOHN KEBLE.

"THE RIGHTEOUS SHALL BE ... ERLASTING

Fundraising for the College

Once the idea of a college or hall was agreed, the organizers began raising the money straight away. E.B. Pusey states: 'Sir W. Heathcote thinks that if we wish the memorial of dear J.K. to take the form of a College or Hall I had better get some promises of subscriptions…' Notices, letters and cards asking for subscriptions were soon sent throughout the country and beyond. The project was noted in newspapers, advertisements were taken out, and letters were written on the subject throughout the fundraising process. The Reverend Edward Kilvert went so far as to compose an acrostic on John Keble's name and circulated it to promote the memorial.

Henry Pellew acted as honorary secretary to the trustees of the fund until 1873, while J.A. Shaw-Stewart was its honorary treasurer. These men, as well as making sure that the project was kept in the public eye, and giving the members of the Council advice relating to the fund, were extremely diligent about corresponding with the fundraisers and contributors, apprising them of the latest progress of the scheme, and answering their questions promptly and helpfully.

It is clear that most of those who had been asked to give did so with a willing heart, and many expressed in their letters the wish that they could contribute more. The Duke of Buccleuch, for example, wrote on 25 June 1866 that he would give £100 because he had 'a great respect for the memory of the late Mr Keble…' Only one letter sounded a sour note, that of the Reverend Charles Guest of Burton-on-Trent, who disagreed with the ideas of the Oxford Movement and wrote that he was not disposed in any way to support the object in hand. Others, such as the Reverend C. Conybeare and Mr Walter, sympathized with the aim of the memorial, but did not think that a college or hall was the best means to choose, while Archdeacon Churton disagreed with the appointment of William Butterfield as architect.

One person who took an active role in the proceedings was

Above: *Cartoon of J.A. Shaw-Stewart*

Charlotte Mary Yonge, the novelist and friend of John Keble. In 1836 Keble became vicar of Hursley, the parish next to Miss Yonge's home in Otterbourne, and was one of the foremost influences in her life, preparing her for confirmation and advising her on her writing. Charlotte Yonge gave £10 towards the memorial herself, and advertised it in her publication *The Monthly Packet*. A letter from Miss Ommaney to Miss Yonge in October 1870 shows that readers had been encouraged to give to the Fund by this means.

Fresh funds were requested in April 1868, after the successful laying of the foundation stone, and in May 1870, Lord Cavendish wrote that Pusey was 'much grieved' that the College would be starting out in debt, and asked if it would be profitable to make any fresh appeal to churchmen on the subject. A letter from Shaw-Stewart in July 1870 indicates that there were several 'bad payers' who had to be chased up.
Marjory Szurko

St John's was sympathetic to the suggestion of a purchase, but questioned the standing of the backers of the scheme. Keble himself had long been concerned with the question of the reform of the Oxford education system and had made it a theme of the Creweian Oration which he delivered as Professor of Poetry in 1839, when William Wordsworth was awarded an honorary degree. The different aim of 'University extension' also interested William Gladstone (the uncle of Lavinia Lyttelton, who became the wife of the first Warden of Keble), Charles Marriott, a Tractarian fellow of Oriel, and Sir John Taylor Coleridge, among others.

However, John Henry Newman's conversion to Roman Catholicism in 1845 caused a crisis among the personalities identified with the Oxford Movement; moreover the idea of extension met with opposition from existing heads of colleges, and Gladstone failed to be elected MP for the University in 1847. Nevertheless, a Royal Commission was set up amid intense disagreements and divisions within Oxford, and in 1854 a bill introduced by Lord John Russell and supported by Gladstone was passed, which successfully began to reduce the dominance of clericalism in the colleges; it was followed in 1871 by the repeal of the religious tests

Above: *Hursley Vicarage today*

which had excluded non-conformists. The restoration of the Catholic hierarchy in 1850 and Wiseman's enthronement as Archbishop of Westminster were followed by the appearance of Charles Darwin's book *The Origin of Species*, and in 1860 the publication of *Essays and Reviews*, containing seven essays on religion, including one by Benjamin Jowett which caused a sensation for its liberal views and its recognition of the new German biblical criticism. Samuel Wilberforce, the Bishop of Oxford, the Archbishop of Canterbury and a large number of other bishops attacked the volume, and two of its authors were indicted for heresy in the ecclesiastical courts; this verdict was later overturned by the Privy Council, but in 1864 Wilberforce managed to obtain a synodical condemnation of the book in Convocation. In 1860, during the meeting of the British Association for the Advancement of Science in Oxford,

Wilberforce had clashed with T.H. Huxley on the subject of Darwin's theory of evolution. By the 1860s the need for University extension was even more pressing, but in the atmosphere of growing religious controversy, the religious aims of Keble and his followers seemed to have become more difficult to achieve.

It was therefore a bold decision to raise money for a new college on Tractarian principles, and the idea of drawing on the name of John Keble was a clever stroke. Liddon and Pusey knew that they could count on a group of like-minded men to help, as well as on large numbers of ordinary people and well-wishers, who would donate to the enterprise because of its association with Keble. The sum of £50,000 was identified at the target for the appeal, and Archbishop Longley was to be its president, with the Earl Beauchamp as vice-president. Beauchamp himself contributed £5,000, as did Pusey, but most sums pledged were much smaller. All involved were connected with High-Church causes, as was William Butterfield, the architect of Balliol College chapel (1856–7), who had already been confirmed as the architect by the end of May 1866.

By the end of 1867, St John's had agreed to sell the site in Parks Road for the sum of £7,047, having been satisfied that the new foundation would not challenge the Church of England. Butterfield drew up plans by the end of the year for a college big enough for 250 students, though only 100 were envisaged in the early stages. This was remarkably ambitious, at a time when there were less than five hundred undergraduates in the University, but the ambition was borne out, and by 1881 Keble was already the third largest of the colleges. However there was as yet only enough money to build a part, and no money for a Chapel, Hall, Library or Warden's Lodgings. For the first six years a temporary chapel and dining hall were used on the south side of Liddon quad, and the first Warden and his wife lived in what were intended as tutors' rooms. The aim was also for the College to be self-sufficient, and it had no endowment. Students paid an all-in annual charge of £81 and this was expected to yield a profit for the College. Three of its first tutors were fellows of other colleges (Magdalen and Jesus), which also helped the finances. The foundation stone was laid by the Archbishop on John Keble's birthday, 25 April, 1868, which was also St Mark's Day, and St Mark's Day was adopted thereafter by the College as the date for commemorations and special occasions; by this time £30,000 had already been raised. By March 1871 the account tendered by Parnells, the builders, had reached £31,233.5s.9d.

Above: *John Henry Newman in 1845, the year of his conversion, by Sir William Ross*

Right: *Canon H.P. Liddon*

The Oxford Movement and Keble College

The Oxford Movement arose out of the religious and constitutional reforms of the 1820s and 30s, which raised important questions and chimed with the longer-term agenda of the High-Church movement. The group was made up largely of young Oxford men who encouraged debate by publishing a series of tracts, by preaching polemical sermons, and by reassessing whole areas of the English religious tradition, especially the teachings of the early church. The principal outcome of that reassessment was an emphasis on the historic, catholic character of the doctrine and practice of the Church of England. The Tractarians surprised themselves as much as everyone else with their extraordinary success, at least in provoking argument. The Movement was characterized not just by controversy, but by controversialism. Previously unthinkable views were being expressed as orthodox Anglicanism by the end of the 1830s. Indeed, the highly controversial Tract 90 testifies to the didactic and rhetorical genius of John Henry Newman, even as he struggled to fit a square doctrinal peg into a round ecclesial hole.

Oxford's undergraduates liked nothing more than taking sides, and those who found themselves drawn to Newman, Palmer, Froude, Keble and Pusey were soon taking their ideas well beyond universities and into the parishes to which they were ordained. Central to Tractarian theology was a robust emphasis on the doctrine of the Incarnation and on the necessity of practical holiness, and gradually changes were brought about, not just in the content of preaching and teaching, but in the practice of Christian worship. Thus the intellectual mission of the Tractarians became, a generation later, the sacramental and ceremonial mission of the Ritualists.

According to some (including Dean Church), the Oxford Movement ended with Newman's reception as a Roman Catholic in 1845. However, the battles to which it gave rise continued. The Gorham Judgement of 1850 saw a judicial committee of the Privy Council overturn the decision of Bishop Philpotts of Exeter not to institute a clergyman on the grounds that he rejected the key High-Church doctrine of baptismal regeneration. W.E. Gladstone was among the 63 eminent lay persons who protested against the judgement and its legitimization of secular over ecclesial power. It also led many to leave the Church of England, Archdeacon (later Cardinal) Manning among them.

Above: *Dr E.B. Pusey*

Above right: *Newman in old age*

The years preceding Keble's death in 1866 were no more theologically peaceful. Pusey and Liddon had sought the prosecution for heresy of Benjamin Jowett (then Regius Professor of Greek), who championed the new Biblical criticism in his contribution to the 1860 volume *Essays and Reviews*. At the same time, the Ritualist disputes – theological, legal and even occasionally violent – had come to dominate much of what we now call Anglo-Catholicism. Keble himself, though certainly not a Ritualist (despite the shameless attempts to claim him as such in some of the popular Anglo-Catholic obituaries), had not retired from controversy whilst in Hursley, but with his 1865 letter 'On the ritual of the English Church', he had weighed into the battle to defend the Tractarian Bishop Alexander Forbes of Brechin, accused of teaching Romanist eucharistic doctrine. The year that Keble died saw the publication of S.J. Stone's *Lyra Fidelium*, twelve hymns, one of which included the lines 'Though with a scornful wonder / Men see her sore oppressed, / By schisms rent asunder, / By heresies distressed', lines directed against the Biblical teaching of John William Colenso, Bishop of Natal.

It is in this cauldron of ecclesiastical polemic, and radical change that we must place the decision to found a college in Keble's memory. The intention was that the foundation would be a bastion of 'orthodox' Anglican teaching against opponents such as Jowett, and a defence against 'papal aggression', which caused such intense scandals as the reception into the Roman Catholic Church of four Oxford undergraduates (among them Gerard Manley Hopkins) six months after Keble's death. (Newman was, at the same time, contemplating the foundation of a Catholic college in Oxford.) Pusey had hoped that Liddon, his chief lieutenant, would be Keble's first Warden. Following his refusal and the appointment of Edward Talbot, the College was able to establish itself at a helpful remove from the centre of the theological brawling that surrounded it.
Peter Groves

Left: *The Oriel Fathers, featuring left to right Manning, Pusey, Newman, Keble and Wilberforce*

William Butterfield (1814–1900) was a well-known ecclesiastical architect whose other most notable achievement was the church of All Saints, Margaret Street, in London (finished 1859), a building clearly related to his later Chapel at Keble. He was a member of the Ecclesiological Society and had evolved a very distinctive personal style, a form of Modern Gothic. In Oxford he had already worked on Balliol chapel, and his connections with the Tractarians and his experience in church building made him the obvious choice for Keble. Though Lavinia Talbot described him as 'very delightful ... so sound and intelligent', he had strong opinions and could be difficult to deal with. The early stages of the building process continued throughout 1869, and a new road, Keble Road, was created between Parks Road and St Giles. H.P. Liddon was offered the post of Warden, but rightly excused himself on the grounds that his High-Church views made him too controversial a figure. The founders lighted on the Reverend Edward Talbot, a young fellow of Christ Church and the younger brother of J.G. Talbot, one of the memorial committee members. At the end of June, 1869, before his appointment was due to be confirmed, Talbot surprised the committee by announcing his engagement to the Honourable Lavinia Lyttelton, one of the twelve children of Lord Lyttelton, a niece of Mr Gladstone and with a sister married to Edward Talbot's brother. Lavinia's youngest brother Arthur (tutor and Precentor at Keble, 1879–82) became the first Master of Selwyn College, Cambridge, founded along similar lines to Keble in 1882. A married Warden was not what men like Pusey had expected, but they accepted it with a good grace. Lavinia was extremely well connected and threw herself wholeheartedly into the Keble project, keeping an enthusiastic diary of the Talbots' time at the College.

The new College was controversial. In December 1869 the Reverend John Wordsworth of Brasenose wrote to Talbot in response to the latter's publication of the aims of the new College and appeal for applicants, hoping that Keble, with its religious principles, might act as a lighthouse when existing colleges seemed threatened by a complete removal of religious restrictions. Dr Pusey spoke in similar vein at the meeting in the Sheldonian on the day of the laying of the foundation stone in 1868: the aim was to found a college 'which would react upon the rest of the University'. Keble's foundation was indeed a reaction to the fact that the University was becoming secularized, and when the Royal Charter was granted on 6 June 1870, it allowed Keble College, as a 'corporation', a freedom in relation to its property and its religious policy which was

Above: *The temporary Hall and Chapel*

not granted to other colleges. The founders hoped to ensure its religious future by investing the religious and internal affairs of the College in the Warden and giving its governance to a Council rather than to fellows. The *Gazette* of 7 June 1870 published the text of a Convocation decree recognizing the Charter and allowing the Vice-Chancellor to matriculate its students in advance of legal arrangements yet to be agreed about the status of New Foundations in the University. The decree was passed on June 16, not least through the weighty influence of Keble's supporters. It was opposed passionately by H.A. Pottinger, who described it as 'a sham decree', and 'a marvellous specimen of legislative confusion', on the grounds that Keble was technically neither a college nor a hall, and Convocation had no power to enable the Vice-Chancellor to matriculate its students. When in November 1870 (after the first students had been admitted) the expected Statute about New Foundations was

The First Council

The Rt Hon. the 4th Earl of Carnarvon (1870–82)
The Rt Hon. the 6th Earl Beauchamp (1870–91)
The Rt Revd Samuel Wilberforce, Bishop of Winchester (1870–3)
The Rt Hon. Gathorne Gathorne Hardy (1870–98)
John Archibald Shaw-Stewart (1870–1900)
Mountague Bernard (1870–82)
Henry Edward Pellew (1870–3)
The Very Revd Henry Longueville Mansel (1870–1)
The Revd Dr Edward Bouverie Pusey (1870–80)
The Revd William Bright (1870–1891)
The Revd Henry Parry Liddon (1870–90)
The Revd Peter Goldsmith Medd (1870–1908)

Earl Beauchamp and Keble

Above: *Frederick Lygon, sixth Earl Beauchamp*

Below: *Madresfield Court*

Frederick Lygon, sixth Earl Beauchamp (1830–91) was a leading Anglo-Catholic Conservative politician, sitting in the Commons from 1857 until he succeeded to the title in 1866. His friendship with Liddon, formed as an undergraduate at Christ Church, made him a natural choice for membership of the memorial fund, of which he became vice-president at its inception. He subscribed £5,000 in the first year of the appeal, a sum only matched by Dr Pusey; another donation of £1,000 followed on the College's opening. Beauchamp was a key member of the College Council from 1870 until his death, and a wealth of correspondence makes it clear that he was consulted at every stage. The Bursar consults anxiously about the arrangements for the opening of the Hall and Library, and wants him to intercede with the Duke of Marlborough over the sale of land for the cricket ground; Walter Lock writes to get him to secure a school inspectorship for a Keble graduand; Talbot writes to explain his proposals on reform of Chapel services; Butterfield writes about the placement of the pictures on the dado behind High Table, and is keen that Dr Shirley be placed there because he had 'very earnestly urged the use of brick'. His intervention was crucial in securing a key amendment in favour of the College at the passage of the Mortmain Bill in 1888, much to the chagrin of the College's opponents, who were vociferous in the press.

Beauchamp was reportedly very keen on the notion of 'economical' living – somewhat belied by his own pleasure house at Madresfield Court, near Great Malvern, which he was remodelling as Keble was founded – and insisted on the 'exceeders' in expenditure among the undergraduates being reported to Council. There were tensions with Warden Talbot, who had different notions of what economy might mean in practice. A rather formidable figure, dismissed by one of his fellow peers as 'the most strait-laced and pompous old prig', Lavinia Talbot (whose aunt was Mrs Gladstone, while Beauchamp was serving in Disraeli's government) found him rather easier going when visiting Madresfield in 1871: 'he is certainly pleasanter as a host than he is in any other capacity… Played at absurd card games. Ld B. seems to delight in all manner of toys and tricks'.

promulgated, it was made retrospective to 1 January 1870, and thus included Keble and its students in its scope. It was nevertheless argued that the foundation of Keble College was 'due wholly and solely to the dissatisfaction of its promoters with the proceedings of Parliament of late years', in particular the 1854 Act. Although Warden Talbot had been formally admitted at Commemoration on 23 June, in the presence of the Marquis of Salisbury, the Chancellor of the University (and, like Gladstone, a member of the Council of King's College London), this was merely 'a piece of harmless acting' and the College could not in fact be part of the University.

Nevertheless the new Statute was approved by Congregation on November 28 by 58 votes to 26, and confirmed on 31 January 1871, with Keble College included. It was passed by Convocation on 18 June 1871, by 30 votes to 2. Three years later Edward Talbot alluded to these problems in his speech on the occasion of the laying of the foundation stone of the new Chapel, saying that the offending Statute had been supported by 'the great bulk of the Liberal party of the University', and that it 'practically admitted all members of Keble to the same position and rights as members of all other colleges'. The opposition, he felt, had been 'exaggerated in the country'.

Edward and Lavinia Talbot

When Edward Talbot asked the Honourable Lavinia Lyttelton to marry him in June 1869, they had already known each other for years. After Charterhouse, Edward obtained a first in Greats in 1865, and a Studentship at Christ Church and a first in History the following year, when he also decided to become ordained. Lavinia went to Oxford to visit him with his mother, Mrs Caroline Talbot, and her father, Lord Lyttelton, the fourth Baron Lyttelton, and heard Liddon preach. Edward was already in love with her, but anxious about his prospects of success; however, when he was offered the headship of Keble 'out of the blue' in 1869, his courage rose. Lavinia had already turned down Arthur Acland, but Edward was accepted, and a year later the families were in Oxford again when Lord Lyttelton was given an honorary degree in the Sheldonian on the day before the official opening of Keble College. Shortly afterwards, Edward and Lavinia were married in the church at Hagley in Worcestershire, near the Lyttelton home at Hagley Hall, and moved into their newly built rooms at Keble.

Lavinia was the third of four daughters (there were also eight sons) of George William Lyttelton and his wife Mary Glynne of Hawarden in Yorkshire, whose sister Catherine also married William Gladstone in a double wedding ceremony in 1839. The Talbot family also belonged to this network of high-minded religious families, and Edward and Lavinia had a common bond in that he had lost his father at the age of eight, while Lavinia's mother had died after the birth of her 12th child when Lavinia was a similar age. Mrs Talbot ('Ganma') and Mrs Gladstone ('Aunt Pussy') both helped to nurse Mary Lyttelton and mothered the Lyttelton children after she died. Edward, then aged thirteen, was very upset himself. Mrs Talbot and Aunt Pussy also advised Meriel, Lucy and Lavinia, as each in turn took on the formidable role of managing this large household. When Meriel was married to John Talbot, Edward's older brother, and Lucy to Lord Frederick Cavendish (both in Westminster Abbey), it was Lavinia's turn, at the age of fifteen, to take over. Hagley and Falconhurst in Kent, the Talbot home which Edward's father had built

but not lived to see completed, were the settings of Lavinia and Edward's lives before their marriage, and remained places for frequent visits afterwards. After Lucy's marriage, visits also took place to Chatsworth, the seat of the Dukes of Devonshire. Lavinia's grandmother Sarah, born a Spencer, spent four years as Lady of the Bedchamber to Queen Victoria and eight as Governess to the royal children, and Lucy also became a Maid-in-Waiting, which was a matter of some importance since the appointment carried a salary. The diaries kept by Meriel, Lucy and especially Lavinia, and the family letters, which sometimes use 'Glynnese', the Glynne family language, give a vivid impression of the concerns of this close and affectionate circle.

Above: *Edward and Lavinia Talbot*

Left: *Cartoon of Talbot as Warden*

The controversy and the uncertainty at first also extended to Talbot's own position, since he was neither the head of a college nor the head of a hall, and the heads of new institutions were not to be given the same privileges as those of existing ones. Lavinia Talbot wrote at the time: 'I shall never see Edward take his place as Head of a House at St Mary's or elsewhere, rather sad'. Many also feared that Keble would be a mere 'clerical seminary', and Talbot sought to assure his listeners that its first students were already going in different directions; he recognized that this issue was 'delicate ground', but argued that success on the river surely proved his point. However, the arguments and the sensitivities of the founders of the College did not go away.

It was in these circumstances of controversy that Talbot was installed by the Chancellor on 23 June 1870. What later became Liddon quad was dotted with ladies in colourful dresses, and the visitors included Charlotte M. Yonge, 'a striking-looking, grey-haired woman with beautiful eyes and an expressive face'. The installation, with all wearing their academic robes, took place in the temporary chapel, where the Warden was put into his stall and the service was in Latin.

From its opening until the granting of its new Statutes in 1952, Keble was governed by a Council of not more than 12 and not less than nine, who were appointed for life. The Council, whose first members were drawn from the committee of the Keble Memorial Fund, was chaired by the Warden and usually met three times a year, one of the occasions being during the St Mark's Day celebrations, which also included a Gaudy. Lavinia Talbot often refers to the arguments that took place in the Council about the future direction of the College, and its meetings were frequently a source of tension to the Talbots. Only very gradually did the tutors, and later the fellows, gain an official say in the College's affairs, and the latter were required on admission in the Chapel to make a solemn declaration that they were communicant members of the Church of England and would uphold the religious aims of the College.

Once the new College had been formally 'opened', whether legally or, in the opinion of some, not, the challenge was to find undergraduates and tutors and to put in place the domestic arrangements for the start of business at the beginning of the new academic year. At the end of September Lavinia wrote that she and Edward had spent most of the last days shopping or arranging books and furniture in the College. The committee voted £100 to the Warden to furnish the common room and library.

Above: *The opening of the College, 23 June, 1870, watercolour*

Left: *The Archbishop of Canterbury and Talbot, thinly disguised as workmen, argue over accusations of the College's alleged affinities with Rome*

She was worried about the poor standard of the food, and the servants were on 'board wages'. There was also a real concern that not enough applicants would come forward, or that those who did would not be up to scratch. In fact there were too many, and she was relieved (though also sad for the persons concerned) that nine in all were 'plucked' in the second matriculation examination on 13 October; 'one nearly burst into tears, another pleaded piteously, and as a climax one fainted dead away. I was sitting in the drawing room when I heard Edward loudly call me. I rushed into the study and saw the unfortunate on the ground, Edward saying "he is in a fit". However, it proved to be a fainting, and he soon came to with water &c.'

From then on Lavinia was always to feel it acutely when undergraduates failed their exams. On this occasion the number was successfully reduced to 30, and these all moved in with their luggage and pieces of furniture on 15 October. The food was still a worry: 'dinner was a failure the first night – one bit of beef – one batter pudding. A little speech of explanation had to be made.' Lavinia shared in everything. She loved the fact that she was given a special place 'under the stalls' in the temporary chapel and was thrilled at the suggestion made soon after that she might take part in the College choir and the Glee Club, and wrote in her diary that first evening, 'The very look of the quadrangle lighted up, the bell ringing, the sounds along

Below: *The first undergraduates with Warden and Mrs Talbot*

the corridor, most exciting. How many months we have looked forward to this day!' The number of under-graduates who came to the chapel services was also anxiously counted – 24 out of 30 to Holy Communion at eight the next morning, but all of them to morning prayers at 9.30am. There was yet another service at 4.45pm, with Edward's first sermon; again all the 30 attended, and one even asked to be allowed to copy out the text. Finally, 'the little evening service' at 10pm, again all came, and 'Well ended this happy day.'

The young College had to contend with many hostile jibes; partly for its architecture, so unlike the traditional colleges and so bright and gaudy to unpractised eyes; partly through suspicions that it would simply be a kind of seminary for High-Church ordinands, and partly simply because it was new and different. It was very important to Edward and Lavinia that Keble should seem 'normal', and play its full part in the University. They were invited out, Lavinia going to dine at the Provost of Oriel's 'in a bath chair!', and went to dinner with Benjamin Jowett, of whom she wrote 'his face rather tires one than offends – it remains exactly the same always – & his voice and manner smooth and unvaried.' The bruising experience of the Congregation debate about new foundations made them all the more anxious. However, success on the river would, it seemed, provide the proof that Keble had properly arrived on the scene. Within days of the Congregation debate in November, the first Keble VIII was competing with other colleges on the river, coached by Mr Mylne, one of the first tutors and the future Bishop of Bombay. They rowed 'very steadily but slow', but things had improved by February 1871. Mr Mylne was very pleased, and while in Torpids 'meek little Keble' came last, they bumped Merton easily and quickly and Mr Mylne was beside himself with delight; in October of the same year they also bumped St Edmund Hall. Such things evidently mattered. It is interesting in the light of what happened later to read that the Talbots were invited to dinner by Thomas Combe, another Tractarian supporter, and his wife Martha ('dull'), but Lavinia noticed the 'beautiful pictures by modern swells' in the Combes' house, including paintings by Holman Hunt, Millais and others. The first Keble concert took place in December 1871, with Lavinia's own rendering of *Fair Maid of Northumberland* receiving an encore. But February 1872 brought a 'horrid discovery of delirium tremens in the new cook'.

In 1874, on one of Gladstone's visits, the Talbots gave a luncheon so that he could meet Liddon ('so happy and velvety') and Dr Acland. Gladstone then went to visit

Above: *The College's disputed status in the University is captured in this cartoon of the scholar flogged by the Statutes*

Prince Leopold and was later much impressed by Mr Mylne's sermon at Keble on the present state of the College. By 1875 the Talbots were themselves entertaining Prince Leopold to tea, after he had inspected the new Chapel.

During the first years, Talbot was occupied with building up the student body and getting the College more firmly established in the University. At the beginning of the second year another 26 undergraduates were admitted, with 20 'plucked'. He also engaged in University issues, daring to oppose Pusey and Liddon by supporting the proposal that examination in the 39 Articles of the Church of England should not be compulsory for Pass Schools for Divinity. Lavinia wrote admiringly of how famous Edward had become for siding with the Liberal party; in the same entry she recorded her impressions of having heard Jowett preach in St Mary's the Sunday before, for the first time in 22 years: 'it was a vague dishonest sermon – too vague to do much harm I still hope, and too dishonest not to set people on their guard.' These were heady years in Oxford as the hold of the Church over the University was gradually loosened. The School of Theology was created in 1870, the very year Keble opened, with the battles over the removal of religious tests and the abolition of clerical fellowships already underway. It is worth noting that 1870 was also the year of extreme ultramontanism, with Pius IX declaring himself a prisoner in the Vatican and asserting papal infallibility.

The Gibbs Family and Tyntesfield

The grandest elements of the Butterfield ensemble were made possible by the generosity of one merchant family, the Gibbses of Tyntesfield in Somerset. The octogenarian William Gibbs (1790–1875), the wealthiest commoner in England, according to *The Times*, had asked Butterfield how much a chapel would cost, and was told between £25,000 and £30,000, which he agreed to donate. Gibbs himself laid the foundation stone on 25 April 1873, declaring his hope that the Chapel might be the means of 'upholding and spreading the true principles of the Church of England as professed by moderate and yet thoroughly catholic churchmen, as much opposed on the one hand to extreme views of doctrine and ritual, as on the other to those of the very low Church'. Gibbs backed Butterfield in the controversy over the theme of the mosaic over the high altar, and his name, along with his wife's, is inscribed beneath the image of the Christ in majesty, which was chosen in preference to the Crucifixion. He did not live to see the completion of the project, but at the Chapel's opening on St Mark's Day 1876, his sons Antony (1841–1907) and Martin Gibbs (1850–1928) announced a donation large enough for the dining hall and Library, completed two years later. William's nephew, Henry Hucks Gibbs (1819-1907), first Baron Aldenham, Governor of the Bank of England and advocate of bimetallism, was also closely associated with the College as a member of its Council from 1873 until his death.

William Gibbs had spent much of his early life in Spain, building up the trade connections with the Spanish colonies in South America on which the family's fortunes were to be based. But it was a hard slog, and William and his nephew Henry were profoundly conscious of the need to efface the shame of Antony Gibbs' (father to William and grandfather to Henry) bankruptcy in 1789, by pursuing both mercantile respectability and landed status. *Tenax propositi*, 'tenacious of purpose', was the family motto, and a portion of the profits each year was marked DS, *deudas sagradas*, 'sacred debts', to discharge the money owing to Antony's creditors. By the 1840s they were making loans to the newly independent government of Peru on the security of concessions to sell guano, bird droppings rich in nitrates and much in demand as fertilizer in England: by the 1850s profits were as high as £125,000 per annum. 'The house of Gibbs made their dibs by selling the turds of foreign birds', quipped the City wags. Originally dissenters, the family was by this time powerfully aligned with Anglo-Catholic currents in the Church, and William's philanthropy involved the building of a number of churches, for which he patronized the leading architects of the Gothic revival.

Originally resident in London, William, taking advantage of the new rail connections to London in which the family were major investors, had purchased the estate at Tyntesfield in 1843. The existing Regency house was rebuilt between 1863–5 to designs by John Norton, its remarkable chapel by Blomfield (albeit with some input from Butterfield, who may have influenced the mosaics) being added in 1875. 'That beautiful house is like a church in spirit', remarked the novelist Charlotte M. Yonge, friend of John Keble. Gibbs' extraordinary gift is recorded in the 'Keble oak' aligned with his study.

Above: *William Gibbs and family*

Below: *Tyntesfield House*

In the debates at Oxford, Liddon was on the side of the conservatives, and Talbot showed courage in his stance, perhaps encouraged by his association through his wife with Mr Gladstone, who, as Prime Minister, promoted the University Tests Act of 1871, which opened the way for non-conformists to enter the universities. The irony by which Keble, as a New Foundation, aimed to uphold religious tests just when they were abolished by law was not lost, and the legal status of the College as a New Foundation with its own very particular charter was of central concern to its Council. Talbot himself was to prove a skilful diplomat, able to manage his relations with the more conservative founders and Council members while maintaining his own more liberal ideas about the right direction for the College.

Early in 1872 the Council agreed that from October that year Keble should have five tutors, and that one of these posts should be offered to Arthur Acland, who was at that time merely a lecturer. He was the third son of the 11th baronet, destined for the Church, but later resigned his orders and went into politics, becoming a member of Gladstone's fourth cabinet. Keble was also fielding a cricket team, and St Mark's Day was kept with a choral service in the morning following an early communion service attended by Lord Beauchamp and Mr Shaw-Stewart. Thirty people, including Lord Lyttelton, dined at High Table at what was already referred to as a Gaudy (though there were as yet no old members). But the great excitement of the year came in July when it was announced that William Gibbs of Tyntesfield in Somerset had given the entire amount necessary to build a proper Chapel, whose cost Butterfield estimated at £25–30,000. Two weeks later the Talbots travelled by train via Nailsea, and then by carriage to Tyntesfield, where they met Mrs Gibbs and two of their many children, both girls, 'one a dwarf, the other consumptive', according to Lavinia.

William Gibbs himself was already 83 years old and confined to a wheelchair. As on her visit to the Combes, Lavinia noticed and admired the paintings in the house, though these were old masters including pictures by Zurburán, Rubens and Canaletto. Gibbs had rebuilt a much earlier house in the Gothic Revival style, which included a new chapel with mosaics by the Venetian glass firm of Salviati, which also worked at Westminster Abbey. He was able to lay the foundation stone of Keble Chapel on St Mark's Day, 1873, but he did not live to see it opened three years later. By the beginning of September 1872, Talbot, Sir John Coleridge and William Butterfield went to Tyntesfield

Left: *William Gibbs, donor of the Chapel*

Below: *The plaque commemorating Gibbs's gift at Tyntesfield ('the Keble oak')*

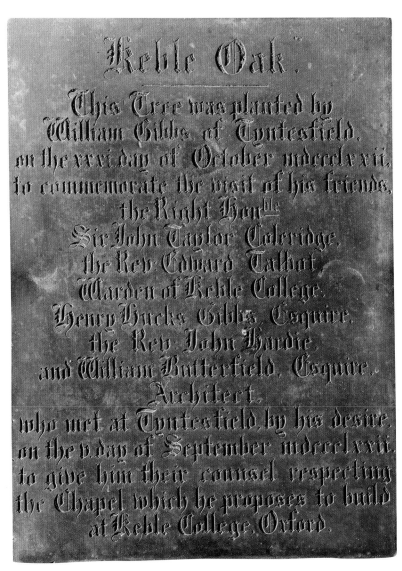

Keble Oak.

This Tree was planted by William Gibbs, of Tyntesfield, on the xxi day of October mdccclxxii, to commemorate the visit of his friends, the Right Honble Sir John Taylor Coleridge, the Rev. Edward Talbot, Warden of Keble College, Henry Hucks Gibbs, Esquire, the Rev. John Hardie, and William Butterfield, Esquire, Architect, who met at Tyntesfield by his desire on the v day of September mdccclxxii to give him their counsel respecting the Chapel which he proposes to build at Keble College, Oxford.

for a meeting to discuss the Keble plans, and the 'Keble oak' was planted in the grounds of Tyntesfield on the axis of William Gibbs's study in the presence of all three, together with Mr Gibbs and the Reverend Hardie, the chaplain of Tyntesfield. It is there to this day, with a plaque commemorating the occasion. With his experience of Butterfield, Talbot was already well aware that there might be arguments with the architect over the Chapel and its decoration, but by the end of the year the plans had been drawn up and it was decided that the foundation stone would be laid on St Mark's Day.

The number of new applicants in 1873 was lower than hoped for, and even fewer passed the necessary examination. However, the Council soon set about discussing the question of providing a decent house for the Warden. Butterfield started on the design and a site was found, but money had to be raised and the project had to wait several years before coming to fruition. Meanwhile, the laying of the foundation stone of the Chapel in 1873 and its opening in 1876 were great days in the history of the College. The former occasion, on 25 April 1873, was preceded the night before by a long meeting of the College Council and a Gaudy dinner for seventy – 'half Oxford', and a good many others besides, including Lord Lyttelton. The following morning a large crowd attended the early communion service, including Charlotte M. Yonge. A cold lunch for 19 preceded the ceremony and more guests arrived: Lavinia's sister Meriel, Edward Talbot's mother, Beresford Hope, Lord Beauchamp and the Dean of St Paul's. In a howling wind, amid sleet and snow showers, the choir, Council and members of the College processed round Liddon quad and stood around the site in the cold, with hymns, prayers, speeches by Lord Beauchamp and Mr Gibbs and a half-hour address by Edward, which he used to describe the College's progress so far and to appeal for more donations, all in the presence of several hundred people. Talbot's speech, especially the part where he thanked William Gibbs for his munificence, was punctuated by applause and cries of 'Hear, hear'. Mrs Combe's gift of Holman Hunt's painting *The Light of the World* had been accepted in the previous month. The Keble Memorial Fund was wound up, with total receipts of £50,025.10s.10d, and a Keble College extension fund proposed, with a target of £15,000, in order to build 36 more student rooms, a hall and library, a house for the Warden, and undergraduate scholarships. The twin aims of the College were again stated as economical education and religious education, and in both the College had succeeded.

Left: *Antony Gibbs, joint donor of the Hall and Library*

Below: *The original Warden's study in Liddon quad, 1870s*

Nor was it the college of a clique or party, as many had predicted. There were now 86 men in residence, some from major public schools such as Winchester, and Keble was doing well against other colleges in cricket and on the river. It is hardly surprising that when it was all over, and everyone, including Miss Yonge and the Gibbs family, had all left, Edward and Lavinia were tired out. A few weeks later the foundations were being dug, and by September, in what seems remarkably fast progress, the walls were several feet high and arrangements were being put in place for raising stone by means of scaffolding. In October the Council was sufficiently satisfied with Talbot to propose raising his salary to £750, which drew from Lavinia the comment 'so we really are rich people'.

By the time of the grand opening of the Chapel in 1876, William Gibbs had died. He was followed shortly before the opening by Lavinia's father, Lord Lyttelton, who had fallen into a depression after the death, in March the previous year, of his daughter May, whom Lavinia had nursed in her illness. He committed suicide soon after

Easter, 1876, by throwing himself down the stairs at home. The long awaited opening of Keble Chapel was overshadowed for the young Talbots by the fact that it took place only three days after Lord Lyttelton's funeral, with few of Lavinia's family present. Only six weeks later Edward's mother died too. The Talbots' first child had been born on 2 October 1875, a girl whom they named Mary (May), but it was a dark year for Lavinia.

The opening of the Chapel was even grander than the laying of the foundation stone had been. Antony Gibbs formally presented the key and the deed of gift, signed by his father, to the Warden, and it was announced that the anonymous donors had also made it possible to build a Hall and a Library. Not until 1878, when these buildings in turn were formally opened, was their identity revealed as Antony Gibbs himself and his brother Martin. In order to preserve its independence against possible ecclesiastical threats, the Chapel was not consecrated; the Bishop of Oxford produced a memorandum on the non-consecration of the Chapel and the Warden obtained a licence for it as a private chapel. Today its status is that of a peculiar, an extra-diocesan place of worship. The interior was at once recognized as extraordinary in its use of stone, marble, alabaster and brass, though Lavinia noted that 'the wretched thing was that hardly anyone heard Dr Pusey, first from the great echo, then because he coughed incessantly. I hardly made out one sentence.' A few weeks later the same thing happened; she could not hear the last sermon preached at Keble by Mr Mylne, about to depart for India as the Bishop of Bombay. To try to deal with the problem, a 'sounding board' was put in over the pulpit in 1879. But when Gladstone was shown the Chapel by Butterfield in 1878, his admiration was 'unbounded'. Reporting the opening, the *Pall Mall Gazette* listed the many guests, who included, according to *The Rock*, 'the chief of the old Tractarian celebrities and the most notable of the present sympathizers'. But *The World* complained of the Chapel's 'unspeakable ugliness', and opined that the spirit of the College was antagonistic to the spirit of the University. Keble's uncompromising architecture and its defiant stand against change went side by side. The real accolade came in November 1879, when Cardinal Newman paid a visit to Lavinia in the Lodgings, bringing with him a bag containing the last lot of Keble's letters to him, which he wanted to deliver personally to the Warden of Keble. He assured Edward that the erasures in the letters were of the painful passages where Keble blamed himself quite

Anglican connections

E.S. Talbot had close connections with like-minded men such as Charles Gore and Henry Scott Holland, who were more liberal in their views than Dr Pusey. In addition to editing *Lux Mundi*, Gore was involved in the initiative of Edward King (a member of the College Council 1873–1910) in the founding in 1880 of the Oxford Mission to Calcutta, run by a new Anglican Brotherhood of the Epiphany, whose Rule he drew up. Edward Talbot was a supporter of this initiative and later contributed the preface to the history of the Oxford Mission to Calcutta by G. Longridge (1910). A Sisterhood of the Epiphany was founded in 1902, and although the Brotherhood came to an end, the Oxford Mission still continues its work in Calcutta (Kolkata) and Bangladesh. A related missionary initiative to be run by a new Anglican order was the Delhi Brotherhood, set up in 1877 from Cambridge, now the Brotherhood of the Ascended Christ and part of the Church of North India. The Reverend James Stuart, Liddon Student 1938, fellow, tutor and Chaplain of Keble, 1939–49, junior dean 1940–4, dean 1947–9, joined the Brotherhood in 1949 and remained in India until late in his life, where he was also editorial secretary of the SPCK in India (ISPCK). In the latter capacity he played an important role in the liturgical development of the united Church of North India, inaugurated in 1970.

Above: *Cartoon of the dedication of the Chapel, with banner depicting John Keble*

wrongly, even for Newman's own conversion; Newman felt that these were unworthy of his old friend. As he left he said that 'he thought Keble College was *the* hopeful thing about Oxford now', at which (after he had gone) Edward and Lavinia 'quite burst'.

The Chapel

Above: *East window*

Below: *Early watercolour of the Chapel interior*

The Chapel stands tall at 90 feet from the ground to the ridge of the lead roof. The internal width is 35 feet, and the length 124 feet. On the exterior, the west entrance is decorated with the *agnus dei* within its arch and a pelican feeding its young on the porch, symbolizing the sacramental union of Christ with his people. Above is a nine-foot statue of St Michael the Archangel with the dragon under his feet. Beneath the niches of the buttresses at the east end are two larger niches with Gabriel the archangel on the left and the Virgin Mary on the right, with Saints Peter and Paul in the smaller niches above. At the west end is a statue of Archbishop Longley, who laid the foundation stone of the College in 1868, and in the northern niche, the Marquis of Salisbury, the Chancellor of the University.

The oak pews face eastward to the altar, in contrast with the arrangement in other college chapels, and are designed to hold 212 undergraduates. In the choir the southern stalls were reserved for the Warden, the tutors and the choir, while the northern stalls were for the ladies associated with the College.

The interior is dominated by an Old and New Testament mosaic cycle (cleaned by vacuum in 1949), and by Butterfield's familiar polychrome. Butterfield went to Venice to study mosaics in situ, and the mosaics and glass for the Chapel were executed under his close supervision by Alexander Gibbs. The inspiration is clearly Byzantine, although the wan colours and the naive realism of scenes such as that of Noah and the ark, with its large camel in the foreground, are anything but Byzantine.

The mosaic panels on the north and south walls of the nave illustrate the stories of Noah, Abraham, Joseph and Moses, and the typology indicated by the inclusion of Christian symbols recalls Ruskin on St Mark's, Venice: 'the whole church [is] a great Book of Common Prayer; the mosaics were its illuminations, and common people of the time were taught their Scripture history by means of them' (*Stones of Venice* II.4). The stained glass windows in the nave portray the twelve minor prophets, and the themes in the nave are sacrificial offering and prophecy.

In the choir and sanctuary the mosaics depict events in the life of Christ. The windows at the west end depict David and Solomon with the major prophets, as well as Samuel and Elijah, with the Ascension in the stained glass windows at the east end.

Below: *Detail of east window*

Right: *Noah's ark, nave mosaic*

Below right: *The controversial Christ in Majesty over the altar*

An interesting feature in the Ascension windows is the focus of the apostles' gazes on Mary, mother of Jesus, who is also the type of the Church.

Over the altar is a controversial depiction of Christ in judgement. As Michael Wheeler emphasized in a lecture given at Keble in 1996, and as Talbot underlined in his farewell sermon in the Chapel on Advent Sunday, 1888, judgement is the overall message of the Chapel. In the mid- to late-nineteenth century this was controversial and uncompromising. Like Keble itself, the Chapel was intended to stand *contra mundum*, against secular values and against the society around it.

When he designed Keble College, Butterfield was at the height of his maturity, and it would not be incorrect to say that its Chapel is the culmination of his life-long search for what J. Mordaunt Crook has called the 'architectural holy grail.'

Allen Shin

2 THE EARLY YEARS

If Lavinia Talbot was enthusiastic and excited about the new College, not all of its first undergraduates were so positive. One of the first cohort in 1870, the Reverend Harry Ward McKenzie, a cricketer and later headmaster of Uppingham, published in 1930 a memoir of his experiences entitled *The First Thirty from Within*. It ends with a plea for the College to free itself from the Council and become self-governing: 'is it surprising that more than twenty colleges should hold aloof from one which is not considered worthy to govern itself?' He had no illusions about the composition of the College's first under-graduates: 'many of them were healthy folk – but many hardly seemed the sort of people to represent the start of what the College was supposed to stand for. It was always a wonder how they were chosen. Was there a shortage of applicants? Did parents wait to see what was going to happen? Without a question, we were a very mixed company and hardly likely to be pillars of the Church.' It was partly that he felt their academic standards left much to be desired; only one of the first 30 reached as high as a second in Greats, and while two got firsts in history and one rose to become a bishop, 'as a whole we were passmen at most and some of us ploughmen'. Unbeknown to the tutors, and surely to the Warden and Mrs Talbot, some of them spent Wednesday evenings in one particular set of rooms, watching boxing matches between one of their number and a professional boxer brought in from outside; 'the liquid refreshment was not tea'.

The ideals of the authorities were strict and chapel attendance punctuated every day, but sport was encouraged as promoting vigorous endeavour. Cricket was on the whole a success; football and 'rugby' were also played, and fives, on courts which faced the yard of the Lamb and Flag, as was the Winchester game, between canvas. Keble rowing had auspicious beginnings, climbing to fourth in Summer Eights in 1879 and 1888, and even gaining headship during the week in Torpids in 1881 and 1882, before being displaced by the end of the week. Keble also had two rowing blues in this period, G.F. Burgess (1878) and F.M. Hargreaves (1880). Keble would only register only one more rowing blue and two more blues coxes in the following 75 years and would not have two University rowers up at the same time again until 1959.

Above: Cartoon of 'The Keble Eight coxed by the Principal', all wearing birettas

Right: MS 49, f 74v: St Helena discovers the Cross

contradictio apud aliquos
In inventione sancte crucis

lcō .i.
E L E
N A
constan
tinu
mat.
femi
nai
compabilu fide· religiōe

But Keble's student body continued to identify strongly with rowing. In 1902, the captain complained in his captain's book when 'only' half the total number of freshmen signed up to row, a complaint repeated in 1912. Smaller colleges were sometimes lucky to be able to put out one eight-man crew for Torpids in the spring (a race reserved for second crews through 1908) and one for Summer Eights (the highlight of the intercollegiate racing calendar). In 1875, Keble made history by being the first college boat club to introduce a second torpid due to strength of numbers. Keble would routinely field several boats for Torpids and, when it became accepted practice, multiple boats for Summer Eights as well.

College life was full of rules, even more than at school; the rooms were small and unlovely, the furniture hard and meagre and the long, stone, Butterfield corridors draughty in the extreme, the food 'just adequate and badly cooked and poorly served'. The story was that 'the only way to know if the meat at dinner was beef or mutton was to look round and see if there was any mustard on the table.'

In McKenzie's view, it was the first Warden who was responsible above all for raising the College above this inauspicious beginning; through his warmth and humanity, the welcome he always gave to returning undergraduates, his willingness to bring his new wife to live in such uncomfortable and inadequate circumstances, his ability to guide the College through the inevitable quarrels and disagreements of the early years, his insight into people and his uprightness of purpose. Others, too, were praised: the early tutors L.G. Mylne (with his long clerical coat, which flapped about as he ran along the towpath), F.J. Jayne, J.R. Illingworth and Walter Lock, who served the College for fifty years and became the third Warden. But Edward Talbot was the one who had to deal with everyone, from the individual undergraduate to the difficult architect or member of Council. His portrait in the Hall shows him as a young man with reddish hair and heavy beard, trying to look solemn and serious; his great-grandson, recalling him as he was when he was much older, still recalled the softness of his beard.

There were regular reading parties. In July 1874, six undergraduates, with Edward, Lavinia, Mr Illingworth, Mrs Talbot and Lavinia's sister, May, spent several weeks at Abendberg, near Interlaken in Switzerland, with reading in the mornings (Lavinia read Theodor Mommsen's *Rome*), expeditions in the afternoons and music in the evenings. Smoking was allowed at the outdoor reading sessions, but only to those who sat on the windward side. A reunion took place at Keble in November that year, with much lawn tennis being played. In the first decade of the College's existence, not only was its magnificent Chapel built, marking the end to the services in the makeshift temporary building (though, like Lavinia Talbot, Harry McKenzie comments unfavourably on the acoustic of the 'wondrous' new building), but also the Hall, Library and Warden's Lodgings. The Hall and Library (1878) were paid for, at first anonymously, by the generosity of Antony and Martin Gibbs, two of William Gibbs's sons. Antony's portrait, with gun and dog, hangs today at Tyntesfield and in the Keble senior common room. While there had been earlier plans for a Warden's house, there was not enough money, and in September 1875 the sum of £8,000 or even £9,000 was mentioned.

Above left: *Keble Eight bumping, 1905, and the crew of the 1905 Keble VIII*

Above: *The crew of the 1871 Torpid*

Sport: The Early Years

Keble College was founded during the period when sports assumed a recognizably modern appearance inside the University and in the country at large. In the first half of the 19th century, Oxford sports, including rowing, cricket and field sports, were expensive and socially exclusive, organized around private clubs. But from the 1850s onwards, sports gradually became more inclusive, losing their association with particular élite schools. They were increasingly organized around colleges, many of which acquired their own grounds and staff, in addition to those of the University as a whole. These were often funded through newly-founded amalgamated clubs, channelling subscriptions and other income into sports, but regulated by college-appointed treasurers. Inter-collegiate competition, including fixtures with Cambridge colleges, flourished. And the rules of many sports, notably football, were standardized, ending the variety of school-based practices. Pursuits once regarded as rowdy and élitist were viewed more positively; rowing was widely regarded as an excellent discipline, while football brought together young men from across the social spectrum.

Although at Keble there was some anxiety that subscriptions to the amalgamated clubs might be a drain on the poorer students' finances, and at the outset they were not compulsory, there was no doubt that the college clubs had the first call on their cash: 'The credit and reputation of the College is an object which each may rightly prefer to his own private taste and indulgence and is unquestionably affected by the position of the College in amusements'. An early priority was the acquisition of a sports field. The land opposite St Edward's School was leased from the Duke of Marlborough in 1871, and purchased in 1893 at a cost of £2,750. The present cricket pavilion dates from 1903, replacing the inferior structure of 1872.

In Keble's early decades there were clubs for cricket, rugby ('rugger'), athletics and football ('soccer'). Other students played golf. Participation rates were high: 69 of the 167 men entering the College between 1891 and 1893 played for a first team, but Keble did not enjoy noted success in

Above: *Cricket XI, 1873*

Above right: *Rugby XV, 1889*

Right: *The XIII Club (for sportsmen), 1910*

inter-collegiate competitions. In addition to playing other Oxford colleges, there were regular fixtures against Cambridge colleges and against non-university teams, both in the region and occasionally on tour. Between 1906 and 1915 27 Keble students won blues, in running, high jump, cross-country, rugby, football, hockey, swimming and water polo.

It was not uncommon at the time for Oxford students to represent their country or to play at a higher level, often while at university. There was a steady stream of Keble rugby players in the home counties, alongside the odd footballer, hockey player and athlete. William Pollock-Hill (1886) held the English record for 1,000 yards and Sydney Sarel (1882) competed in the 3,500-metre walk at the 1908 Olympics. Keble's finest sportsman of the 19th century was undoubtedly Gilbert Oswald Smith (1892), described as 'the greatest centre-forward of all time' by *The Times*. Capped over 20 times for England, starting when he was still up at Keble, G. O., as he was popularly known, scored a hat trick against Ireland in five minutes and led the side that beat Germany 12-0 in 1901. He played for the country's leading amateur side, the Corinthians, scoring a record 113 goals in 141 matches. Keble produced another England international footballer, Robert Topham (1886), who played alongside Smith for England.

Although Keble gained a reputation for its footballers, if there was one dominant sport in College, it was probably rugby. Keble was strong in the 1910s: the XV reached the Cuppers final in 1914, and there were four Keble students in the Oxford side in 1912. The rugby club enjoyed the support and coaching of F.W. (later Canon) Matheson, who was a Keble undergraduate in 1902 and stayed on to be Dean of the College. The most outstanding player of the time was Arthur James ('Jimmy') Dingle (1910), capped three times for England and nicknamed 'The Mud'. After a memorable try against Cambridge, *The Clock Tower* said of him that 'You are, perhaps, the most popular Rugger man in the Varsity with the "townees", and equally popular with members of the fair sex.' Dingle joined the East Yorkshire Regiment in 1914 and, now captain, perished at Gallipoli.

Alisdair Rogers

Left: *Designs for stained glass windows celebrating sporting heroes, G.O. Smith on the left, E.M. Baker on the right, from the JCR cartoon album*

domestic crises, as when three of the Lock children came down with scarlet fever, a serious illness in those days, and one that required isolation. As this happened at Christmas, their father did his best to make this more bearable for them during their recovery by composing a poem:

Hark! St Giles's bell is pealing
And I hear its soft tone stealing
Through the panes, along the ceiling
Telling me I should be kneeling
Where the Christ child is revealing
News of Christmas joy and healing
But alas! I sit here feeling
Lonely – for I too am peeling!

Seen from Parks Road and Museum Road today, the Lodgings can look grim and forbidding, but it is still a family house, which comes into its own at Christmas and on social occasions. Henry Scott Holland called it 'the big great house' and recalled 'the crowded drawing room' and the 'friends from London'. The Warden's study, looking out across the length of Pusey Quad to the Chapel, with the great beech tree in front of the window, must be very much as it was in Edward Talbot's day. Walter Lock's daughter Mildred remembered it as 'a large oak-panelled room which opened off our enormous hall'; it was a room which the children never dreamt of entering without knocking or being invited.

The Council was very concerned about the finances. There was no endowment and the books had to balance each year, or better still, make a surplus. The expenditure of the undergraduates was also restricted, and a careful watch was made for 'exceeders', those who had gone beyond the limit set for extras on their battels bills, while 'economizers' were duly appreciated. But economical though it might be, life in the College was far from being as serious as that might suggest. Shaw-Stewart ceased to be Bursar in 1880, and on 5 January 1881 he held a dinner for the college servants in the senior common room. Running a large institution in the late nineteenth century was very labour intensive, and there were 80 people present. There were speeches, and the evening ended with some 'capital songs'. However, the critics of the College had not been silenced, and Dr Pusey intervened in a debate in the letter pages of *The Times* to defend the College against charges that the monies subscribed for its foundation had been used, not to found a true memorial to John Keble, but rather a 'home of Ritualism'. In 1876 *The World* had noted the contradiction inherent in the support the College received from Gladstone, who had wished the religious

In the event, the Lodgings was built with the help of a loan of £3,000 from Edward Talbot's mother, which was eventually converted into a mortgage to her of £4,000. Mrs Talbot believed that Edward and Lavinia should have a decent place in which to live, as befitted an Oxford head of house. Not surprisingly, the Lodgings, on the corner of Museum Road and Parks Road, recall Butterfield's many rectories.

Edward and Lavinia moved in in 1877, after two years in the modest set of tutor's rooms which had seen the birth of their first child and the deaths of Lavinia's father, Edward's mother and Lavinia's sister, May. Though substantial, the house is not large in comparison with the lodgings in some of the older colleges, but in view of Keble's claims in relation to frugal living, it attracted adverse comment in the press for alleged extravagance, and *The World* complained that 'the home of asceticism and prudential sanctity has built its Warden a "lordly pleasure house"'. There was certainly fun in the house as the family grew, and the diaries of three generations who lived there in the early period record regular theatricals, social occasions and music; we may suppose, however, that the tone was never allowed to get out of hand. At times there were also

Keble Stamps and Postcards

In 1871 Keble originated a system for colleges to run their own postal services, using special stamps sold through the Lodge. The result was a highly efficient, inter-college communications network, or it was until the Postmaster General clamped down on it just 15 years later, on the grounds that it infringed his monopoly. At a meeting held on 11 February 1886, under the chairmanship of the Vice-Chancellor, college representatives led by the Warden of Merton capitulated.

While the system was in operation, letters and postcards were delivered seven times each day by the college messenger (the first of whom was John Waite, 1870–1), with a speed and regularity quite as effective as modern email. The earliest specimen of these stamps so far recorded was used on 29 November 1871, and Keble was eventually joined by Merton, Hertford, Lincoln, Exeter, St John's and All Souls colleges. Balliol was just about to be added in 1886 when the Postmaster General intervened. Oriel dabbled with it, as did the Oxford Union, while Selwyn, Queens' and St John's at Cambridge all had a go too. Keble also issued College postcards embossed with the College arms, printed by Emberlin and Son, Oxford, and the College ordered at least 1,000 of these between 1875 and 1881. These cards were sold at a half penny each and hand-carried without being cancelled. A message on one sent on 22 July 1885 reads: 'Wednesday morning. Dear Rigaud, Our servant will call this afternoon for the books, prob. about 3. Will you leave orders for them, if you will be out? Yrs sincerely and gratefully, W. Lock'.

By 1876 stamps were being ordered in stocks of 15,000 a time, and through obscure stamp auctions over recent years, Christopher Meakin (1962) managed to acquire a complete sheet of the final Keble stamp issue of May 1882, of which only 1,000 complete sheets were printed, as well as an even rarer complete sheet of the St John's College stamps of January 1884. Stamps on cover are rare, and used postal stationery even rarer. There are Oxford college stamps in the Royal Collection, and the stamps, in particular a unique block of eight 'parcel stamps', are of great interest to modern philatelists. In recognition of this part of Keble's history an issue of commemorative stamps was also issued to celebrate the centenary in 1970.

With thanks to Christopher Meakin and Don Aver

tests to be removed, and its own desire to keep them. Anxieties remained about the legal status of the College as a New Foundation, in relation to the removal of the tests by the Universities Tests Act of June, 1871. The Council took counsel's opinion in 1879, as to whether the College fell within the purview of the Act and, if so, about the status of scholarships and exhibitions established after its passing. The advice given was that Keble had indeed been a college in June 1871, and therefore was not exempt from the Act, but that awards resulting from private donations could have religious limitations attached.

However, counsel had also stated that, not being a head of house, the Warden of Keble could not be an Elector for the Bampton Lectures, and other uncertainties continued into the 1880s in relation to the College's capacity, under its charter, to accept gifts of property. The question again

Left: *Edward Talbot, Warden, 1870–88*

was whether, by its charter, the College had been incorporated into the University, and counsel's opinion, obtained in 1887, advised that the decree admitting Keble College as a New Foundation clearly did not incorporate it in the University, and indeed, that the College 'appears studiously to have avoided obtaining such incorporation'. There were certain legal questions which were important for the transfer of advowsons to the College, and as a prominent member of the Council, a doughty supporter of the College and the person largely responsible for the transfer to the College of St Barnabas, Jericho, in 1886, Earl Beauchamp was much involved in its legal problems. He consulted the Duke of Buckingham, writing that Keble did not wish to be incorporated, and after a private bill had been rejected by the Commons on a second reading, he succeeded, by a move which gave rise to disapproval in some quarters, in proposing an amendment exempting Keble from the Mortmain and Charitable Uses Act of 1888. The question of the College's charter had aroused unfavourable comment earlier, and the *Church Times* in 1876 noted that Keble was a 'gypsy college', because the suspicion which its founders entertained towards both the University and the Church had led them to provide for the institution to be moved elsewhere, should sufficient cause be given.

The Finances in the 1880s

1887–8 was Edward Talbot's last full year as Warden. It was also the last of Henry Wakeman's eight years as Bursar and tutor in history. Wakeman had become a fellow of All Souls in 1873 after gaining a first from Christ Church (Keble's first four Bursars had been undergraduates at Christ Church, as had Talbot). He returned to All Souls, aged 36, as Estates Bursar, in which post he remained until his death eleven years later.

Talbot and Wakeman were leaving behind a well established and financially sound college. Undergraduate numbers had stabilized around an average of 150, thereby ensuring full occupancy. Total income for that year amounted to £16,167 and a surplus of £964 was reported – a good year: the average profit margin achieved during the 1880s was five per cent. Terminal payments – the £27 fee paid each term by undergraduates to cover tuition, university dues, lodging and full board – accounted for 78 per cent of all income. Buttery sales contributed £2,520 (16 per cent) and college dues, paid by the Warden, Bursar and tutors, £724 (4.5 per cent). The sale of 'refuse and beer' to college servants added £229. There was no investment income, but the College earned £44 from the rent of a house in Blackhall Road, which it held on a long lease from St John's.

Foodstuffs and drink were the largest item of expenditure, amounting in total to £5,575. The salaries of the Warden, Bursar and seven tutors cost £4,145, and the wages of the servants £1,913. No provision was made for the payment of pensions: a fund for fellows was not started until 1894 and the first pension payment was made in 1906 (£300 per year to the Reverend Canon Spurling, who retired after 31 years as a tutor at the College). The College was heated by coal fires and lit with gas lamps. The coal bill was £628, added to which was a £76 bill for faggots (wood kindling) and a £36 payment to the chimney sweep, who had 364 chimneys to keep in good working order: he last appears as a separate item in the annual accounts for 1908, still being paid just £37 for the year. The gas bill was £148.

Wakeman's successors must have looked back on his term of office with something approaching envy. Just three years later, the College recorded a loss, the first in its history, of £175. This was not because of any exceptional items: rather it was the sum of several relatively small adverse changes. The obvious course was to raise the terminal payment, but the College Council was opposed to this both in principle, as it would 'discredit the calculation upon which the College was founded', and in practice, as it might deter applicants. Instead, the Council opted to impose, from October 1892, an entrance fee of £5 per undergraduate.

In 1886 the College had invested £114 in a stock of curtains, which it proceeded to hire to undergraduates at 3s. per term for window curtains and 1s.6d. for door curtains. Such was the demand for privacy and warmth, that a year later the stock had increased to £294. By 1896 the College was earning £122 per year from this trade, a return on investment so outrageous that even the finance committee felt moved to concede, in April of that year, that the rental charge might be reduced by a third, 'when the finances of the College make it advisable'.

Roger Boden

Living in the Lodgings

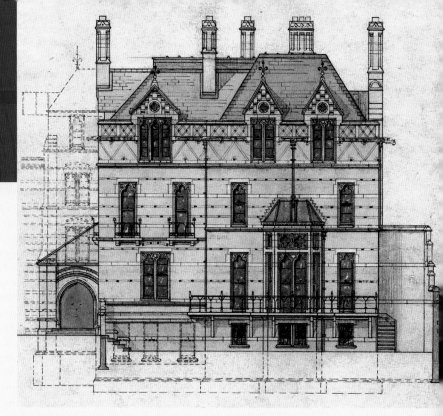

Butterfield's drawing for the garden elevation of the Warden's Lodgings.

Life as it was lived by the families in the Warden's Lodgings in the early days was recorded in the diaries, not only of Lavinia Talbot, but also of her eldest daughter Mary (May), and by Mildred Lock, the youngest of the five children of Walter Lock, who kept a family diary himself which passed eventually to his daughter Lucy. May Talbot, born in 1875 and the eldest of Edward and Lavinia Talbot's two daughters and five sons, kept a diary which continued until the Talbot family left for Leeds in 1888. Her husband became Dean of York and her son, Sir Edward Ford (1910–2006), was assistant private secretary to George VI and was the originator of the phrase 'annus horribilis', used by Queen Elizabeth II in a famous speech in 1992. May's diaries tell of the life of a Victorian child, with frequent references to 'Fraülein' (who was prone to bad headaches) and Miss Packer, who taught the girls 'awfully well' and was succeeded by Miss Powell, who explained the Reformation to them, including the power the Pope had over the kings of England before Henry VIII; May thought it was horribly cruel of Henry VIII to dissolve the good monasteries as well as the bad ones.

There were often theatricals. In June 1888, a musical performance of *Andromeda* was put on in the Hall, with the Honourable Mrs E. Lyttelton as Andromeda, Miss Hilda Wilson (whose voice was too loud for May's taste) as Cassiopeia and Mr Wright as Perseus. Mr Harper led the male chorus, who seem to have been singing the parts of the Queen's maidens. The quad was lit up for the occasion with Japanese lanterns and ices were served in the interval. The social life of Lodgings children included walks, picnics, social occasions with the undergraduates, visits to other colleges for concerts, lawn tennis, croquet, and cricket and riding for the boys. They went to watch the procession at Commemoration in June and to the Keble garden party, again with ices, and 'a great many children'. May's visit with Fraülein, at the end of June 1888, to Felstead House in Banbury Road, then a 'school for the middle class' and owned by the College since 2004, was occasioned because her mother was presenting the prizes to the pupils. A keen interest was taken in results, and joy felt when friends including Mr Wright and Mr Trench of Keble got firsts, but great disappointment that 'darling Mary' only had a second, though it was explained to May that 'brilliance' was needed as well as 'the actual facts'. The family also visited the Talbot and Gladstone houses at Falconhurst in Kent, a journey which involved changes at Didcot, Reading, Redhill and Hawarden. On the Falconhurst visit in the summer of 1888, a famous ladies' cricket match took place in which May played, and which was reported admiringly in the local press. But later that year Edward was appointed as vicar of Leeds. On 13 November, May went to Oxford station to see off Uncle William (Gladstone) and Aunt Pussy, remarking how jolly it was to see a great statesman like that, 'though I'm a Conservative', and the next day the Council chose the next Warden. May's comment was 'I *do* hope that he will be a good Warden to my darling College'.

When Mildred Lock (b. 1905) wrote her memories of her childhood in the Lodgings nearly twenty years later, she recorded that there were still ten servants working in the house. The rooms were heated by coal fires, for which the coal had to be carried up from the basement, replenished at regular intervals, and then cleaned out; this produced a great deal of dirt, and there were no modern cleaning appliances. All food was prepared in the basement kitchen and, if necessary, had to be carried up to the top floor where the children spent most of their time with their nurse or governess, only coming down to tea with their mother in the drawing room if she was neither out nor entertaining. Mildred recorded her mother's horror at learning, after the First World War, that one of the tutor's wives had no one to help her with her baby and enable her to carry out her duties in supporting her husband, and defended her own mother, saying that it would have been out of the question for her to give a tiny baby the attention it needed. Visits to the basement by the children were forbidden, except on Shrove Tuesday for pancake-making and on 'stir-up Sunday' to stir the Christmas puddings. However, an exception was made during the First World War, when all the household went down to the servants' hall after an air raid was announced. The Warden started praying and there was no raid either then or later. Mildred also tells of the electric lights, which were newly installed in 1910, and the words 'God save the King' in lights which the College electrician fixed up outside the Lodgings for the coronation of George V. Family plays in the Lodgings at Christmas, and the children playing outside in 'the Pit' were also features of this period, as was a coming-out party for Mildred's older sister May in 1912, with dancing in the drawing room of the Lodgings and 'gentleman's relish' sandwiches, much enjoyed by the younger children.

The Manuscripts

Keble Library contains about 90 manuscripts, some of them early modern. Unlike most college collections, Keble's is remarkably focused and is the product of a very brief period, about 30 years (1881–1911).

The collection focuses almost exclusively on what could broadly be described as 'liturgical books', and, most frequently, quite lovely ones with ornate, painted decoration. These were books used as the tools for divine service on a daily basis in the medieval church. Thus, the collection includes missals (with the daily order of the mass), breviaries (with the readings for the full Christian year) and lectionaries (groups of devotional readings for various occasions). The Keble collection is also rich in books of hours, the most common surviving medieval book; such volumes contain readings for individual private devotion laid out in a sequence, which corresponds to the daily monastic round of prayer.

The books speak to the same concern for revitalized devotion that guided the founders of the College, and communicate that same interest in a reformed and ornate devotion.

Above: Ms 49, f235v: Christ in majesty with all the saints

Below: Ms 47, f 9r: the Virgin and Child adored by a layman and a laywoman

All the books were donated to the College by early wellwishers and the majority of the books came from two sources. The largest group, 41 books in all, was donated by the Reverend Charles Edward Brooke (1847–1911), a noted 'Ritualist' vicar; he had been able to cream off the most relevant volumes from a collection formed by his brother, Sir Thomas Brooke, a noted Victorian book-collector. H .P. Liddon provided the second largest donation, some 26 volumes, in addition to a vast amount of non-manuscript material.

Among the College's relatively few books copied in England, Ms. 47 is perhaps the most important. This is a small and relatively unassuming book of hours, although with superior illustration. The heraldic swan on the shield of a Roman soldier associates the book with the distinguished group of late 14th-century illuminated books produced for the Bohun family at their castle at Pleshey in Essex.

Ms. 49 represents perhaps the College's greatest book treasure. Known as the Regensburg Lectionary, it was produced in south Germany in the late 13th century to provide devotional readings for a group of Dominican nuns. This glorious volume was designed to enhance reading with intense visual stimulation.

Another hyper-illustrated volume is Ms. 20. Vast numbers of late 13th-century Paris-produced bibles survive, but few can rival this one for the frequency and quality of the illustrations accompanying the sacred text.

One of the few text manuscripts in the Library is again a book produced in the late 13th century, in this case the basic primer for introductory theology students in a medieval university. Its author, Peter Lombard, attempted to offer a comprehensive guide to and resolution of all theological topics, the *Sentences* ('Opinions'), *c.* 1140. For several centuries, theologians took up his work as a set text and, to gain their degree, were required to write a critical commentary on it.

In addition to this impressive collection, the College has also been distinguished as a place where manuscripts are studied. Several early members have gone on to distinguished careers as manuscript scholars, for example Noel Denholm-Young (1923, History), T.A.M. Bishop (1926, Classics) and Alan J. Piper (1964, History). In addition, for 35 years the College was home to an international expert in the area, Malcolm B. Parkes (lecturer and fellow, 1961–97). Parkes's meticulous and detailed catalogue of the Keble manuscripts is exemplary, and various of his students, among them Vincent Gillespie (1970), Alastair Minnis (1971, visiting graduate student in English), and Jeremy Griffiths (supervised by Parkes in the 1980s) have, in their turn, become leaders in this field of study.

Ralph Hanna

Oxford House in Bethnal Green

Above: *Oxford House today*

Oxford House in Bethnal Green was the first 'settlement' to open in what used to be called the East End of London. Founded from Keble in 1884, it was built as a home for graduates, tutors and those intending to enter the Church. They could learn at first hand about the problems of disadvantaged areas and provide practical support for the local community, but most importantly, its purpose was to promote 'the preparation of character for ... the reception of the religion of Christ'.

The movement for founding Toynbee Hall, building on the work and ideas of Samuel and Henrietta Barnett, had already begun in 1884, but it seemed to Talbot and to those around him that the plan was not sufficiently religious in character, and Oxford House was seen explicitly as a church settlement, carrying the ideal of the Oxford Movement to a deprived area of London, and with an explicit attachment to a parish (St Andrew's, Bethnal Green).

Oxford House opened its doors on 8 September, in the old day-school of St Andrew's, with Talbot as chairman of the executive committee in Oxford. Early heads included the Reverend E.E. Jackson, the Honourable J.G. Adderley, the Reverend H. Hensley Henson and the Reverend A.F. Winnington-Ingram (later Bishop of London and a member of the Council of Keble), who stayed for nine years and was at the same time Rector of St Matthew's, Bethnal Green. W.J.H. Campion (tutor at Keble, 1882–92) was its Secretary in 1890–1.

The work focused from the first on clubs, lectures and instruction for men and boys. By 1892 there were 28 residents and workers, 22 of them from Oxford; in the 1890s, attendance on Sunday nights had reached over 200. An appeal for the new building was launched at a meeting held in the Mansion House in 1891, at which Henry Scott Holland made a witty speech, in which he claimed that the needs of east London were not the only social problem to be tackled: there was also the question of the 'surplus of educated gentlemen' who had nothing to do but fill up their time with horse-racing and so on. Accordingly, Toynbee Hall and Oxford House had been founded as 'labour refuges or shelters for congested gentlemen in the East End'. New buildings were inaugurated in 1892 and 1894 by the Duke of Connaught and the Duchess of Teck. The present-day Oxford House is a community and arts centre, which works in particular with youth programmes and with the local Somali community. It still occupies the same site and its former chapel bears brass plaques with names familiar from the early period of Keble's history.

The first decade saw Lavinia Talbot attending lectures for ladies in Oxford, together with other young University wives, and both she and Edward were enthusiastic about the cause of women's education, as were her father, Lord Lyttelton, and her uncle, Mr Gladstone (although it would not have occurred to them that ladies of her own social standing might have a serious academic education or go to university). Both Liddon and Pusey opposed the idea of women's halls at Oxford, but it was mainly due to Edward Talbot's initiative, in which he was supported by Lavinia, that Lady Margaret Hall opened in 1879, with nine students, as a definitely Church of England college for women. Edward and Lavinia had the idea of founding 'a Keble in this sort of Education' in April, 1878, while on a visit to Girton in Cambridge. By June, Edward had summoned a meeting at Keble attended by several University wives and by sympathizers, such as Henry Scott Holland. Both Edward and Lavinia were members of the committee set up to carry the project forward, which included another leading Tractarian and Oriel man, Edward King. The moves which resulted in the founding of Lady Margaret Hall quickly provoked others to set up Somerville, as a rival women's hall on secular principles. But a further venture was the founding of Selwyn College, Cambridge, Keble's sister college, though *The Times* of July 1878 noted that Selwyn 'would not be like Keble'. Selwyn opened in 1882 with Arthur Lyttelton, Lavinia's brother and fifth of the 'old eight' (the eight sons of George and Mary Lyttelton), a Keble tutor and later contributor to *Lux Mundi*, as its first Master. Appointed at only thirty, 'little pig Arthur' also acted as dean and tutor, and was a supporter of the Liberalism of his uncle, William Gladstone.

In the 1880s Keble was to the fore in the founding of an Oxford branch of the Church of England Purity Association, a kind of crusade designed to combat sexual licence. The moral and social dimensions of Oxford Tractarianism also found expression in the aim of bringing the message of High-Church religion to the poor in London's East End.

Walter Lock

Above: *Walter Lock, Warden, 1897–1920*

Top: *The Warden and tutors, 1888*

When Walter Lock retired from Keble in 1920, after 23 years as Warden, he was one of the longest-serving heads of house, and he could count 50 years of unbroken association with Keble College.

An undergraduate at Corpus and a fellow of Magdalen from 1869 (and, on ordination in 1873, tutor in theology until 1891), Lock became a tutor at Keble in 1870. From 1882 to 1897 he was Sub-Warden and, while Warden, from 1897 he was also Dean Ireland's Professor of the Exegesis of Holy Scripture. His retirement was prompted by his election in 1919 as Lady Margaret Professor of Divinity, a chair attached to Christ Church. This chair he resigned in 1927, aged 81. His publications on the New Testament are numerous, but it is through his contribution *to Lux Mundi* (1889) and his biography of John Keble (1892) that he found a wide readership.

It was not widely known that Lock's grandfather was a butcher, nor is it sufficiently known today that in the 1870s and 80s the reformed and renewed Oxford was acknowledged for its openness to talent, and its relative indifference to birth or status. Walter's father, Henry Lock, son of a Dorchester butcher, had become a solicitor in 1835. Henry had three sons, Walter being the second; he attended the school in Dorchester of the poet and scholar William Barnes and went on to Marlborough College and thence to Oxford.

At the age of 46, Walter made a socially advantageous and symbolically appropriate marriage. His wedding to Miss Jane Campion took place in September 1892, at Newick Park, near Lewes, the home of Jane's uncle. The Campions and the Heathcotes belonged to the landed gentry of Hampshire and Sussex: Sir William Heathcote (1801–81) had in his living the parish of Hursley, which in 1836 he offered to his former tutor at Oriel, John Keble. Thus, through his marriage, Walter Lock's association with Keble extended beyond the College founded in his memory to the rural world of Hursley. Just one month after the wedding, Walter completed his biography of Keble, published in 1892 in the centenary of Keble's birth.

Charles Lock (1974)

From early in 1884 there was talk of starting some kind of outpost there, and a meeting held in the hall was attended by Bishop Walsam How and the social reformer Octavia Hill. By St Mark's Day these ideas had become clearer, and former undergraduates were invited to help. Oxford House in Bethnal Green was founded from Keble later in the year 1884, a hair's breadth earlier than the more secular Toynbee Hall, founded from Balliol. Although the work of Oxford House included a boys' club, it did not represent muscular Christianity; rather, it gave an opportunity to high-minded young men from Keble to live in the East End while working in the civil service or the city, and at the same time leading a 'simple and religious life' and doing their best to alleviate the dreadful conditions they found around them. Oxford House opened in the disused school of St Andrew's Church, with a boys' club, a library, Sunday afternoon lectures and 'a chat and smoke' on Sunday evenings. As at Keble, when the main house opened in 1892, the conditions were fairly spartan, but the venture succeeded, forming the beginnings of the wider settlement movement. It is still functioning today, albeit without its high Victorian flavour.

Dr Pusey died in 1882, and the College received manuscripts of John Keble's sermons and other writings from his estate to add to John Keble's own library, which had formed the basis of the College's own collection. Pusey's memorial was the foundation of Pusey House in St Giles in 1884, in which Liddon and Earl Beauchamp were much involved, and whose first Principal was Charles Gore. Its library contains Pusey's own books.

Talbot's more liberal understanding of Christianity in comparison with the views of Pusey and Liddon was demonstrated in his participation, together with many others with a Keble connection, in the publication of *Lux Mundi*, a collection of essays edited in 1889 by Charles Gore.

The Servants in 1870

The College establishment at the opening was limited, just 12 men in all, though it was to expand rapidly in subsequent years. It may not have been easy to recruit suitable persons, in spite of the evident mobilization of the Keble network, as only the Steward, porter and head scout remained three years later. William Davies was dismissed after just a few months, having tried to commit suicide; in December 1871, Powell Washellier, the Polish bootman, was caught trying to steal a pair of boots and sentenced to 14 days' hard labour. The Steward clearly gave satisfaction, serving the College until 1883, by which time his salary had risen to £140 per year. One of the prototype loyal retainers was James Warrell who, at the age of 23, joined the staff in September 1871 as under-butler at £25 per year, rising to be 'common room man' at £80 per year. In 1914 he was superannuated at 20s per week, but kept on as Chapel attendant, finally being pensioned off in 1921.

All the servants were answerable to the Bursar, who exercised tight discipline. Being absent without leave or drunk on duty would be likely to lead to a suspension of 'leave out', the equivalent of gating. Tight though the Bursar's control was, when Shaw-Stewart left in 1880, no fewer than 80 turned up at a farewell party the College organized. The servants were quick to develop a collective identity, Lavinia Talbot recalling her amusement at the intercollegiate servants' sports teams. There was a servants' hall on the ground floor of the Clock Tower, and their dormitories were located on the top floor. In 1885 it was agreed that they could have a reading room.

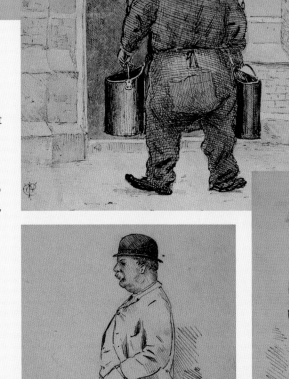

Caricatures of College servants from the JCR cartoon album: the coal carrier, porter and Steward

The original servants

Office	Name	Age at appointment	Terms	Previous employer	Testimonial from
Steward	Walter Gray	24	£50 per year with board	Station master with GNR	Mr Gamlen
Porter	William Green	48	£60 per year with board and lodgings	Staff Serjeant with Lancashire Militia	Colonel Legge
Cook	Alfred Church	29	£30 per year with board	Cook with Newport Market School	Shaw-Stewart
Head scout	Henry Tebby	21	£40 per year with board	Footman to Admiral Wellesley, Nova Scotia	Rev. N. Byron
Scout	Henry Denyer	19	£18 per year with board	Footman to J. Talbot, Esq. MP	Rev. E.S. Talbot
Scout	Richard Histed	18	£15 per year with board	Deputy Warehouseman at Clarendon Press	Mr T. Combe
Scout	William McLeod	17	£15 per year with board	Servitor	Shaw-Stewart
Scout	Harry Stringfellow	16	£15 per year with board	Page	Rev. Binney
Boots and coachman	Powell Washellier	43	2s. per day	Labourer	Rev. Robert Chamberlain
Waiter	Thomas Brooks	19	2s. per day	Servant	Mr Taylor, plumber in High Street
Scullery boy	John Gittons	13	Board and washing	Schoolboy	Shaw-Stewart
Assistant cook	William Davies	18	Board and washing	Usher to Mrs Rogers, Stevenage Park, Herts.	Mrs Rogers

Gore was also a fellow of Trinity, which had given Newman an honorary fellowship in 1878. The book went into ten British editions and several American ones in the first year, and was seen as a key attempt to bring together Christian faith and contemporary thought. Since 1875 Talbot had been a member of a group of more liberal churchmen led by Gore; other contributors from Keble included Walter Lock, who was then Sub-Warden, W.J.H. Campion, J.R. Illingworth and Aubrey Moore, all Keble tutors. Others included Henry Scott Holland, of Christ Church, who was well known to the Keble group, R.C. Moberley, Regius Professor and Canon of Christ Church, 1892–1903, and R.L. Ottley, tutor 1881–3, both of whom later became members of the Keble College Council. Campion also edited the *Economic Review*, the journal of the Christian Social Union, founded in 1889, and the same Christian social commitment also led him to become Secretary of Oxford House. *Lux Mundi* also demonstrated the practical dimension of later Tractarianism; its contributors saw that Darwinism was not necessarily in opposition to religion, but that it could be seen as reinforcing the Christian view of divine immanence, and indeed the contributors argued for a vigorous statement of credal orthodoxy. Nevertheless the book was highly controversial, not least because Gore's own essay seemed to question the divine inspiration of the Old Testament, and one of those who was deeply upset was Gore's patron, H.P. Liddon, who was still a member of the College Council. Liddon went on to the offensive, but the essayists were supported by Edward King, previously Principal of Cuddesdon Theological College, Canon of Christ Church and now Bishop of Lincoln, another member of the Council. Liddon died on 9 September, 1890; however, the controversy continued, and in the following year 38 Anglican clergy signed a declaration in opposition to *Lux Mundi*.

Above: *St Barnabas, Oxford*

Keble Advowsons

By the Second World War, Keble represented the most powerful concentration of 'Anglo-Catholic' patronage in private hands in the Church of England. Particularly in its earliest years, and again in the 1920s and 1930s, the College had been offered livings, usually by people who thought that the College would support the catholic tradition. In the earliest years, key Council members like Lord Beauchamp and Lord Halifax acted as brokers in the transfer of patronage to Keble. Beauchamp was behind the acquisition of St Barnabas in 1886; Halifax was probably responsible for the fateful appointment of his chaplain, Reverend H.H. Leeper, to St Stephen's, Devonport in 1902. Scarcely a meeting of the Council passed without advowsons business being on the agenda. Interestingly, the College Council was perhaps more moderate in its inclinations than the donors; as donor-patrons were sometimes more catholic in their views than the parishes, there were occasional tensions.

Sensitivities over Ritualism, however, meant that Keble was likely to be in the front line of attacks. In 1902–3 the College was subjected to withering criticism in the national press and in a pamphlet by H.V. Bowen, who visited 17 of the then 42 Keble parishes to identify their ritual abuses: H.H. Leeper's ministry in Plymouth was the spring-board for the attack. Bowen observed genuflection before the reserved sacrament, and noted an image of the Virgin and Child with a lamp burning before it, several crucifixes, and the stations of the cross. Bowen's account enumerates the ritual excess in shocked tones: 'After the sermon a hymn was sung, during which sixteen candles were lighted on the altar where the Sacrament is reserved, and the clergyman, who had retired to the vestry, reappeared wearing a gold-coloured cope, and attended by the thurifer with the censer, two acolytes, each carrying a lighted candle, and one or two others, all of whom wore red cassocks and cottas. They all knelt in a group before the altar, and the clergyman drew back to the curtains of the tabernacle. Incense was then lighted, and the clergyman censed the Reserved Sacrament, and verses of a hymn were sung, the curtains still being drawn back, and incense being burnt meanwhile. Some verses of another hymn were sung, and finally the curtains of the tabernacle were drawn to again, and the ceremony concluded, the clergyman, his

Above: *All Saints, Bookham*

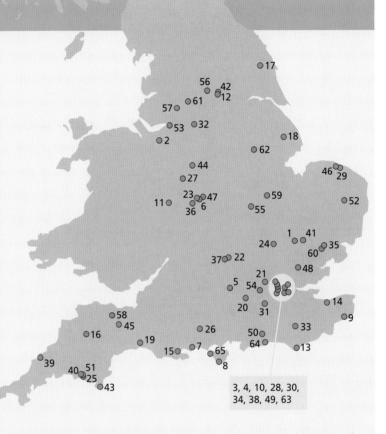

3, 4, 10, 28, 30,
34, 38, 49, 63

attendants, and the choir genuflecting as they left the chancel'. To the blistering attack on the College's patronage in *The Times*, Warden Lock had to reply that many of the clergy identified had not actually been presented by the College, which in some cases had only recently acquired the patronage. But controversy did not go away. In 1906, 27 of the College's 43 livings were informed against to the Royal Commission on Ecclesiastical Discipline, and they included no fewer than 16 former College members; an interesting demonstration of the way the patronage was used to promote the careers of alumni.

In respecting the wishes of the Anglo-Catholic donors, the College might find itself out of step with local sensibilities. C.F. Blood, appointed in 1935 to Chale on the Isle of Wight, described his parishioners who, by and large, rejected his ministrations as being 'descended from smugglers and [having] no sense of honour'. In 1940 the Archbishop of Canterbury wrote to complain about the quality of those appointed to livings in Dover and Folkestone. To be fair to the College as patron, Warden Kidd had already tried to move the absentee priest in Folkestone, and Lord Hugh Cecil (later Baron Quickswood), after visiting in 1928, made it clear that he had no sympathy for this

species of extreme Anglo-Catholicism: 'Services with an elaborate ceremonial are not successful in drawing congregations …. The anglo-catholic movement is suffering from diseases which are quite different from those of which it is often suspected … the diseases are liturgiology and music. Clergymen and organists seem to have lost the old ritualist tradition of doing good to the people, and they have substituted what is really I think the spirit of artistic connoisseurship … I often feel that the Church of England needs more vulgarity'.

1. Arkesden [and Wicken Bonhunt], Essex	18. Fulletby, Lincolnshire
2. Ashton Hayes, Cheshire	19. Hawkchurch, Devon
3. Balham, London	20. Hawley, Hampshire
4. Beckenham, Kent	21. Hayes, Middlesex
5. Beenham Valence, Berkshire	22. Headington, Oxford
6. Bordesley, Birmingham	23. Highgate, Birmingham
7. Bournemouth, Dorset	24. Hitchin, Hertfordshire
8. Chale, Isle of Wight	25. Hooe, Devon
9. Charlton-on-Dover, Kent	26. Hyde, Hampshire
10. Chislehurst, Kent	27. Lapley, Staffordshire
11. Cleobury Mortimer, Worcestershire	28. Lavender Hill, London
12. Cross Green, Leeds	29. Letheringsett [and Cley, Wiveton and Glandford], Norfolk
13. Eastbourne, East Sussex	30. Lewisham, London
14. Eastchurch, Isle of Sheppey, Kent	31. Little Bookham, Surrey
15. East Stoke, Dorset	32. Low Marple, Greater Manchester
16. Exbourne, Devon	33. Mayfield, East Sussex
17. Foxholes [and Butterwick], Yorkshire	

34. Mitcham, Surrey	51. Sutton on Plym, Plymouth, Devon
35. Mount Bures, Essex	52. Tacolneston, Norfolk
36. Northfield, Birmingham	53. Thelwall, Cheshire
37. Jericho, Oxford	54. Thorpe, Surrey
38. Paddington, London	55. Thorpe Malsor, Northamptonshire
39. Petroc Minor, Cornwall	56. Toller Lane, Bradford
40. Plymouth, Devon	57. Tonge Moor, Bolton
41. Radwinter, Essex	58. Upton, Somerset
42. Richmond Hill, Leeds	59. Water Newton, Cambridgeshire
43. Salcombe, Devon	60. White Colne, Essex
44. Salt, Staffordshire	61. Whitworth, Lancashire
45. Sampford Peverell, Devon	62. Winthorpe, Nottinghamshire
46. Saxlingham, Norfolk	63. Woolwich, London
47. Shard End, Birmingham	64. Worthing, West Sussex
48. Shelley, Essex	65. Yarmouth, Isle of Wight
49. South Kensington, London	
50. Storrington, West Sussex	

The Light of the World

Holman Hunt's controversial painting *The Light of the World* (1853) was bought from Hunt for 400 guineas by Thomas Combe, a major patron of the pre-Raphaelites, and exhibited in London in 1854. Early in 1873 it was given to Keble by his widow, Mrs Martha Combe, together with another Holman Hunt painting of 'an early British martyrdom', with the condition that both should be placed in the 'new chapel' as soon as it was ready. She was also willing to give the College a bust of John Henry Newman, with the intention that it be placed in the new College Library; this bust was actually given in 1890 and reached the College only after her death. Mrs Combe's condition attached to *The Light of the World* was accepted in March 1873.

When the picture had first been exhibited it provoked public comment and, indeed, hostility among many, including Thomas Carlyle. In May 1854, when it was exhibited at the Royal Academy, Ruskin defended it in a letter to *The Times*. In *Modern Painters* he wrote that it was 'the most perfect instance of expressional purpose with technical power, which the world has yet produced'. Many saw it as too Protestant, or as 'Roman'. When Butterfield learned of the condition attached to Mrs Combe's gift, he objected strongly to having it anywhere in the Chapel, and the Warden and Council were obliged to backtrack. William Gibbs thought the painting beautiful, but as a result of Butterfield's opposition it was placed in the Library, where it remained for nearly two decades.

The painting's fame was such that arrangements had to be made for people to visit the College to see it in the Library, which was otherwise only open to the tutors. By 1885, when Holman Hunt asked for it to be sent to his studio in London, word had got out that its condition was such that it was in need of repair, which the artist offered to carry out at his own expense. The Council agreed to permit Holman Hunt to have it photographed, but reserved to itself the right of deciding any future requests for photography. In the light of criticism that its position in the Library was dangerously near the hot-water pipes, Liddon proposed that the Council place on record the fact that its position had been decided on the basis of advice from Holman Hunt himself. Working with Holman Hunt, Frederick G. Stephens had made an early copy (1851–56), which is now in the Manchester City Art Gallery, and in 1900–4, with substantial help from his assistants since his eyesight was by now failing, Hunt drew on the help of Edward R. Hughes to make the much larger copy which is now in St Paul's Cathedral. When the St Paul's version was exhibited, the Bursar of Keble objected to Hunt's account of the College's behaviour, and in 1904 there was an exchange of letters in *The Times* on the matter between Hunt and Walter Lock, then Warden. The St Paul's version toured the English-speaking world from 1905–7, attracting huge and unprecedented crowds and attaining the status of a 'Protestant icon'. There was substance, however, to Hunt's complaints of hostility to his

Above: The Light of the World, *Holman Hunt, 1851–3*

original painting from the 'bigoted Goths' of Keble College, whose second Warden, Robert Wilson, dismissed with some scorn a request to allow it to be shown in the Guildhall Art Gallery.

Proposals for creating a side chapel were discussed on St Mark's Day, 1890. Over Butterfield's objections, the Warden and Council proposed that the organ be raised in the long vacation of 1891. The new Chapel would be a memorial to H.P. Liddon (d. 9 September, 1890), and would

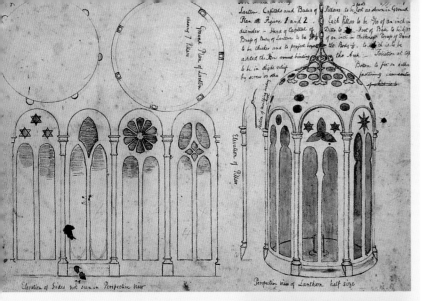

Above: *Original drawing for the lamp in* The Light of the World

Right: *The lamp which Hunt had made when painting* The Light of the World *(now in Manchester City Art Gallery)*

Below: *William Holman Hunt*

Above: *R.J. Wilson, Warden, 1888–97*

Below: *Cartoon of Talbot on resignation from the Wardenship to become vicar of Leeds, 1888*

house *The Light of the World*, which, in any case, had to be removed from the Library in order to make room for the books which Liddon had left to Keble. An appeal would be made, and initial work on the chapel was put in hand by the architect J.T. Micklethwaite; the cost was modest, but even then there was an overspend. Mrs Combe died on 27 December, 1893, leaving £3,000 to general endowment and £1,500 towards the cost of 'removing and replacing in a better position ... Holman Hunt's great Picture known as "The Light of the World"'. Mrs Combe was willing for the legacy to be used towards the completion of the Liddon chapel. Micklethwaite described his new housing of the picture as a 'shrine'; and defended his design, saying that, had he been asked, he could have designed a canopy, and that 'what we have done looks like a cupboard because it is a cupboard'. More elaborate plans for the chapel were drawn up in 1894 at a cost of £1,173.16s. 5d, and by October that year the screen had been completed, and work done on the organ loft so that the organist could sit on the north side of the organ. It was also agreed that there should be a protrusion in the new gallery over the stalls to house the organist. *The Light of the World* has been in the side chapel (which was not, in the end, named after Liddon) ever since.

Whatever its theological weaknesses, some of which were pointed out by Archbishop Michael Ramsay in his book *An Era in Anglican Theology: From Gore to Temple* (1960), with its powerful emphasis on the centrality of the Incarnation the collection was a landmark in the history of 19th-century Anglicanism.

In 1888 Talbot left Keble to become vicar and rural dean of Leeds, and later became Bishop successively of Rochester in 1895, Southwark in 1905 and Winchester in 1911. The children hated the idea of leaving their 'beloved Keble', where they had spent all their lives so far. The thirteen-year-old May Talbot was very miserable at the news, but consoled herself with the idea of the great work to which God had called her father. However, she could hardly concentrate on her lessons with Miss Powell and Fraülein, and wrote that her eyes were red from crying. The last day came on 20 December 1888, and as May waited for the carriage to come, she reflected that she did not know how much she loved Keble, and the 'dear old house' where she had been so happy, until she knew she had to leave it. Talbot was succeeded by the Reverend Robert Wilson (1888–97), a Mertonian classicist who had been an assistant master at Radley and Marlborough, fellow and tutor of Merton, and subsequently vicar of Wolvercote and Warden of Radley.

The Arms of Keble College

The College bears as its Arms of Community the arms of Sir Henry Keble, Lord Mayor of London in 1510, which are *argent a chevron engrailed gules on a chief azure three mullets or*. How did it come to adopt them?

As final preparations for the opening of the College were made in the summer of 1870, it was suggested that the new foundation should adopt as its coat of arms those borne by John Keble. The original idea was to mark each piece of plate or crockery with the new arms, but the cost proved too high. In the end they settled for putting 'KC' on everything. However, the idea of the College bearing arms proved tempting, and so Tom Keble was asked for his ideas.

John's nephew confessed that there was some confusion over the family arms. His uncle had believed that the family arms were *vert a chevron engrailed or on a chief of the second three mullets of the first*, so that the colours were a simple green and yellow. Tom agreed with these arms, except that he had believed that the arms were *azure* and not *vert*. Believing that the family were descended from Sir Henry, he asked the College of Heralds for clarification. The Windsor Herald confirmed Sir Henry's arms to be those that are now used by the College, with the proviso that Tom had to prove his connection or descent from the Lord Mayor before the College should use them. There is no record that this descent was ever proved.

It is difficult to be certain when the College took up its arms, as examples from the early 1870s are represented in simple single colour prints; for instance, the first stamps are in various shades of blue. The earliest dated example of the current arms is on a cartoon of the Warden dated 1878. It all suggests that the College decided, without the approval of the Court of Heralds, to adopt the arms as we see them today.

There is one other example of Keble arms, which John Keble himself would have known. In the parish church of Southrop in Gloucestershire there is a memorial tablet to Thomas Keble erected in 1670. This Keble was an ancestor of our Kebles, and John must have seen these arms every time he took services as the curate of Southrop in the 1820s. Its colours? *Or a chevron engrailed gules on a chief sable three mullets of the first.*

Is it too late to change?

Robert Petre

Wilson later collaborated with two others to complete and publish Liddon's unfinished *Life of Edward Bouverie Pusey* (1893–7). Other traditions continued, in particular the celebration of St Mark's day; in 1892 Lock, then tutor and Sub-Warden, preached in the Chapel on the eve of St Mark's day, not only in commemoration of John Keble but also to mark the recent death of W.J.H. Campion. He was to marry Miss Jane Campion on 28 September of the same year.

The College was by now settled on its course. Judging by schools of origin, Keble's undergraduates were drawn from very much the same backgrounds as those of the older colleges, though skewed somewhat towards the 'fringe' public schools rather than the first division. In the academic years 1895–8, a total of 2,523 students matriculated at Oxford, of which 177 (7 per cent) came to Keble, which by then had the third largest undergraduate population. 45 per cent of the University's matriculands came from the top 22 public schools, compared with 35 per cent of Keble's. Adding the next 28 public schools, the balance shifts: the top 50 public schools provided 57 per cent of Oxford's intake and 55 per cent of Keble's. The next tier, the 54 'fringe' public schools, provided 12 per cent of Oxford's intake and 19 per cent of Keble's.

School origins of Keble students, 1895–8

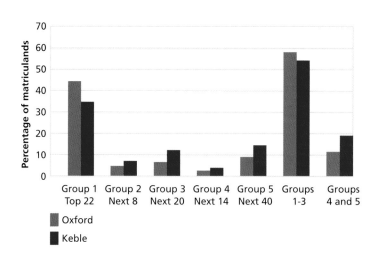

Financial Crises: Challenges and Responses, 1890–1914

The College faced near-disaster in the mid-1890s. In 1875, trustees acting on behalf of Mrs Talbot had granted a mortgage of £4,000 to the College to fund the construction of the Warden's Lodgings, interest being fixed at 4 per cent. In November 1894, the College received a £3,000 legacy from the estate of Mrs Martha Combe (the donor of *The Light of the World*) and felt able to pay off the mortgage. There was, however, a year's delay as Talbot could not find the mortgage deed and an indemnity had to be drafted. Meanwhile the Bursar, Major J.P.E. Jervoise (Eton and the King's Own Hussars) had invested the funds earmarked for the repayment of the mortgage in India 3-per-cent stock. He suggested that the mortgage be redeemed by a transfer of this stock, but Talbot's solicitors preferred cash. So when, in November 1895, the indemnity was delivered, Jervoise gave the College's stockbrokers, Messrs Tatham & Co, a power of attorney to sell sufficient of the stock to realize £3,600, the College having the balance in cash. Tathams forwarded a sale note on 27 November, but said the sale was for settlement on 30 December, and that payment would be remitted that day. The draft never came. On 10 January Tathams' affairs were placed in the hands of the Official Receiver. Almost all the £3,600 was lost: the accounts for 1897 record a dividend on Tatham's estate of just £31.

In response to this disaster, Talbot and his wife offered to cancel the mortgage. Council felt that, as trustees, they could not refuse the offer, but felt they could accept only on the basis that the College shared the loss equally with them. It took until 1901 for the College's share of the loss to be made good. Meanwhile, the hapless Jervoise received a stern rebuke from Warden Wilson, questioning the advisability of the Bursar's making investments independently of the finance committee. But the implied culpability was misplaced, as the loss had arisen, not from the investment, but from the failure of Tathams, who had been brokers to the College for 20 years.

Although there were modest capital projects, such as the creation of the side chapel to accommodate *The Light of the World*, new rooms on the west side of Pusey Quad, completed in 1901, and the provision of electricity and telephones in 1909–10, these improvements were accompanied by continuing parsimony in day-to-day matters. Although the income from curtain rentals had been reduced, it was offset in 1909 by the introduction of storage charges for bicycles. Nor were tutors immune from financial stringency. In 1898 it was revealed that William Hatchett Jackson, tutor in natural science, was paying University fees for his students, 'sometimes in excess of £100 a year', out of his own salary of £300 per year, but the Council was only willing to reimburse up to £25 per term.

In 1907, Jervoise was succeeded as Bursar by Francis Champernowne, a Keble graduate (1884), a barrister and expert in trust law, who had been Treasurer of Oxford House in Bethnal Green since 1888. Having mastered his new brief he prepared, in June 1910, a comprehensive report on the College's financial position. The good news was that 'The cost of the food of each undergraduate per day has been reduced this year to 1s 10d as compared with 2s 6d three years ago, representing a saving of about £800 per annum.' This enabled him to estimate that in a normal year the College 'should shew a surplus of £450'. But he pointed out that this was a very small margin on which to rely, and the lack of endowments made it difficult to compete with those colleges which were able to subsidize living costs. More positively, he sees no serious threat from salary and wage pressures, and estimates that capital expenditures (including the re-pointing of brickwork, repairs to stone-work, the installation of baths and the replacement of earth closets with water closets) can be accommodated within his budget projections. But pensions are a looming issue, and Champernowne recommends that the College should double (to £200) its annual contribution to the tutors' pension scheme, and institute a servants' pension scheme with a College contribution of £100 annually.

Champernowne's analysis proved accurate. In the following two years a full complement of undergraduates generated healthy operating surpluses. A reduced intake in 1912–13 and 1913–14 turned this into a small loss, but this was to be rendered invisible by the sea of red ink that followed.

Roger Boden

Below: *The summary accounts for 1906–7*

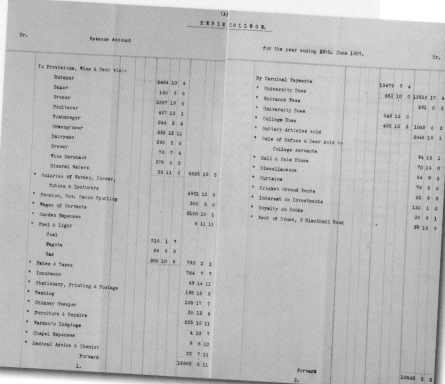

The College Silver

By comparison with some other colleges, Keble is not very rich in silver, but it does possess some items with strong associations with John Keble. When Keble left Oriel, his pupils subscribed to a present of a silver candelabrum, a large silver salver, a tea pot and a coffee pot, all from the workshops of the noted silversmith Paul Storr (1770–1844). It is not clear how they reached the College, but they are recorded in the inventory of 1870. The Paul Storr collection was augmented in 1935, when a Miss Nora Davison gave a candelabrum, entrée dishes, and other pieces that had been presented by undergraduates to her grandfather, the Reverend John Davison, a contemporary of Keble at Oriel. And it was to Storr's work that the retiring Council turned in 1952, when it donated a gilt and silver cup and cover.

Although not matching the Storr pieces in quality, a series of significant gifts by H.O. Roberts (1909) have enriched the collection. In 1924 he gave a cup mounted on three ball-and-claw legs, with emblems of the rose, shamrock, thistle and fleur de lis, which might suggest a Jacobite provenance. In 1960 Roberts gave a silver milk jug,

a replica of a 1742 design, commemorating his 50 years' association with the College. When Leonard Rice-Oxley, a great friend of Roberts, died, his colleagues subscribed to the matching coffee pot still in regular use in the senior common room.

Several pieces have been donated by fellows on their retirement or departure, including a candle-snuffer donated by E.M. Hugh Jones, an 1854 claret jug given by J.S. Bromley, and a pair of candlesticks made by Anthony Hawksley (1967), given by Basil Mitchell. A surprise gift in 1973 was the bequest of over 60 items, mainly of eighteenth- and early nineteenth-century silver from Reverend F.E.P.S. Langton, a St John's, Cambridge man, who had no prior connection with the College.

Above and left: *Silver by Paul Storr, including John Keble's candelabrum*

Right: *Claret jug by Omar Ramsden*

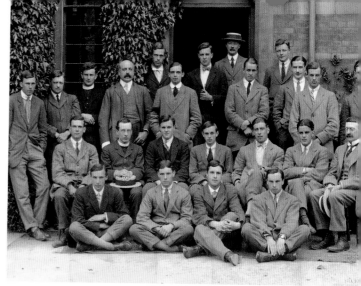

It was Edward Talbot who had had to deal with the arguments between members of the College Council and the architect about the Chapel, and who, having accepted the gift of *The Light of the World* in 1873 on the understanding that it would be hung in the new Chapel, submitted to Butterfield's refusal to have it put there. An unsatisfactory alternative was adopted whereby the painting was placed in the Library when it opened in 1878. By the mid 1880s it had become clear that some other solution would have to be found, and the College's association with Butterfield was broken when he objected vigorously, in 1890, to the idea of altering the Chapel with the aim of housing the picture and commemorating H.P. Liddon. Talbot had by now moved on and his successor was left to manage this awkward situation.

The College also received other donations from its supporters. Its important collection of manuscripts derives largely from H.P. Liddon, many of whose books are also in the Library, and from the gift of Canon Brooke (d. 1911). The Library contains many of John Keble's own books, and other Oxford Movement material, and even before the installation of the first Warden, the College had been offered advowsons (with the right to appoint incumbents) of Church of England parishes, and it also began to inherit them through bequests. This often gave rise to legal and other costs, and the Council did not always agree to receive such gifts. Eventually the total was to reach 67, the largest number held by any other Oxford college except Christ Church. While the College was founded with no endowment, and indeed without sufficient funds to carry out more than a limited part of Butterfield's grand design, it also began to acquire trust funds with the explicit purpose of supporting parishes or assisting ordinands, and thereby helping to ensure the High Church ideals of its founders.

Finance continued to be a problem, but through the long service of Walter Lock as tutor, Sub-Warden and Warden, the College enjoyed an extraordinary degree of continuity in its early period. It also kept its connections with the upper echelons of the Church, and several of its early tutors went on to become bishops. J.G. Mylne, tutor 1870–6, left to become Bishop of Bombay, to the excitement of the Talbots; F.J. Jayne, tutor 1871–9, eventually became Bishop of Chester, and Arthur Lyttelton Bishop of Southampton. R.L. Ottley became vice-principal of Cuddesdon Theological College and the second Principal of Pusey House. Others were equally distinguished: J.R. Illingworth, tutor 1872–83, later gave the Bampton lectures and was the author of many books; Arthur Acland, lecturer and tutor, 1871–5, was a member of Gladstone's fourth cabinet and a privy councillor; Aubrey Moore, tutor and dean, 1881–93, contributed to *Lux Mundi* and was the author of theological books and sermons. The inter-connection between the College and the theological life of the University was strong; Walter Lock himself held the post of Dean Ireland's Professor, 1895–1919, simultaneously with his position at Keble. But across the University there was change, as the number of Catholics and nonconformists grew. Pusey died in 1882, the same year as the new University Statutes were introduced, which drastically reduced the number of clerical fellowships. The era which had seen Keble's foundation and formed the context of its early years was over.

Thirty Keble men served in the Boer War of 1899–1902, of whom three were killed and one received the VC. He was C.H. Mullins (1888), a Johannesburg solicitor who was imprisoned after the Jameson Raid. A major in the Imperial Light Horse in 1899, he gallantly rallied his men and rushed forward under heavy fire at Elandslaagte on 21 October, and was paralysed below the spine.

Above left: *First VIII, 1914*

Above: *Essay Club, 1914*

Below: *John Tracy, Tutor 1887–1915, with Edwin Hughes (1902, Classical Exhibitioner), 1903*

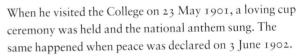

When he visited the College on 23 May 1901, a loving cup ceremony was held and the national anthem sung. The same happened when peace was declared on 3 June 1902.

The company of volunteers which the College had raised was sustained after the war by the enthusiasm of Nugent Hicks, tutor in classics 1897–1909, later Bishop of Gibraltar and then of Lincoln, a member of Council and an honorary fellow, and known to the undergraduates as 'Bumbo' Hicks. It was absorbed into the OTC (Officer Training Corps) in September 1908, and in 1914 there were 133 members of the College fully trained, now under Captain (later Lieutenant Colonel) F.W. Matheson, tutor in theology 1909–21, Bursar in 1921 and later a member of Council and Dean of Carlisle. When the Vice-Chancellor in 1914 drew up a list of men to be recommended for direct commissions, Keble headed the list.

Ralph Kite came up in 1913, the son of Bertie Kite, who had come up to Keble in 1876 and went on to be Dean of Hobart, Tasmania. The College already had electric lighting, with economical 'Keble sockets', but 'practically nothing' was supplied. When he and a friend went to visit someone at Bloxham they rode the 20 miles. In Hilary Term 1914, two Keble men, Ernest Gore (1910) and Edward Talbot (1912) ran a mission lasting a week. But out of the Keble rugby team, which put up a fine performance against University College in the inter-collegiate final played on March 11, seven fell during the First World War, and six from the University side.

Keble in the First World War

Above: *Officers Cadet Battalion officers, 1917*

Below: *Keble freshmen, 1914*

The effect of the mobilization for world war was a radical reduction in the College's income, as student numbers fell dramatically; the income from the billeting of officers and cadets for training did little to offset the losses due to the war, which were estimated at about £17,000. Economies were made to make ends meet: in 1914 the dons had agreed to a cut in salaries by one fifth; the Bursar's plans for more bathrooms were shelved; repairs to the organ were postponed. Several of the academics took up varieties of war service. Billy Reade superintended Red Cross work in Egypt; 'Crab' Owen worked in the Admiralty; the theologian Kenneth Kirk served as an army chaplain. The recently graduated Lieutenant L. Rice-Oxley helped to train the cadets in College, and published *Oxford in Arms*, with an account of the College. The Pusey lecture room was lent for lectures to Belgian refugees in 1915, while a portion of the Fellows' Garden was handed over to pigsties for the war effort.

The human cost was devastating: 966 Keble men served in the war; 172 were killed (17.81 per cent: the University average was 18.36 per cent). 2nd Lieutenant B.H. Geary was awarded the Victoria Cross for his bravery on Hill 60 near Ypres, defending a crater against repeated bombardment on 20–21 April 1915. Although severely wounded, he survived. Another 14 were awarded the Distinguished Service Order, and 76 the Military Cross. Keble's participation rate in the services was relatively high because of the popularity of the cadet forces on the eve of war.

It was agreed, even during hostilities, that some memorial to the sacrifice of Keble men should be established, and a war memorial and endowment fund was established in August 1917, helped early on by the collection of £1,000 in the USA with the energetic support of Frederick Kinsman, Bishop of Delaware. The first American gift came from Katherine Buckley of Philadelphia, who donated $5 'as a small thank offering for the life of Blessed John Keble and beloved of memory in America. I wish my mite could be $500 and that would in no wise express my thankfulness for the upbringing I have had in the knowledge and possession of some of his writings'. By 1919 the fund already stood at £8,804. Various proposals for an appropriate memorial, including a stone cross in the centre of Liddon quad, were considered before determining on the war memorial chapel at the west door of the Chapel. The memorial was dedicated by Edward Talbot, now Bishop of Winchester, at a meeting of the Keble Association on 27 June 1922.

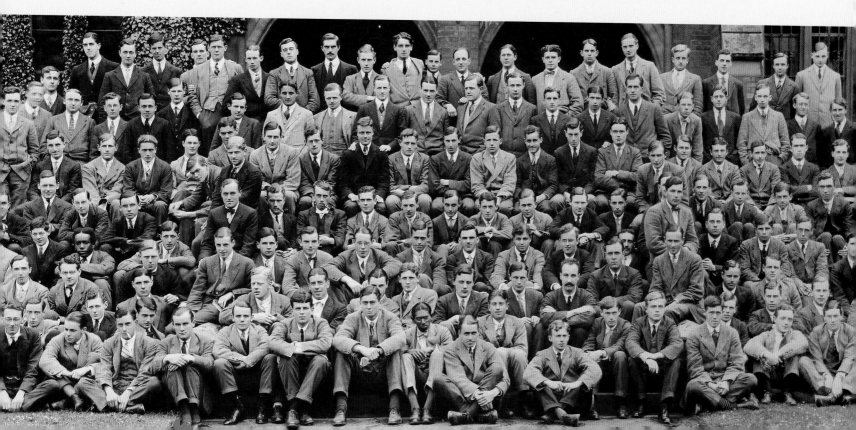

3 THE DEVELOPMENT OF THE COLLEGE

Walter Lock held the Wardenship through the First World War and until 1920, when he was succeeded by Beresford Kidd (1864–1948), who had read Greats and theology at Keble, achieving a first in the latter in 1887. Kidd was Warden from 1920 until 1939 and he was also a distinguished ecclesiastical historian; his collections of primary documents relating to the continental Reformation and the history of the Church from the beginning up to AD 1500, and his three-volume history of the Church up to AD 461 (1922) remained standard works for decades. The College Council remained powerful. It met three times a year, on or near St Mark's Day and at the beginning of the other two terms, and while the Warden had authority over the staff and the buildings, and control of the College as a religious and educational body, he could not independently institute any changes involving additional expense. The 1898 Statutes allowed for a consultative body consisting of the tutors and such lecturers as the Warden chose to select, but the latter was above all to retain 'in his own hands the control and direction of the religious training of the College and of the services and religious instruction given in the College Chapel', and to deal personally with all serious matters of discipline and government. The Warden appointed tutors and lecturers, subject to the Council's ensuring that they were sufficient in number to maintain the Chapel services and that enough of them were resident in College to fulfil its needs. The Warden and Council fixed their salaries, as well as those of other officers, in consultation with the finance committee, a sub-committee of the Council. It was established that the Warden was entitled to the use of the Lodgings free of rent, rates, taxes and repair costs.

Above: *Beresford Kidd, Warden 1920–39*

Right: *Ironwork at the top of the Hall stairs*

The College Council in 1918

Arthur Winnington-Ingram, Bishop of London

The Council of 1918 comprised 12 members, six laymen and six ordained persons, by and large sharing Anglo-Catholic convictions. The most distinguished clerics were Vincent Coles, former Principal of Pusey House, Arthur Winnington-Ingram, graduate of the College, and Bishop of London (1901–39), and Edward Talbot, the first Warden and now Bishop of Winchester (1911–23). The lay members were equally distinguished, including George Talbot, a prominent barrister, Vicary Gibbs, a partner in the family firm of merchant bankers and the owner of renowned botanical gardens at Aldenham in Hertfordshire, and George Russell from the distinguished whig family, who had retired from politics in 1895 to become an enthusiastic promoter of purity movements and a committed social activist.

Charles Wood, second Viscount Halifax, was in 1918 the longest serving member of the Council, to which he had been appointed in 1880 (he would retire the following year at the age of 80). Halifax, a former groom of the Prince of Wales' bedchamber, was an activist in Church politics and president of the English Church Union from 1868 until 1919, in which role he pursued Pusey's ecumenical vision of corporate reunion with Rome.

Hugh Richard Heathcote Gascoyne-Cecil, later Baron Quickswood, had joined the Council in 1898. He was the youngest son of the third Marquis of Salisbury, serving an apprenticeship as personal secretary to his father when he combined the roles of Foreign Secretary and Prime Minister. As MP for Oxford (1910–37), he earned a reputation as an accomplished orator, Lord Curzon remarking that his words 'combined the charm of music with the rapture of the seer'. But the strength of his convictions sometimes made him a difficult man to deal with. He remained on the Council until it was dissolved in 1952, and he had not been an enthusiast for the reform, fighting a strong rearguard action.

Anglo-Catholic sympathies provided an important bond between these men. Vincent Coles and Viscount Halifax, for example, both counted Liddon among their closest friends. But family connections were also important. George Talbot was the first Warden's nephew; Vicary Gibbs was the third son of Henry Hucks Gibbs, who had himself served on the Council 1873–1907; Viscount Halifax was succeeded on the Council by his son, the future Viceroy of India and Foreign Secretary; also joining that year was Sam Hoare, Conservative MP, who had married Lady Maud Lygon, daughter of the sixth Earl Beauchamp.

Charles Wood, second Viscount Halifax

Hugh Richard Heathcote Gascoyne-Cecil, Lord Quickswood

The finance committee's agreement was required for any expenditure proposed by the Bursar on fabric or property over the sum of £25 and it was required to audit the termly accounts and to present an annual financial return, for which it was enjoined to employ a professional auditor at an annual cost not exceeding 30 guineas. There was also a pension fund for the tutors, into which the College would contribute up to £100 per year. The 1899 by-laws concluded by laying down a list of precedence for the entire College, from the Warden down to the least senior undergraduate.

The Great War had an immediate impact on Keble's finances. Numbers plummeted. The Michaelmas intake in 1914 was down to 42 (from 57 in 1913) and many of these men had left for the army within a term or two. Twenty-four matriculated in 1915–16, 10 in 1916–17 and 15 in

1917–18. By the end of the war, a revenue surplus of £4,995, patiently accumulated over 44 years, had been turned into a deficit of £10,347. It was to take the College a further three years to return to break even, by which time the accumulated deficit had climbed to £24,000.

Peace brought a flood of new matriculands: 38 in Hilary 1919, 43 in Trinity and 96 in Michaelmas. The surplus of students necessitated the building of 'hutments' in the fellows' garden, at a cost of about £1,000. By Michaelmas 1920, the new intake was down to 60 and thereafter stabilized at 57. But undergraduate numbers alone could not restore the College's finances. The cost of living had doubled during the war. Bursar Champernowne addressed himself to the task of putting the College's finances in order, and in March 1920 submitted his assessment of the situation in a memorandum to Council, estimating that, compared with 1913–14, costs other than salaries had risen by about £9,000. The Council eventually – and quite bravely – settled on a figure of £50 per term with a remission of £10 'for sons of necessitous clergy'. This rate was reviewed in 1927 and found to be 'substantially lower than the average cost elsewhere'.

Champernowne also reviewed the salaries. The Warden's salary had been fixed in the by-laws at £1,000, 'reducible when other emolument amounting to £500 or more are receivable'. This was confirmed as Warden Kidd's commencing salary when he took office in 1920. Salaries of the tutors were dependent on length of service, starting at £250 per year for the first three years of service, and rising in steps to £500 per year after 19 years of service. Given the war's inflation, the Bursar proposed either a 20 per cent increase plus £50, or a 10 per cent increase plus £100. Fund-raising offered little salvation. The Memorial Appeal launched in 1917 was struggling. The target was £100,000, but by March 1920 only £10,500 had been given or promised, four-fifths of it from old members. Champernowne suggested that 'it is desirable if possible that the services of someone of experience in raising money and in dealing with the press should be secured', but this does not seem to have been acted upon.

Champernowne's 1920 memorandum reads like the work of a man exhausted by the unequal struggle to balance the books. Whatever the reason, he died the following year at the age of 55. *The Clock Tower* summed up his contribution to the College: 'His power of grasping problems as a whole, and, above all, his art of endearing himself without effort to all kinds of men breathed new life into the old routine of office-work.'

Above: *The Clock Tower, Jubilee edition, 1920*

The Oxford and Cambridge Act of 1923 necessitated further changes to the Statutes by the University Commissioners in 1925, approved by the Privy Council in 1926 and further amended by Visitor's Statutes in 1930. The College now had an administrative body, referred to as The Warden and Fellows, with college meetings held twice a term. In the 1930 Statutes, the number of fellows is laid down as not less than six or more than 12, and the ten first fellows, who had much greater security of tenure than before, were the Bursar and the tutors, in order of seniority: they included Owen, Jolliffe, Rice-Oxley, G.D. Parkes (the only scientist), Lieutenant-Colonel O.R.E. Milman, the Bursar, and the young Russell Meiggs. Honorary fellows were also provided for, the first of whom to be elected was the first Warden, E.S. Talbot. Fellows were to be admitted at a service in the Chapel and were required to declare that they were communicant members of the Church of England, although by a later resolution this did not apply to professorial fellows. The Warden must still be in orders, and if a new Warden was elected by the College Council at Keble rather than in London, the election must be preceded by the celebration of Holy Communion; the name of the person elected was to be announced by placing a notice with the College seal on the Chapel door. The new Warden was to be inducted into his stall in the Chapel by the senior member of the Council present, the Te Deum was to be sung and the Warden was then himself to celebrate Holy Communion in the Chapel. The position of the Warden and fellows was strengthened, and the Council became a trustee body rather than an administrative one.

In the 1920s the lecturers at the College included Gregory Dix, the future monk, Prior of Nashdom and liturgist, and the tenor Peter Pears spent a year at Keble as an undergraduate in 1928–9. An undergraduate who came up in 1930 and in whose affections Keble ranked very high was Chad Varah (1911–2007). He was the son of a vicar in Lincolnshire and an exhibitioner in science (he was later proud of his honorary D.Sc from City University), who left Keble with a third in PPE; he was ordained in 1935. In order to fund his increasing range of activities he was a writer for *Eagle* and *Girl* in the 1950s, and in 1953 he

founded the Samaritans. Chad Varah was made an honorary fellow of Keble in 1981 and a Companion of Honour in 2000. One of his contemporaries at Keble was Douglas Henchley, who read Engineering and reached the rank of brigadier in his military career. Henchley was later to play a major role in fundraising for Keble and in the running of the Oxford Union. The 1930 intake also included a Serb from Belgrade, Rhodes scholars from Alberta and South Carolina, a mature undergraduate from Hong Kong who also read PPE, A.W. James, who was President of the Debating Society and Tenmentale,

The Jubilee and the Centenary of the College

1920: 'Brilliant weather, perfect organization, generous hospitality'

The College jubilee of 1920 was celebrated with a series of events, some more serious than others. So many attended that the students had to give up their rooms, sleeping in bell tents pitched in Pusey quad and in the College garden.

The fun side of the jubilee could be found in the sports contests and the dinners. A cricket match between 'past and present' ended in victory for the students. There was a rag regatta on the river, with VIIIs races (including the 66-year-old Reverend Herbert Hunt in a veterans' boat), scratch fours, punt races and double punting in canoes. The last was particularly chaotic, as everyone ended up in the river, with 'survivors' trying to avoid crews training for Henley while swimming across to the College barge. A memorable dinner was one at which the

staff were served by the undergraduates; it was also the only dinner of the week where speeches were not recorded in the local press.

The main events took place on 22 June, beginning with three communion services at 6.30, 7.30 and 8.30. One feature was the sermon of Edward Talbot, Bishop of Winchester, in which he reminded his listeners of the triumphs and trials of the years since the College opened under his guidance. He managed to raise a laugh by reminding them of the optimism of the early years: 'I remember dear old Dr Pusey's childlike hopefulness in contemplating a college in which no-one should be ploughed for an examination, a hope which we must own has not been realized'.

1970: 'Formalities to be kept to the minimum'

The centenary celebrations of 1970 stretched out over five weeks, beginning with a concert in the Sheldonian Theatre on 23 May and ending with a dinner for subscribers to the centenary appeal on 1 July. As Douglas Price emphasized in his centenary address, the festivities were to be as much about the future as about the past.

The central point of the celebrations was the laying of the foundation stone of the new buildings by HRH Princess Margaret on 11 June. At her insistence the ceremonies were brief and informal, with the Warden's and Chancellor's speeches being timed at three minutes only; parts of the tour were curtailed to allow the Princess to leave on time; but in her speech she praised the College authorities, stating that the new buildings were 'an act of faith in the future in line with that so boldly made upon its first foundation'.

The fine weather of June 1970 was in sharp contrast to the dank and dreary May morning in 1977 when Princess Margaret returned to open officially the Hayward and De Breyne buildings, thus inaugurating 'a new era, a re-foundation of Keble College'.

Robert Petre

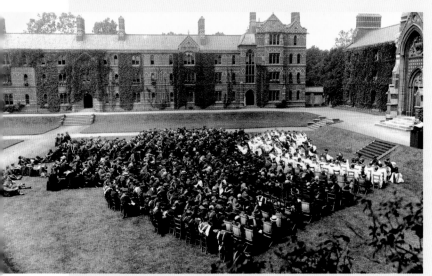

Above: *Jubilee celebrations in 1920*

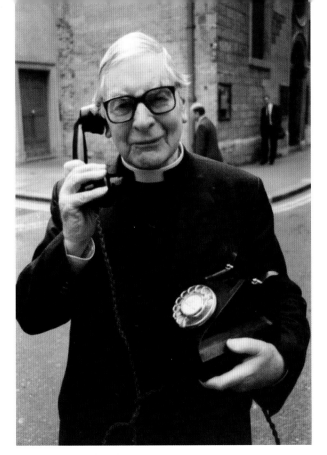

Above: *Chad Varah (1930)*

leader-writer for the *Manchester Guardian* and editor of the *Times Educational Supplement*, and Nicolas Zernov, perhaps an influence on Chad Varah, who was President of the University Russian Club; Zernov arrived as a graduate student from Belgrade and went on to become Spalding Lecturer in Eastern Orthodox Culture and a distinguished scholar of the Russian and eastern churches. In 1934 W.H.C. Frend came up from Haileybury with an open scholarship; he was to become a well-known historian of the early church and held a chair at Glasgow.

The loyalty displayed by men like Chad Varah and Douglas Henchley towards the College throughout their long lives is perhaps somewhat surprising, given what the College was like at the time. Warden Kidd could seem a stern and forbidding figure. There were few dons and all undergraduates lived in College, in conditions which were still frugal. The 50th anniversary of the College's foundation was celebrated, and the Keble Association founded in the aftermath of the First World War. The College continued to feel the human and financial effects of the war throughout the 1920s, though it attracted some notable tutors, including the Roman historian and Oxford character Dacre Balsdon (1926–7) and Russell Meiggs (tutor 1928–38, fellow 1930–8), who had come up to Keble as an exhibitioner in 1923 and who went on to become a famous ancient historian, expert on trees and timber in the ancient world and on the Roman port of Ostia, and fellow of Balliol.

Oxford Movement Celebrations

As one of the most solid memorials to the Oxford Movement, in the city of its inception, it was only natural that two of its major anniversaries would be celebrated in the College.

Both celebrations involved an open air mass. In 1933 this was held in Liddon quad, with a large temporary altar being constructed in the corner by the side-chapel; in 1983 a pilgrimage mass was celebrated by the Archbishop of Canterbury, the Visitor of the College, in the Parks. The earlier celebration concluded with a procession to Christ Church, to the grave of Dr Pusey; the later one with a buffet lunch in Hall.

In 1933 the College used the anniversary to launch an appeal for funds, producing a 'newspaper' of *Keble College Past Present and Future*. This celebrated the whole of life in the College, from David Talboys, doyen of the scouts, to the Keble plays; from the oldest inhabitant of the College (an apple tree) to the Henley VIII.

The years between the anniversary celebrations produced many changes in the Anglican church, not least a rapprochement with other denominations and faiths. The 150th anniversary saw 'an historical reassessment and critical appraisal' of the Oxford Movement at a five-day conference. The papers given formed the basis of *Tradition Renewed*, which not only had a foreword by the Visitor, but an open letter from Pope John Paul II and contributions from both Evangelical and Methodist scholars.
Robert Petre

The 100th and 150th anniversary celebrations of the Oxford Movement: right: 1933; below: 1983

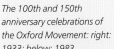

Above: *Harry Carpenter, Warden, 1939–55*

The Keble Association

The Keble Association is a registered charity, run by volunteers and based on the membership and subscriptions of Keble old members. Founded in 1920, it continues a close association with the College, giving significant grants to individual students, and supporting student activities.

The association began its life just after the First World War, in the context of the College's 50th Jubilee celebrations, when some 600 former students of the College congregated in Liddon quad on 21 June 1920. The experience of the war and the original aims of the College were clearly very much in the minds of the proposers of the new association, and it was unanimously agreed by those present that its first aim should be to provide financial help for those would not otherwise be able to afford to study at Keble. Two further aims were also agreed: to provide financial help for former students and their families who were in need, and to maintain links between Keble men who joined the association, and the College. The first chairman was the Reverend H.W. McKenzie, a member of the First 30 in 1870, who had been headmaster of Lancing and Uppingham and was a notable rower and cricketer. Its first secretary and treasurer was H. Purefoy Fitzgerald (1889), who served on the committee for 28 years and was the Association's President in 1946.

The list of presidents of the Keble Association, from its inception in 1920 until the present day (with a gap only during the Second World War, when meetings were suspended), includes previous Wardens, a Sub-Warden and a number of fellows, including Vere Davidge, Douglas Price and Eric Stone, as well as a distinguished array of bishops, judges, lawyers, academics and other Keble men prominent in public life and in a wide range of fields.

Above: *The London dinner, 1937*

The 1930s were still a difficult decade, despite the celebration of the centenary of the Oxford Movement in 1933. Money was still very short, and a further attempt at fund-raising was conspicuously unsuccessful. For the undergraduates, coal and hot water for baths were limited and there was always financial anxiety, though by the end of the decade the Bursar, C.R.E. Hillman, had managed to balance the books. But all in all, Douglas Price could describe Keble in the 1930s as a 'happy society'.

This relative stability was to end with the advent of the Second World War. Harry Carpenter, tutor in theology and Chaplain since 1927, succeeded Kidd as Warden in 1939 and held the post until he became Bishop of Oxford in 1955. The College was requisitioned and occupied by female staff supposedly of MI5, who were bussed to work at Blenheim Palace; they later remembered how very cold they had been while at Keble. Like many other Oxford academics, the fellows who were not called up were drafted into government or intelligence work. Some degree of normality remained, including the election to an honorary fellowship in 1944 of the poet Walter de la Mare. His son Richard had come up to Keble in 1920 to read history and went into publishing, eventually becoming chairman of Faber and Faber. Walter was a friend of Leonard Rice-Oxley, who took him the news of the honorary fellowship.

An Unsuccessful Appeal in the 1930s

In May 1933, the Council agreed to the recommendation of the Warden and fellows that an appeal for funds should be launched, and it was agreed to employ a Mr Duffas for a year to run it, and a firm of solicitors for three months to manage publicity in the press. The College produced an illustrated appeal publication and the Archbishop of Canterbury wrote an initial letter to *The Times*, which was supported by a leading article. However, the appeal was not a success, raising only £9,104.5s.10d, against expenses of £2,569.7s.6d. It had also targeted chiefly clergy, including the many former undergraduates who had gone into the Church, as well as current Keble incumbents and members of the Anglo-Catholic Congress. While it had probably benefited from the fact that it coincided with the centenary of the Oxford Movement, this was not a promising strategy for raising money. An appeal to priests in the London, Canterbury and St Albans dioceses was, for example, so unsuccessful that it was abandoned. Russell Meiggs took an exhibition of personal relics of John Keble to the Catholic Congress of the Episcopal Church in Philadelphia in October, and received a sympathetic reception there and elsewhere in the USA, but the Warden and fellows were forced to admit that the financial result of this initiative, which coincided with the effects of the depression, was 'nugatory'. The College concluded that it was been a mistake to expect support from the general public, but consoled itself by recording its gratitude for two significant donations, from a member of Council and an honorary fellow, and with the view that the paid agents had done their best.

At the end of the war the College received government compensation for the use of its buildings, and this helped to pay for rewiring and the installation of electric fires. The student population immediately after the war was very mixed; at least one GI, who had married an English girl and decided to stay in Britain, was admitted by Warden Carpenter after knocking on the door of the Lodgings, and for several years the student body continued to contain demobbed soldiers, as demobilization was staggered. Some undergraduates had not yet been demobbed; Henry Maddick came up to Trinity in 1946 and remembers being one of five undergraduates, still in uniform, who were summoned by the proctors and fined five shillings for drinking in a public place. Another who arrived in 1946 after serving in India was Leolin Price, who had been at a grammar school in Tonbridge; he was taught by Jolliffe and A.G. Dickens, and later became a distinguished barrister and QC. Food rationing intensified in the late 1940s and the College seemed a depressing place to Bryan Magee when he came up in 1949, although the presence of the young Humphrey Carpenter (b. 1946, Keble 1964) propelling himself round the quad in his pedal car did something to alleviate the gloom. John Zehetmayr (1941) returned from naval service in 1945 and was surprised to find Carpenter married. Michael Ranson, who came up to read English in 1948, found it a 'low period in the College's fortunes'.

Many undergraduates were in their mid 20s, and Keble's policy was to require schoolboys who were awarded scholarships to do their national service before coming up. The College was far from being a centre of privilege, and most undergraduates came from state schools on grants. A distinguished Keble student of the period was the poet Geoffrey Hill, who arrived from

Geoffrey Hill

Geoffrey Hill (1949) is one of the most distinguished of post-war English poets. His early poem 'Genesis' was written when he was still an undergraduate and published in *The Clock Tower*; the manuscript version is in the college archives. He also published in *Isis* and *The Oxford Guardian,* the magazine of the University Liberal Club, and his first published collection came out with Fantasy Press in 1952, the year of his graduation. It was followed by *For the Unfallen* (1959), *King Log* (1968) and *Mercian Hymns* (1971). His poetic output is prolific, including *The Triumph of Love* (1998), *Speech! Speech!* (2000), *The Orchards of Syon* (2002) and his 14th collection, *A Treatise of Civil Power* (2007). Hill's work is dense, permeated with religious imagery and with memories of his Worcestershire origins. He has won many awards for poetry, is a major critic and essayist, and was co-director, with Christopher Ricks (Professor of Poetry at Oxford, 2004–9), of the Editorial Institute at Boston University.

Bromsgrove County High School in 1950 and was already writing poetry as an undergraduate, some of which Bryan Magee published as editor of *The Clock Tower*. Another who arrived from a poor background via grammar school at Ashby-de-la-Zouch was James Martin, who remembers the time spent at Keble as one of his happiest and most exciting periods. Martin's subject was physics, but he attended lectures by C.S. Lewis and heard Bertrand Russell; an organ-playing friend took him on a tour of the organs of Oxford, and memorable aspects of Keble included for him the kindness of Warden Carpenter and the mathematics tutorials given by E.G. Phillips, with his long beard.

At this time there were nine fellows besides the Warden, and two lecturers (the Greek scholar Spencer Barrett and the historian John Bromley), neither of whom was willing to declare himself a communicant member of the Church of England and so could not become a fellow. One of the more eccentric Keble fellows was the moral philosopher Donald MacKinnon, later Regius Professor at Aberdeen, who had become a fellow in 1937 and was renowned for playing with razor blades in tutorials, climbing up the curtains, or even hiding under the table ready to surprise an unsuspecting pupil. He was succeeded in 1947 by Basil Mitchell, senior proctor in 1956–7 and a member of the Hebdomadal Council in 1958, later Nolloth Professor at Oriel, who admitted that he would have liked to have gone to one of the older established colleges and found it hard to get used to the polychromatic brick-work of Keble.

Keble in the Second World War

At the outbreak of war the age of conscription was set at 20; although courses would be cut short, students could still begin their studies. Those facing the call-up were examined on the shortened course, and received a war degree, which they would be entitled to convert into a full honours degree once the war was over. But as the war progressed, the age of call-up was progressively lowered. From December 1942 matriculands had to be under 18; the effect of this was mitigated by the introduction of six-month short courses for service cadets, some of whom were taught at Keble by the Warden, MacKinnon, and Rice-Oxley.

There was initially an attempt at normality. Numbers did not plummet at once: there were 126 undergraduates on the books in Michaelmas 1939, and in 1940 the organ scholar, Meredith Davies, organized a small choir which sang a Dvorak mass in the Chapel, and this choir later joined up with the Bach Choir to sing the *St Matthew*

Passion. But numbers soon fell: in 1940 there were just 89, and in 1941, 68 undergraduates. By 1941 Davies' absence meant that the Warden and G.D. Parkes shared the duties of organist on Sundays.

The requisitioning of the College by the Ministry of Works meant that Keble's undergraduates had to be dispersed, although a handful of dons continued to live in college in splendid isolation. In 1940, 16 Keble men were at Wadham, 20 at Trinity, 10 at Christ Church, 10 at Hertford and 33 at University. Their connections with the College became attenuated, though 35–40 were still taking communion in Keble Chapel (in spite of the suspension of the chapel rule), and their identity as Keble men was reinforced by the requirement that they dine on separate tables in their host colleges, who may well have looked down upon them. Forestry student John Zehetmayr (1941) recalls that the Keble scholars in Wadham 'occupied one end of a table in hall, played squash and brewed coffee together and in the summer of 1942 hired a punt for £5 for the eight-week term'. The College games teams were amalgamated with Wadham for the duration of the war.

Academics over the age of 25 were in a reserved occupation, but several were recruited into government service. The historian Geoffrey Dickens took out a commission, becoming a lieutenant in the Royal Artillery in 1942; the economist Maurice Hugh-Jones worked at the Ministry of Food, where he was in charge of the import and distribution of rice; law fellow Vere Davidge was at the Treasury and the Cabinet Office. Spencer Barrett spent the war in Oxford as a member of the Geographical Survey Unit, which pieced together holiday photographs and incidental bits of information to build up an accurate picture of the French coast, with a view to identifying invasion sites.

Left: *Keble and Wadham joined forces for sports: the joint Torpid crew, 1940*

The Blenheim Girls

Five Oxford colleges were requisitioned for various purposes during the Second World War. Keble was requisitioned in September 1940 by Department J of the Ministry of Works, following the bombing of Wormwood Scrubs, where women from that department had previously been working. Keble accommodated around 250 women who were bussed out to work at Blenheim each day. From the College's viewpoint, the requisition 'was acquired by guile and was promptly executed'.

The women were accommodated by doubling up in the undergraduate sets. Although the College was not officially supposed to know where they worked or what they did, the destination of the buses which rolled up at the College each morning was an open secret. The Blenheim bus left early and Keble's male students describe coming to College for tutorials only to meet the girls going to catch the bus in various stages of dress or undress.

College papers record the requisition, the amount paid to the College, the cost of relocation of Keble's male students, the number of additional staff required to serve, the thinness of the mattresses and the apparent disappearance of substantial quantities of college crockery and cutlery. Efforts to enforce undergraduate discipline on the women had to be relaxed, and gate hours were extended. The women were welcome at all Chapel services, and in March 1941 a late evensong at 7.40 p.m. was instituted to accommodate their timetable. Warden Carpenter took many under his wing and to some became a life-long friend.

Above: *Blenheim Girls' reunion, 1998*

In 1998 the College arranged a reunion lunch for the Blenheim Girls; 96 had been traced and 65 attended. Many had not seen each other since the war and all remarked that they had never seen the Hall without blackout curtaining across the stained glass windows. They told of their ration of one bucket of coal per week, of scouts bringing hot water, and that a bath was a luxury rarely experienced as there were so few in College. They all declined to discuss what they had done during their time at Keble, saying that they had signed the Official Secrets Act.
Isla Smith

Above: *The dinner to celebrate the acquisition of full status, 1952*

Writing from a later perspective, however, he added that 'I now realize that I was in fact extremely fortunate', and he had no problem with the religious declaration. The last fellow to have to make it was Douglas Price in 1949. This was also the period when the College purchased part of the Norton Hall estate in Northamptonshire for £35,000, and made the investment decision that one third of assets should be in land, one third in equity shares and one third in fixed, interest-bearing stock.

New Statutes in 1952 finally vested all governance in the Warden and fellows. The Council ceased to exist and religious tests were abolished for senior and junior members, only the Warden still having to be a clerk in holy orders. Barrett and Bromley were accordingly now admitted as full fellows. The new Statutes were drafted by Vere Davidge (lecturer and then fellow in law since 1927, Bursar since 1945) and steered through by Harry Carpenter, who was able to persuade the Council to disband itself. At last they placed Keble on a con-stitutional par with the older colleges of the University.

James Martin (1952)

James Martin read physics at Keble and joined Armstrong Siddeley in 1956 and IBM in 1959. He went on to be an innovator in computer technology, advanced business systems and predictions about the future. He was a founder of CASE (computer-aided systems engineering) and has also pioneered ultra-complex systems for corporations. His 1977 book, *The Wired Society*, predicted the use of computers and the internet 25 years before its time and, in 1987, he foresaw the rise of religious extremism and envisaged a terrorist attack on New York. He is the founder and benefactor, through the largest single donation ever given to the University, of the School of the 21st Century at Oxford, part of a worldwide initiative whose mission is to identify, research and find solutions to the enormous scientific and human problems of the future.

These Statutes were kept simple and there were no by-laws; Spencer Barrett's keen eye made sure the drafting and the punctuation were both impeccable. With the new Statutes, and the gradual recovery from the war, things began to look up. Carpenter was succeeded by Eric Symes Abbott, at the time Dean of King's College London and later to be Dean of Westminster. Abbott was sociable, keen to raise the level of Keble's academic life and to improve the College in other ways, insisting, for example, on a complete redecoration of the cold and gloomy Lodgings. He ensured that Keble fellows were paid as much as fellows in other colleges, and established an alliance with Davidge based on

a mutual love for rowing. There was also expansion in the fellowship and undergraduate numbers began to rise. M.R.D. Foot, the historian of the SOE (Special Operations Executive) in France and editor of the Gladstone diaries, was lecturer in politics from 1952 to 1959 and was elected as a Labour member of the Oxford city council in 1955. He encouraged David Penwarden to stand as a Liberal for West Ham North, even though he was an undergraduate and chairman of the ball committee.

Though he tried hard as they returned together from Henley in 1959, Basil Mitchell did not succeed in persuading Abbott to prefer Keble over the offer of Westminster. In the College, real expansion took place during the Wardenship of his successor, the philosopher and theologian Austin Farrer (1960–8). It was partly a product of the general expansion of university education and changes in government funding following the Robbins Report of 1963. Within Oxford, the Commission of Inquiry led by Lord Franks (Provost of Worcester 1962–76) was set up in 1964 and reported in 1966. Franks had been Provost of Queens, and was the candidate in 1960 of Maurice Bowra, then acting Vice-Chancellor, for the Chancellorship, which was won in a contested election by Harold Macmillan. The Commission addressed in particular the respective roles of Congregation and the Hebdomadal Council. The somewhat obscure system according to which all Oxford college accounts were presented until the early twenty-first century was also established, and these were known as 'the Franks accounts'. Keble's bid to increase its fellowship was also assisted by pressure from the University to offer college fellowships to scientists holding research positions without college associations. As for the expansion in the 1960s, Douglas Price noted with prescience that, while the advent of shared ('joint') appointments between the University and the colleges enabled the latter to increase their teaching provision to match the rising undergraduate numbers, this advantage came at the cost of dependence on University priorities, which did not (and do not) always suit those of an individual college.

The theological and philosophical dimensions of the College were maintained in the 1950s and 1960s through the membership of Basil Mitchell, Austin Farrer and Christopher Stead (Chaplain and fellow in theology, 1949–71) of the Oxford philosophical group known as the Metaphysicals. Keble students were regularly taught by Iris Murdoch, another of its members, at St Anne's. Basil Mitchell also belonged to the Monday lunch club,

Eric Symes Abbott

Eric Symes Abbott was Warden only for a short period (1956–60), but left a lasting mark on those who knew him. He had previously been Chaplain of King's College London, Warden of Lincoln Theological College and Dean of King's College London, in the days when, under its complex constitution, the Dean was on a par with the Principal of the College, as well as head of the theology faculty and warden of the College's hostel for theology students in Vincent Square. Abbott was also chaplain both to King George VI and Queen Elizabeth II, and had close pastoral links with the royal family. He was at heart a London person, and in 1959 he was invited back to become Dean of Westminster, a post he could hardly refuse and which he held until 1974; for a period during 1959–60, he actually held the two posts simultaneously. His forte was spiritual direction, and his connections assisted the College in persuading Princess Margaret to visit in 1970 and 1977. Eric Abbott was a cultivated and highly social man, and his hospitality, especially to young recently married and about-to-be married fellows, is still remembered. Basil Mitchell was unsure whether anyone so smooth could really be a good man. He had also coxed while at Cambridge, and he encouraged rowing at Keble; he was a particular master of the art of speaking at a bump supper. He was not an academic, although he wrote several books; his real skills were with people, and it was this that led his friends to set up a memorial trust which still provides for an annual lecture in his name.

Right: *Larry Siedentop, watercolour by Bob Tulloch*

otherwise known as the 'holy lunch', a group of eight, half clerical, half lay, which still continues and to which Dennis Nineham and Averil Cameron have also belonged. Members lunch together each Monday in term-time at their various colleges, and, after the reading of Sext from the Cuddesdon service book, enjoy a theoretically modest lunch and some relatively high-minded gossip. To Basil Mitchell, the arrival in the College of distinguished and like-minded colleagues such as Christopher Stead and then Austin Farrer brought a period of great contentment. It was also a time which brought some real intellectual distinction to the College.

The younger new arrivals in the 1960s and 1970s were of a different stripe, though no less distinguished. Academic standards among undergraduates were not high: Peter Iveson (chemistry, 1958) recalls, 'I was barely aware that degrees were classified and that it might be possible to obtain first class honours.... Hardly anyone at Keble was gaining first class honours at the beginning of the 1960s'. This began to change, and when Adrian Darby, an Etonian who had been a lecturer at Christ Church, became fellow in economics in 1963, he set about building up PPE by increasing the number of tutors. A tutor in politics was essential and Paul Hayes was appointed from Nuffield College before he had finished his D.Phil.

In 1966 Darby himself made possible the appointment in philosophy of James (Jim) Griffin, an American Rhodes scholar. In 1973 the PPE tutors were joined by another American, Larry Siedentop, also from Nuffield, and when Adrian Darby became Bursar in 1968, Jeremy Hardie became fellow in economics in yet another appointment from Nuffield. Their arrival coincided with that of a group of younger law fellows, Peter North (1965), David Williams (1963) and Dyson Heydon (1967) with similar ambitions. The first two of these went on to become Vice-Chancellors of Oxford and Cambridge respectively, the third a Justice of the High Court of Australia. On Basil Mitchell's departure in 1968, Farrer was unsure about the choice of Richard Hawkins as his successor, because he was thought to be an agnostic or an atheist, though Farrer allowed himself to be persuaded by the PPE tutors that

the College must appoint him as the best candidate. Inevitably tensions were felt. The PPE and law fellows were the young Turks of the day, and their hopes were shared by Eric Stone, senior tutor for eleven years from 1965. These men wanted Keble to be intellectually distinguished and liberal in outlook. Davidge, however, had different views, Paul Hayes and Denis Meakins valued sport as highly as academic success, and Christopher Stead and Douglas Price wanted to uphold the College's High Anglican tradition. The older fellows were also used to the idea that Keble was a poor college, and some found it difficult to accustom themselves to the idea that it could set its sights higher. There was agreement that the College needed money and that there should be an appeal, but views differed about what its objects should be.

Austin Farrer

Austin Farrer (Warden 1960–8) was an outstanding theologian and philosopher, 'regarded by many people', according to Douglas Hedley (Keble 1981), 'as the greatest Anglican theologian of the twentieth century'. He was a member of the Oxford Metaphysicals, the group which began to meet in 1946, and to which Basil Mitchell also belonged; the latter has written eloquently about Farrer on several occasions. Farrer is remembered in his capacity as Warden of Keble for his distinctive hurrying walk (undergraduates dubbed him 'the White Rabbit'), his high voice, and as a figure rather remote from the average undergraduate; his wife Katharine, a writer of detective novels, was in some ways a more forceful presence.

Austin Farrer's reputation has grown steadily since his death. To his own books, published in his lifetime, which included his Bampton Lectures (*The Glass of Vision*, 1948), and the Gifford Lectures (*The Freedom of the Will*, 1958), as well as *Love Almighty and Ills Unlimited: an Essay on Providence and Evil* (1962), were added the posthumous publication of many of his remarkable sermons, as well as several volumes resulting from conferences held to discuss his contribution. Characteristic features of his thought were his theory of downward causation and his insistence on the importance of images as a way towards the understanding of God. He also had a characteristic literary style: clear, arresting and unimpeded by footnotes or theoretical apparatus. A sermon preached in Keble Chapel on St Mark's Day, 1963, opened with the sentence 'When I was a freshman in this College – dear me, it's three years ago, and it seems like yesterday – a lot of things happened which surprised me'. All the freshers came individually to meet him in the Lodgings, and 'we had a sort of extemporary and ragged party, which lasted most of the day'. In another sermon preached in the Chapel, he described John Keble as a most gentle, unassuming man, perhaps not fully appreciated by Wilberforce, Pusey and Liddon. But he also said, 'Today we cheer for John Keble, and Dr Pusey, but tomorrow, which of us will want to walk in these men's steps? And why should we? Every generation must solve its problems in its own way.'

Farrer's thought was profound, and he could be uncompromising, but he had a sharp awareness of human nature which perhaps not all undergraduates of the day appreciated; 'the worship of the heart' was all well and good, but what mattered in life and in relationships with God were good habits, set customs, a pattern of life; a steady marriage rather than an exciting love-affair.

Electing a Warden, 1960 and 1969

The formal position under the 1952 Statutes was that the Warden would be nominated by the Archbishop of Canterbury in his capacity as Visitor, but the idea was that the Visitor would be acting on the basis of a consensus of the fellows. Achieving that consensus was not, however, a straightforward process, as the elections of 1960 and 1969 reveal.

The Wardenship became vacant when Eric Abbott accepted the Deanery of Westminster in 1959. The name of Austin Farrer, then tutor in theology at Trinity, and just passed over for the Regius chair, emerged at an early stage in the proceedings (Basil Mitchell, philosophy don and fellow 'Metaphysical', was a leading advocate), but there were serious misgivings among some of the fellows (including Spencer Barrett, who was adamantly opposed, and, more tentatively, Douglas Price, Dennis Shaw and Denys Potts) about his suitability: although his scholarly credentials were unquestioned, his abilities as an administrator were doubted (it was said that, during Governing Body meetings at Trinity, it was his habit to read *The Times*), and some found his manner somewhat distant. The other candidates were one G.M. Styler, and a youthful Dennis Nineham, then Professor of Divinity at King's College London. As Douglas Price confided to his diary: 'Styler [was] safe but unexciting, Nineham exciting but dangerous, Farrer undoubtedly the strongest claimant as a scholar, but doubtful as regards personality …. I cannot believe that the CofE is so utterly destitute of men with both the humour and intellectual qualifications requisite in a Warden as has been pretended'. When it came to the straw vote at the College meeting on 27 January 1960, there were six votes for Farrer, four for Styler and one for Nineham (that came from Price, who had decided unusually to live dangerously); at the formal resolution to put Farrer's name to the Visitor, the voting was six to five in favour. Although this was only a bare majority, Leonard Rice-Oxley, the Sub-Warden, decided not to indicate the figures to the Archbishop, in Price's disgusted words, 'a piece of political chicanery more to be expected of a town council than a Governing Body meeting'.

When Farrer died of a brain haemorrhage in December 1968, his successor was elected under the old Statutes rather than the new ones under discussion (which would have enabled the election of a non-cleric). The Governing Body consulted Abbott and Carpenter, and came up with 17 names, soon whittled down to four or five. Spencer Barrett, Douglas Price and Jim Griffin (replacing Peter North, who was in New Zealand) constituted the committee to consider them. The front runners emerged as Henry Chadwick, Jack McManners, the ecclesiastical historian, Robert Mortimer, Bishop of Exeter, and Dennis Nineham, now Regius Professor of Divinity at Cambridge. But some were not reconciled to a clerical Warden, and, according to Price, a group he identifies as 'the PPE tutors' wanted to elect an older man (Mortimer, whose powers were

Above: *Dennis Nineham, Warden, 1969–80*

failing) on the grounds that his tenure would be short and a new lay Warden could then be elected under the revised Statutes then under consideration. On the straw vote taken at the meeting on 27 March 1969, there were 19 for Nineham and 11 for Mortimer; on the second vote, 23 for Nineham and 6 for Mortimer. Price considered the meeting well conducted, apart from the behaviour of Paul Hayes (who showed 'the mind of a mere politician and the manners of a boar') and Roy Harris, who had absented himself from all meetings and turned up only to vote at 4 p.m. (for the older man), 'the most gross impropriety that I have known in my 20 years on the Governing Body'. Whatever anxieties the PPE tutors may have held about Nineham (and the recollections of at least one of them differ from Price's contemporary testimony), they were soon reconciled to him, emerging as key allies in his reform programme.

63

It was a sign of these disagreements that Davidge's fellowship was not extended until the age of seventy, for which his own Statutes had provided. All agreed, however, that more rooms were needed, not only for the rising numbers of junior members but also for the increased fellowship. A middle common room was created for the first time, and a new boathouse, shared with Jesus College, had been opened in 1964, paid for by a substantial loan.

The idea of raising money from old members in connection with the 100th anniversary of the inception of the building of the College in 1968 had begun spontaneously in 1950, with a target of £20,000. By 1965, the total raised stood at £15,808, after a deduction of £1,019 for expenses. Covenanted money was still to come in, bringing the amount to £23,000. The College asked for another £45,000, £40,000 of which would go into the endowment, £22,000 to complete work already in hand, £5,000 to 'rehabilitating' the organ, and £13,000 to clearing an existing loan on the boathouse. The appeal brochure noted that 'No money can be looked for from government sources, which make grants only to the University, never to the colleges, nor from Oxford's own appeal, which is for the repair and restoration of buildings'. It was also noted that more space was needed, as there were now more graduates, and there was pressure on undergraduate numbers from the Commonwealth and overseas. Dennis Shaw proposed a new building on the Museum Road and Blackhall Road site, and in 1968, André de Breyne, then chairman of Pearsons, was brought in to dine by Kenneth Mills, a member of an old Keble dining club called the Apple Tree. De Breyne took to the atmosphere of the College so much that he offered to contribute £50,000 if the College could match it. Dennis Shaw was dispatched to North America to try to raise the money when Austin Farrer ('deeply religious, fastidious, highly intelligent and at times as maliciously waspish as a saint is allowed to be', according to Adrian Darby) had declined to go on grounds of health; in fact he found the 'window-dressing' necessary for an appeal distasteful.

However, Shaw's was a successful visit. Edmond du Pont (1928) offered $50,000 and Hiram Kennedy Douglass (1919), donor of the gates between Liddon quad and the fellows' garden, the equivalent of $500 annually by legacy. The visit also resulted in an agreement with the University of the South to endow scholarships at Keble for graduates of Sewanee. Once the Ahrends, Burton and Koralek buildings had been commissioned, a much bigger appeal was launched under the secretaryship of Dennis Shaw, with

a view to marking the centenary of the College's actual opening in 1970. The major needs were identified as facilities, and teaching and research posts. The target was set at £1m, of which £220,000 was already pledged; the new building would cost £405,000, including a site mortgage of £55,000, and when the appeal was closed in 1974 it had considerably exceeded its target.

For all his misgivings, Farrer was chairman of the appeal; he described Keble's dilemma in satirical verse. He died unexpectedly on 29 December 1968, and Spencer Barrett was appointed Vice-Warden. A recording of Farrer's last sermon, preached in Keble Chapel days before he died, calls to mind his distinctively high voice and uncompromising style. In the interregnum which followed his death, it was agreed that the Statutes should be changed in order to remove the stipulation that the Warden must be in holy orders, and Spencer Barrett, Douglas Price and Peter North were given the task of determining the view of the Archbishop of Canterbury, then Michael Ramsay, whose consent was needed as the Visitor. Neither he nor Eric Abbott (who was also consulted) had any objections, and the change went ahead.

It was agreed that the election of Farrer's successor should proceed during the interregnum and before the new Statutes took effect. The change to the Statutes was drafted with typical exactness and in some detail by Spencer Barrett as Vice-Warden. Peter North argued in contrast for brevity, but in the end the change was made while the latter was away on leave in New Zealand. The choice of Warden fell on Dennis Nineham, who was at the time Regius Professor of Divinity at Cambridge. Nineham was a radical theologian, known for his classic commentary on Mark's gospel (1963). He was a contributor during his Wardenship to *The Myth of God Incarnate* (1977), a collection of essays edited by John Hick, which caused as much

Above: *André and Victoria de Breyne, watercolour by Bob Tulloch*

Right: Sir Charles Hayward

Below: HRH Princess Margaret with Dennis Nineham, Harold Macmillan (Chancellor of the University) and the architect viewing the model of the ABK buildings at the centenary celebrations, 1970

Below right: Harold Macmillan with Princess Margaret at the opening of the ABK buildings, 1977

controversy in the late 20th century as *Lux Mundi* had in the late 19th. In the previous year he published *The Use and Abuse of the Bible. A Study of the Bible in an Age of Rapid Cultural Change*, a central work in the contemporary turn to narrative theology. He was to prove as progressive in his Wardenship as in his theology.

The arrival of Dennis and his wife Ruth at Keble in October 1969, brought a new liveliness and vigour to the College. Adrian Darby, fellow in economics since 1963, succeeded Davidge as Bursar in 1968, with Charles Bourne, who had previously been chief clerk, promoted to Domestic Bursar. When Charles Bourne died in 1969, Air Vice-Marshal Jack Maggs succeeded him as Domestic

Bursar and served until 1977. The combination of Nineham and Darby was well calculated to see the College through some major changes. The appeal was launched at the Oxford and Cambridge Club, with support from John Betjeman, and the next milestone was that of the centenary celebration itself in 1970, when the foundation stone of the new Hayward and De Breyne buildings was laid by Princess Margaret, thanks to her connection with Eric Abbott; she also opened the new buildings in 1977. After the centenary it was decided to employ a full-time secretary for the appeal office and this role eventually went to Douglas Henchley (1930). The De Breyne quad was completed in 1971, after the houses on Museum and Blackhall Roads had been demolished and after a term's delay in its occupation, caused by a builders' strike, had necessitated sending freshers out to live in lodgings. More funds were needed before work could start on the rest. Partly through the good offices of Adrian Darby's father-in-law, Sir Alec Douglas-Home, then Foreign Secretary, a visit was arranged to the home of Charles Hayward, formerly chairman of Firth Cleveland, on the small Channel Island of Jethou, as a result of which he donated £700,000. Adrian Darby recalls that Hayward's wife told him afterwards that they had intended to turn the request down. This resulted in the naming of Hayward quad.

A further initiative that marked the centenary was the publication of the Keble College Centenary Register, compiled by Basil St G. Drennan, exhibitioner in history (1922), president of Tenmentale and editor of *The Clock Tower*, a civil servant and Principal Clerk of Committees, House of Commons. The *Register*, which took nine years to produce and which Jack Maggs was employed after his retirement to update, contains complete records from the first 100 years of the College. It has been of the utmost value in the writing of this book. The Bursary and the College accounts were also computerized, after years of relying on card indices and Dickensian high desks; this involved Adrian Darby combining efforts with the then Bursar of Trinity to write an accounts programme in BASIC, for nothing suitable existed at the time.

The state of the College finances – or rather its dire lack of money – shocked Dennis Nineham, who found the conditions 'straight out of Dickens' and set about doing something about it, including asking some of the richer colleges for contributions. The Ninehams had been warned off the move to Keble by Harry Carpenter's wife, Urith, on the grounds that the Lodgings were impossibly cold. The

Keble Proctors and Assessors

The colleges elect proctors in rotation according to a scheme laid down by Archbishop Laud. Their role is to ensure that the Statutes of the University are upheld, which they do by hearing examination complaints, investigating and prosecuting breaches of the disciplinary code and sitting on university committees. The assessor, whose role is more concerned with student welfare, is a recent addition to the team.

Walter Lock	Senior Proctor, 1882–3
William James Heathcote Campion	Junior Proctor, 1890–1
John Tracey	Senior Proctor, 1901–2
W.H.V. Reade	Senior Proctor, 1912–13
David Simpson	Junior Proctor, 1923–4
George Parkes	Senior Proctor, 1934–5
Vere Davidge	Senior Proctor, 1945–6
Basil Mitchell	Senior Proctor, 1956–7
Gordon Smith	Senior Proctor, 1968–9
Paul Hayes	Junior Proctor, 1980–1
Michael Mingos	Assessor, 1991–2
Ian Archer	Junior Proctor, 2003–4

Below: *The procession at the installation of Ian Archer as Junior Proctor, 2003*

buildings were shabby and the beer cellar, established in 1958, was condemned as unfit by the health authorities. Ruth Nineham also set about improving the social side of the College and offered friendship and encouragement to the wives of young fellows, who often felt very excluded. Increases in student numbers continued to be opposed by Douglas Price in the 1970s, but Nineham successfully argued that the size and scale of Keble and its Hall, Chapel and Library, were such that they could only be maintained if there were enough students and fees to pay for them. With Nineham's encouragement, Darby raised the student

fees from the college average to the highest of all the colleges, justifying this on the grounds of poverty. He was also a founder member of a new committee chaired by Roger van Noorden, the Bursar of Hertford, to look at prices and charges across all the colleges; this produced the formula for increases known as the Van Noorden Index, which remained in use for decades. Dealing with the junior members about increases to their board and lodgings charges could be difficult, but, with the help of the JCR, Darby contrived to keep the overall charges within the level of the then maintenance grant. Keble also became a beneficiary under the new college contributions scheme, which taxed richer colleges in order to build up the endowment of the technically 'poorer'; it ceased to be a recipient early in the Wardenship of Averil Cameron, and later even became a minor contributor.

Desmond Watkins (1952) remembers the optimism of the early 1950s, as well as the sense of a divide between the glamorous Oxford of *Brideshead Revisited* and the realities of Keble, though the latter he found egalitarian and friendly. Tony Turner's poems about his undergraduate years in 1953–7 record that, in April 1956, Krushchev and Bulganin visited Oxford, after the 20th Party Congress, but six months later sent Soviet tanks into Hungary. The musical 'Salad Days' of the same year expressed the bittersweet personal experience of Turner and others in the 1950s, but the events in Hungary and the Suez invasion of 1956 were also key events for the undergraduates of the time. National service ended only at the end of 1960, and Roger Sainsbury (1959, President of the JCR 1961–2) remembers that there was still a mixture in the College of 'callow youths' and older men who had far more experience.

Both senior and junior members across the University protested against the Vietnam war. In the 1950s gowns were still worn for tutorials, and undergraduates of both sexes dressed as if they were in their 30s, but this, too, now changed. In 1968–9, when Gordon Smith was senior proctor and Peter North pro-proctor, student unrest compelled them to patrol the streets with the bulldogs several nights a week, and in Broad Street, the wall of Balliol was plastered with posters attacking them. The failure of the Franks Commission in 1966 to recommend student representation in governance provoked a petition to the Privy Council against the new University Statutes, and when the recommendations of the committee on relations with junior members set up under H.A.L. Hart also failed to accept the more radical student demands, there were sit-ins in 1970 and 1973 at the Clarendon Building and the Examination Schools, and attempts to attack other university buildings. The protesters wanted an end to privilege and paternalism, and demanded a central students' union and a say in university and college administration; there were calls for the admission of more working class students, more mature students and more women. In 1972, junior members at Keble were at last given a voice in the affairs of the College by the creation of a standing committee, but they did not yet become full members of college committees or of Governing Body, and when Chris Perrin (1975), as president of the JCR, was invited to attend a Governing Body meeting in 1977, he found the attitudes of fellows dismissive in the extreme. However, privilege was not a real issue at Keble:

The College Parishes Today

Today the College continues to exercise the patronage of its 65 benefices, although in recent decades, due to increasing reorganizational schemes of the dioceses, the College's right of presentation of new priests has often been suspended. The Advowsons Committee usually carries out one or two appointments each year. In order to nurture the patronage connection, the College organizes two biennial events. The Keble Parishes Day is held in September every other year, and over a hundred people usually attend. Some distant parishes hire a bus to bring as many as 30 or 40. The day includes lunch in hall and a tour of the College followed by tea, ending with choral evensong in the Chapel. Every other year in January, the College also invites the clergy for a three-day clergy conference with guest speakers, who have recently included Professor Keith Ward, Dr John Muddiman (Keble 1964), Professor Martin Percy and Bishop Stephen Cottrell. Some parishes are also invited to the corporate communion service held in Michaelmas and Hilary terms. They come for an evening service and a

Above: *All Saints, Thelwall*

formal dinner in hall, followed by a drinks reception hosted by the Warden. The College also maintains the Harlow Trust Fund, which was set up to help poor catholic parishes in the diocese of Birmingham, and in recent years has given out about £25,000 each year.
Allen Shin

Above: *Keble freshers, 1979, the first group to include women*

undergraduates in the early 1960s still included many from grammar schools who had state scholarships, worth £300 a year, to which a college exhibition might add another £50; tuition was free, though not much was left over for spending after battels had been paid.

In 1971, the Chaplain, Christopher Stead, left to become Ely Professor of Divinity at Cambridge, and a canon residentiary of Ely. Nineham supported the idea of a five-year chaplaincy but was defeated, and Geoffrey Rowell was appointed in 1972, as both Chaplain and fellow in theology, a position he held until 1994.

The College was not one of the more progressive. In the late 1960s, the fellows were still debating whether to have a ladies' night and, if so, on which evening. However, within a few years Dennis Nineham used his casting vote in favour of an amendment proposed in Governing Body by Jim Harris to allow women to dine on any night of the week. Junior members now sat on committees and adopted a trades unionist approach to negotiations about rents. But by 1978, encouraged by an interview with the chaplain, Geoffrey Rowell, and a meeting with Chris Perrin, the President of the Keble JCR, the journalist Graham Turner remarked in the *Sunday Telegraph* on a marked shift towards the right at Oxford: the only issues which now stirred students were those that offered some discernible personal gratification. In 1977, one of these involved a student request for the installation of a condom machine at Keble, which, when denied by the Governing Body (who did not take it seriously) threatened to disrupt the impending visit of Princess Margaret. Persuaded by Denis Meakins, the Governing Body thought again, held an emergency meeting and reversed its decision. Judging by the stories of her repartee on her visits to the College, the Princess herself knew very well what students were like, and would have been well able to deal with the situation.

The *Record* of 1979 recalls the changes to the College during the 1970s, 'culminating in the most radical of all (undreamt of in 1950), that providing for the admission of women'. Dennis Nineham, as chair of the Conference of Colleges, was much involved in the debates across the University about the admission of women to the men's colleges, of which he was very much in favour. In 1971 a motion put to Keble's Governing Body opposing the admission of women for the foreseeable future, whatever scheme was proposed, was lost by 19 votes to 6, but the necessary two-thirds majority was not reached. In 1972 Keble and Selwyn debated the position about reciprocal facilities, should one college become co-educational before the other. The issue gathered momentum and, in 1973, it was necessary to emphasize that the College's position derived from the report of a special committee of both senior and junior members. However, the first five men's colleges admitted women in 1974, and a 'straw' vote at Keble in 1976 produced a clear majority in favour. Changes to the rules about women guests on guest nights were introduced in 1975, and the Sex Discrimination Act was passed in the same year, with concomitant effects on the filling of joint posts and the terms of college scholarships and endowed fellowships. The University wished to stagger the admission of women and in 1977 Keble agreed to participate in a ballot about the phasing, if all men's colleges in the same position also agreed to take part. When University College broke ranks, Keble decided to go ahead and admit women from 1979. It was agreed by the majority of colleges that there should be a 30 per cent ratio of open awards given on the basis of the 1978 entrance examination, but the question of closed awards caused some difficulty. The women's colleges were nervous that they would no longer be able to attract the best women candidates or offer sufficient open awards, and the College

agreed to contribute £500 per year for five years to a fund for scholarships at women's colleges proposing to admit men. It was also decided to investigate the practicality of inviting a group of schoolmistresses to the College in order to explore how best to attract women applicants.

After ten years as Warden, Dennis Nineham resigned to return to academic life as a professor at Bristol, and was succeeded in 1980 by Christopher Ball, a specialist in linguistics and fellow in English language at Lincoln College. Ball was active in university and external issues, and was knighted in 1988. One of the early events in his Wardenship was the 150th anniversary of the Oxford Movement, celebrated in 1983 with a procession of the Keble parishes and a service in the Chapel. Ball also encouraged moves to raise academic standards in the College, for instance, introducing reporting on the quality of tutorials from the undergraduates. Ed Balls (PPE 1985) was then President of the JCR; Julie Willcox (Hutton) felt she had made a gaffe at a lunch in the Lodgings when she told the Warden that she disagreed with his idea of including Blues in the Norrington Table, but when Keble came ninth in the Table in 1987 and 1988, it excited comment in the national press. Further initiatives during the 1980s, while W.W.M. Allison (physics) was senior tutor, led to the College acquiring a fellow in Japanese (Brian Powell) and a

further fellow in English (Nigel Smith), at first shared with Queen's and wholly a college appointment, but later becoming a university lecturer. Attempts to attract women fellows were not very successful in producing long term appointments, but the College had some success in appointing junior research fellows, including David Eastwood, who was to become the chief executive of the Higher Education Funding Council, the source of the annual grant of public money to the University, and its regulator as a charity in the early twenty-first century. The influence of Geoffrey Rowell, Chaplain and fellow in theology from 1972 to 1994 and the author of many works on the nineteenth-century Church, the Oxford Movement and other topics, who, on leaving Keble, became suffragan Bishop of Basingstoke and Bishop of Gibraltar in Europe, was powerful during the 1980s. However, a significant number of fellows kept Chapel and religious matters very much at arms' length, or were even hostile.

By the end of the 1980s, internal divisions had made the situation in the College difficult. Ball was deeply involved in national educational bodies, in particular NAB (the National Advisory Board for Public Sector Higher Education, covering polytechnics, local education and church colleges) and was felt by some to have become detached; he resigned in 1989 and there was an interregnum of a term.

69

The Growth of the Conference Business

In 1920, Bursar Champernowne had suggested that Keble might follow Balliol's lead and 'systematically' fill the College during the long vacation. There is little evidence of such a strategy being implemented in the interwar years and, given the state of the rooms and the low opinion in which Keble's architecture was held, little reason to suppose that it would have been successful.

After the Second World War, however, things began to improve, as rooms were redecorated, electric fires installed and more bathrooms provided. With such luxuries, the conference business began to grow. A landmark was the arrival, in the summer of 1948, of the first cohort of 'the Drapers', a week-long summer school for shop managers. Now organized by The British Shops and Stores Association, the summer school has recently celebrated 50 years at Keble. It is a relationship that has given Keble one of its quirkier features. The dinosaur on the boundary wall on Blackhall Road appeared overnight during the Drapers' conference in the early 1970s. It quickly became iconic, and when the Arco building necessitated rebuilding of part of the wall its head was carefully redrawn by a group of undergraduates headed by Leo Lewis.

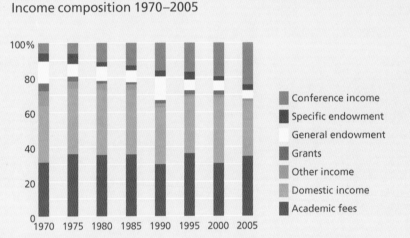

Income composition 1970–2005

Legend:
- Conference income
- Specific endowment
- General endowment
- Grants
- Other income
- Domestic income
- Academic fees

Building the conference business was a slow process. By 1970 it contributed 6 per cent of the College's annual income. The introduction of washbasins into the Victorian bedrooms and the construction of Hayward and De Breyne quads gave it a boost, and during the 1980s it grew steadily, accounting for 16 per cent of total income by 1990. But the market was changing and in the early 1990s income began to fall. Shared toilets and bathrooms might be tolerated by American and European summer schools, but corporate clients and organizers of academic conferences expected better. So when the specification for what became the Arco building was being drawn up, en suite facilities in all rooms were a key requirement. At the same time, the College embarked on a rolling programme to convert the Victorian sets from study and bedroom to study-bedroom and bathroom/dressing room. The investment paid off and the growth in the business resumed.

By the end of the 1990s Keble had over 250 en suite rooms and the largest conference business of any Oxford college. A Hall that could seat 250 in comfort was a great asset, but the College did not have a lecture theatre that could hold that number, nor enough seminar rooms for 'break-out' groups. These became a priority in the design of what became the Sloane Robinson Building, opened in 2002. By 2005, conference revenues accounted for 24 per cent of total income.

The vacation conference business has transformed Keble in more ways than one. The financial contribution is critical. Net income averages 30–35 per cent of revenues and is equivalent, in its impact, to a near doubling of the endowment. The impact on Keble's buildings is equally profound, with enormous improvements in the quality of student accommodation, and new facilities like the theatre and the café. The business also sustains a team of up to 30 students who are housed, fed and paid during the Easter and summer vacations to augment the permanent staff.

Roger Boden

Right: *Ken Lovett*

The many difficulties surrounding the initiative also led in 1993 to the resignation of the music fellow, John Caldwell.

Finance was also still difficult, and Ken Lovett, who became Bursar in 1991, kept a very tight control on expenditure. John Seagrave had left in 1990 and a brief spell during which Alan Corney, fellow in physics, took on the Bursarship, had been marked by a student rent strike which proved difficult to handle. The College had sold its farms, mainly in 1982, the last being sold in the 1990s.

Jean Robinson

Jean Robinson was an important presence in the College from 1966 until 1994. She was successively assistant librarian, Librarian, adviser to women and executive secretary of the appeal in 1989–92. She knew nearly all the undergraduates and graduates and was a very good administrator; moreover she knew how to deal with actual and potential donors. She was also for years the only woman with a recognized place in this very male group, and after women had been admitted she was concerned for and protective of them. Since she could also be decisive and outspoken, some fellows, unsurprisingly, resented the position she had built up, and felt she overstepped her place. But James Griffin says of her that she helped to make the College a 'bright and humane place', and Ed Schneider (1971) has preserved what he calls a 'typically charming note' written to him in 1974, in which she concluded, 'If you have an idle moment visit the Robinson castle sometime – there is always coffee bubbling or a glass of something handy'.

Fortunately for the College, George Richardson, economist, fellow of St John's and recently retired as secretary to the delegates and chief executive, Oxford University Press, in which capacity he had turned around the latter's fortunes, agreed to become Warden. Richardson was to regret the fact that he had only five years in post (Wardens of Keble retire at 70). Healing was necessary, and he and his wife Isabel could offer that, but there were also new challenges and the College needed to move forward. One legacy of the previous few years was that, extraordinarily in view of his recent achievements, George Richardson inherited a situation in which the Warden was not allowed to be the chair of the College's finance committee; this only changed when Averil Cameron had been in post for a year.

The College's inability or unwillingness to look after the Chapel organ resulted in a major crisis which extended into Richardson's Wardenship. This was perhaps the episode which reflected least well on the custodianship exercised by the Governing Body. It was decided to replace the original organ, already failing in 1965, with something more classical, and an appeal for funds for a new one was launched in 1986. An organ scholars' reunion dinner was held in 1988 at which the courses were labelled as the Pedal, the Positive, the Great and the Swell. However the fundraising was unsuccessful and the issue of the organ acted as a surrogate for deeper divisions between those who supported the Chapel and those who were opposed to it.

But overall the picture was improving. Ken Lovett also brought in Roger Boden (PPE, 1965) with the twin brief of raising the income from conferences and setting up a modern development office. Jean Robinson had recently died in post. She had been Librarian since 1965 and was executive secretary of a further appeal in 1989–92, with James Griffin as Director and a target of £5m. She knew everyone, old members as well as students. Eric Stone also died in 1993, and the College was still recovering from both of these events when news came that Paul Hayes had been diagnosed with Hodgkin's Disease; he died in Trinity Term 1995, teaching and examining to the end. But the Arco building by Rick Mather, named after the then Atlantic Richfield Oil Corporation, was opened in the same year, providing a further 93 student rooms. It had originally been planned on a smaller scale, but a bold move by Keble, in maximizing its possible gain through a tax break known as the Business Expansion Scheme, enabled the College to put up a much larger building, with additional public rooms, which could also bring in letting income and attract conferences to the College.

Averil Cameron was elected as the first female Warden late in 1993 and took up the post after George Richardson's retirement, in time for Michaelmas Term, 1994. Three women had all been elected to head colleges that had previously been all male, the others being Marilyn Butler at Exeter and Jessica Rawson at Merton. Interestingly, all three were academics: Marilyn Butler had been Professor of English Literature at Cambridge, Jessica Rawson came from a career at the British Museum, and Averil Cameron had held chairs of ancient history and late antique and Byzantine studies at King's College London.

Their arrival caused a stir in Oxford, and at Averil Cameron's first Governing Body meeting at Keble, there was only one woman besides herself: Claire Lewis, a senior research fellow, who subsequently moved on to Sheffield University. Jane Hanna, fellow in law, had resigned, and while the College had succeeded in the 1980s in appointing three women to research fellowships, these were short-term appointments. The Librarian, Marjory Szurko, attended

Above: *Averil Cameron, Warden since 1994, portrait by Mark Roscoe, 1999*

Below left: *Sloane Robinson Building, 2002*

Below: *Arco building, 1995*

Above: *College staff, 2008*

one of the first Gaudy dinners held after 1994 so that the Warden would not be the only woman present. Some of the female graduate students, in particular, were excited by her arrival and a hearteningly large number of old members, many of them men of the older generation and, indeed, in orders, wrote to express their pleasure when the election was first known. Gradually, though only gradually, some women fellows were appointed, and the number noticeably grew once the College started to take on more young research fellows; in 2007–8 it had 13 of these in all, a very considerable shift from the old-style model. In 1999 Keble gained a record 38 firsts in finals. Its finances also began to improve significantly.

The Arco building was complemented by the Sloane Robinson Building, also by Rick Mather, in 2002, and the former fellows' garden landscaped and renamed Newman quad. The O'Reilly Theatre in the Sloane Robinson Building, and Newman quad itself, were named by Sir Anthony O'Reilly, and the main site of the College attained its present and final form. Ken Lovett had also initiated the far-sighted policy of buying more houses in prime Oxford locations near the College. These housed students, in particular the growing number of graduates, but the College also benefited from the Oxford property boom, and the substantial profit made by the sale of these houses was an important factor in enabling it to buy the former Acland Hospital and adjacent buildings on Woodstock and Banbury Roads in 2004. This was a bold move. Some of the site has been restored and adapted and the former hospital functions as a residence for graduate students, but its long-term development is one of the main challenges currently facing the College.

The last three decades of the 20th century saw a steady improvement in Keble's fortunes, both absolutely and (with the exception of endowments) relative to colleges generally.

Income per student (in 2007 values)

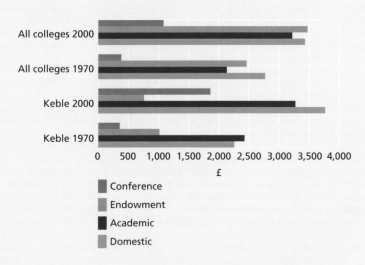

In real terms Keble's income per student increased by 59 per cent over the 30-year period. Within this total, conference income grew five-fold, domestic income by two thirds and academic income by one third, whilst endowment income actually declined by one quarter. The growth in domestic income reflects the higher proportion of students housed in college accommodation, following the addition of the Hayward, De Breyne and Arco buildings. The apparent decline in endowment income is in fact a sign of the College's financial prosperity: in 1970 Keble's investments were managed to generate much-needed dividend and interest income, but by 2000 it was managing to balance its books without substantial endowment income and the strategy was designed to achieve capital growth.

In relative terms, Keble's domestic and conference incomes per student have both grown significantly faster than those of the colleges generally. But Keble's academic income per student, which in 1970 was 14 per cent higher than the average because of higher-than-normal college fees (then paid by Local Education Authorities on behalf of their students), had, by 2000, fallen into line.

The increased percentage of students accommodated in Keble is reflected in shifts in the balance of costs.

Costs per student (in 2007 values)

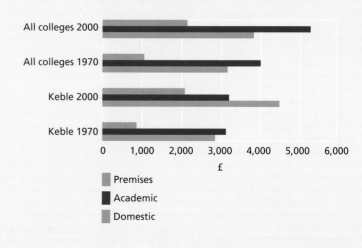

Domestic expenditure, which in 1970 was only 90 per cent of the average, had by 2000 climbed to 115 per cent. Meanwhile, expenditure on premises, 76 per cent of the average in 1970, rose to almost 100 per cent. By contrast, Keble's academic costs per student remained virtually unchanged in real terms, whilst the average for all colleges climbed by 30 per cent. This does not necessarily imply any reduction in Keble's teaching provision relative to the average. The main reason for the growth in the all-colleges figure is a higher spend on research activity by those colleges that have the endowment income to support it.

Income per student in 2007

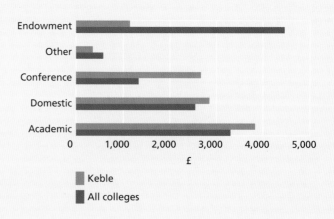

Endowment income per student remains far below the average, reflecting both the modest level of Keble's endowment (a respectable £25m at the beginning of 2008 – the highest in its history but still less than 1 per cent of the total for all colleges) and the modest rate of drawdown. The College now draws a maximum of 3.15 per cent of the average value of the endowment over the prior 3 years: in 2006–7 the actual drawdown under this rule amounted to 2.5 per cent of the year-end value of the endowment. The average drawdown for all colleges in that year was 3.3 per cent.

In other respects the College continues to out-perform. Conference revenues per student are now double the average and both domestic and academic incomes are above average. The latter may appear curious, given the drive to harmonize fees: the explanation lies in the dramatic increase in graduate students across the University as a whole – up 54% from 4,805 in 2000 to 7,380 in 2007. Keble has shared in this growth but not to the same extent (157 in 2000, 204 fee-paying in 2007 – an increase of 30%). Fee income flowing to colleges from graduate students is roughly half that earned for undergraduate students.

The cost picture is no less encouraging.

Costs per student in 2007

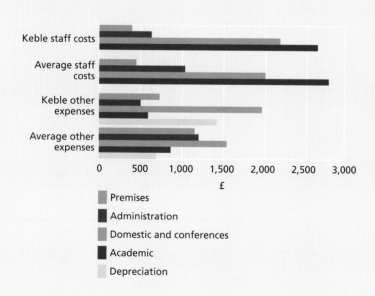

- Premises
- Administration
- Domestic and conferences
- Academic
- Depreciation

By most measures Keble can claim to be considerably more efficient than the average college. With the exception of domestic and conference activity, staff costs per student are lower in all areas – dramatically so in administration. A similar pattern is present in non-staff

costs, with one notable exception: Keble's depreciation charge per student is more than double the average. Depreciation is a non-cash charge against income, which is intended to measure the rate at which buildings, plant and machinery are being used up. More than 90 per cent of the charge relates to buildings. Keble's charge is so high, not because its buildings are expected to wear out faster than other colleges –- brick is, in fact, a lot more durable than stone. Rather, the charge reflects a very conservative approach to maintaining our buildings: the faster we depreciate them (and Keble depreciates over 25 years, where 40 years is nearer the norm), the more quickly we build up cash reserves to fund renewal of the fabric. This is in stark contrast to the College's first hundred years.

Roger Boden

BUILDINGS AND GARDENS

Keble is more fortunate than many other colleges in that it has reason to be proud of all its architecture. Butterfield's original buildings for the College are nowadays held to be his crowning achievement, and Keble was spared the unfortunate 1960s developments from which some others suffered, although the monstrosity of the Thom building of the department of engineering on the corner of Banbury and Keble Roads sadly spoils the skyline of Liddon quad. The bold Ahrends, Burton and Koralek buildings of the late 1970s are themselves Grade 2* listed, and with the successful landscaping and planting of Newman quad (once the fellows' garden), the two complementary Rick Mather buildings of 1995 and 2002 form a third integrated area, while at the same time speaking to the decorated Butterfield façade which forms one side of them. Indeed, the roof terrace of the Arco building and the upper levels of the Sloane Robinson Building provided spectacular views, with new insights into Butterfield's ingenuity and decorative genius. It is true that in the early twenty-first century, the original architecture has lost that gaudiness that was Butterfield's pride when it was new, and would be transformed if external cleaning could be afforded. But the College buildings as a complex rightly inspire admiration, and the ABK buildings have drawn from the architectural historian Geoffrey Tyack the comment 'Nowhere in Oxford is the language of modernism used with more subtlety'.

This is not how many people regarded Butterfield's creation in the early days. Gerard Manley Hopkins wrote to William Butterfield in 1877 of his 'beautiful and original style', that 'I do not think this generation will ever much admire it. They do not understand how to look at a Pointed [Gothic] building as a whole, having a single form governing it throughout.' Although she was impressed by its scale, Lavinia Talbot's initial reaction when she first saw the new College was doubtful: 'I don't admire the architecture, which is Butterfield's', but by 1876 she described the 'great Chapel' as 'a daily delight'. In 1885 J.D. Sedding wrote 'Keble College can never look mellow.... Mellowness is a quality it must ever lack.... Keble will be a nature-puzzling, time-defying object till the crack of doom, and will stare with its peculiar nineteenth-century stare straight into the eyes of eternity'.

Above: *Aerial view of the main site*

Right: *The ABK building*

Above: *View from the
Chapel roof towards the
Warden's Lodgings*

The public reception was predominantly one of
bewilderment and even hostility, and so far as external
viewers are concerned, the story of the reception of Keble's
architecture is one in which early denigration and later
disregard gave way – very gradually – to appreciation and
respect. Much of the rest of Oxford looked down on this
upstart institution, which was not a real college, and was
built with highly decorated brick rather than mellow stone.
As the first Warden later wrote in his *Memories of Early
Life*, it was not even the 'deep-red brick which (but for
want of money) Mr Butterfield would have liked to employ,
but the pale dull red of the modern builder's work'. Phrases
such as 'a holy zebra' and 'a fair-isle sweater' are expressive
of the somewhat bewildered reactions. Oscar Wilde joined
the chorus, praising Oxford as the most beautiful thing in
the world, 'in spite of Keble College'.

By 1947, however, John Betjeman wrote in *The Clock
Tower* that Keble was the most original building erected in
Oxford in the last century. It featured in his poem
'Myfanwy at Oxford' (1940), and its importance was
recognized by John Summerson in 1949. In the 1960s
Butterfield's 'rich gaudy Gothic' was being praised for its
pioneering use of materials in the interests of modernism.
Champions of Butterfield's architecture included Sir
Kenneth Clark and Sir A.E. Richardson, who in 1959

supported its claim to be recognized as an historic building
of the first class. Clark had not mentioned Keble when his
book, *The Gothic Revival*, came out in 1927, but the
second edition, published in 1950, explained his change of
view, and in a letter to the Governing Body in 1959 in
support of its Grade I Listing, he stated that 'it is one of the
finest buildings of its date in England'. Richardson's view
was that it was 'the most comprehensive of all the buildings
of the Gothic revival', and outstanding for its compositional
arrangement. Nikolaus Pevsner recognized its merits and
Hugh Casson wrote of it in 1988 'you expect drama and
you get it'. Geoffrey Tyack refers to it as 'one of the most
startling, yet also one of the most impressive, buildings of
the Gothic revival'. In Simon Jenkins's *England's Thousand
Best Houses* of 2003 (not, of course, that Keble is a house)
it is downgraded only because its exterior now needs
cleaning. The chapter on William Butterfield and Benjamin
Webb in a recent book by the architectural historian
J. Mordaunt Crook gives Butterfield the serious critical
attention he undoubtedly deserves, and a television
programme with Gavin Stamp as presenter, shown in 2007,
was highly appreciative of Butterfield's Keble. But the old
prejudices linger in Martin Amis's novel, *The Information*
(1995), where the two protagonists are said to have shared
a set of rooms (never the case in the real Keble) in the

Right: *Sir Hugh Casson, watercolour, 1988*

Below: *Detail of brickwork*

'mighty hideousness' of Keble College. In the same year, an article which appeared in the architectural press when the Arco building was opened still says that Butterfield's 'absurdly decorated exteriors hold little interest', and that their use of brick in a city constructed largely of Cotswold stone is 'an act of astonishing arrogance, scarcely imaginable today'.

It has never been easy for artists to capture the scale or the unique combination of grandeur and detail in Butterfield's ensemble, and the attractive watercolours of the gateway and other parts of the College, in Hugh Casson's *Hugh Casson's Oxford* of 1988, soften the Butterfield effect so much that they might even belong to another and more conventional college. It is only more recently, in photographs by Lucy Dickens and others, that Keble's true grandeur stands revealed.

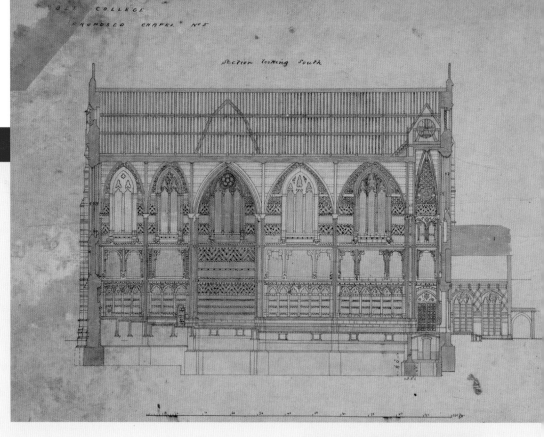

Dealing with the Architect

'Mr Butterfield's refusal about the Tower was annoying & impractical and in matters of this kind we must I am sure be prepared to act without him if he can not be got to act with us'.

This comment, in a letter of October 1870 from Warden Talbot, highlights the tension that arose between an architect with a very strong sense of the final look of a building project and the practical requirements of his clients. In this instance, Butterfield was refusing to put a striking clock in the gateway tower. As in many other examples, the architect's view prevailed.

Butterfield had inspected the site in June 1866 before recommending its purchase; he drew up block plans for the College layout in February 1867, handed over completed designs for accommodation and temporary administrative buildings in December of the same year, and it was his forms for tendering that were used when appointing builders. However, it would be wrong to see Butterfield as imposing his ideas on a reluctant committee: the block plans were drawn up with the help of Lord Beauchamp; his first designs for accommodation were returned with a request to allow for 100 students, rather than 68; and the tenders were considered by a building committee, although they did leave him to draw up the contracts. When Butterfield showed his drawings in December 1867, 'Mr Butterfield stated … that the walls would be faced with stone'. (The minutes do not record when the architect and the committee changed their minds on this.) As a sign of the trust that they had in him, in October 1869 the Memorial Committee decided 'that no presents should be definitely accepted until they have received the approval of the Warden and the Architect'.

Almost all of the letters in the College archives from or about Butterfield relate to the design of the Chapel. As soon as William Gibbs promised the money, Warden Talbot predicted 'a battle royal', and he was not wrong. The use of brick was condemned by some, with Liddon believing that the Chapel represented 'an opportunity for escaping some of the mistakes of the earlier buildings'; he was not pleased with the 'odd designs' that were accepted. The Warden challenged the need to make the practical aspects of the Chapel so obvious, only to be told that 'There are bodies as well as souls in Chapel'. Butterfield was very hurt by the Council's criticism of the mosaics, although 'Of course I made very light of it'. The College archives contain the Butterfield-Liddon correspondence on the choice of Christ in majesty above the altar, which left Liddon complaining that 'he is quite as peremptory on theological & practical questions as on purely architectural ones'. The deciding factor in Butterfield's favour was that he had the support of the benefactor: 'Of all the many architects with whom I have had to do, he is the only one who seems to me to conduct his business in an effective and conscientious manner'.

Robert Petre

Top: *Butterfield design for the Chapel*

Left: *Plan showing the circulation in the chimneys*

Right: *William Butterfield*

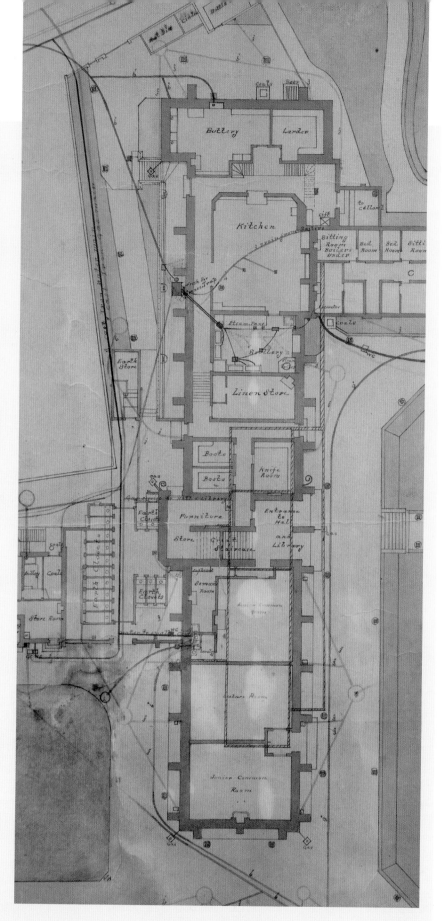

Above: *Section of an early drainage plan, showing the west Liddon ground floor range, including the SCR, JCR and the 'cloaca maxima'*

Butterfield is remembered at Keble as a famously difficult man, even if Lavinia Talbot thought otherwise. In 1868 he was in his mid 50s, but All Saints, Margaret Street, to which Keble Chapel is so clearly related, was begun when he was only 35 years old. He visited northern Italy, with its striped brick buildings, in 1854, and built the chapel at Balliol in 1856–7. He was in fact a contemporary of Pugin (b. 1812), who, since the late 1830s, had been hectically employed in designing new Roman Catholic churches and cathedrals. The two met in 1844 with a group of Camden Society (founded 1839, later known as the Ecclesiological Society) and Tractarian friends. In the same year Butterfield was invited to join 'The Engagement', a group of high-minded supporters of the Tractarians who were also liberal in their political views; other members during the group's lifetime from 1844 to 1852 included W.E. Gladstone, A.H.D. Acland and J.T. Coleridge. Influenced by the ideas expressed in Ruskin's *Seven Lamps of Architecture* (1849), Butterfield's church of All Saints, Margaret Street marked a transition from Puginism, and polychrome seemed the style of the future. G.E. Street's *Brick and Marble Architecture of the Middle Ages in Italy* (1855) set out Street's ideas on the subject, and Butterfield later justified his choice of polychromic brick both in terms of an honest approach to the use of local materials and as a reference to medieval brick patterns. Interestingly, Butterfield

Above: *All Saints, Margaret Street*

81

himself declined to worship at All Saints as he felt the style of worship to be too 'high'. In 1851, when Pugin published his *Earnest Address on the Establishment of the Hierarchy*, in which he veered back from the orthodox Roman Catholic position towards the High Anglicanism of the Tractarians, he was supported by Gladstone, Benjamin Webb and Butterfield himself.

Pugin died in 1852, only forty years old, after a tragic stay in Bethlem hospital. Butterfield went on to become the architect who transformed romantic into 'modern' Gothic. His connections with the Tractarians meant that he was already part of the circle which provided the founders of Keble, and he was the obvious choice to design a new foundation on Anglican lines which needed to be bold and assertive enough for its position, 'like a Christian sentinel facing the besieging armies of science', in Hugh Casson's words, directly opposite the University Museum. The Museum was designed by Benjamin Woodward in Bath stone and also influenced by Ruskin, and had been the scene in 1860 of the famous debate about evolution between Thomas Huxley and Samuel Wilberforce. But with the abolition of the brick tax in 1850, together with advances in railway transport and in technical areas such as colour, the shift from local stone was already underway. Butterfield had begun the Chapel and new quadrangle at Rugby School in 1867, and still more relevant to his Keble commission, the muscular brick of his design (referred to by J. Mordaunt Crook as 'its bricky glory') fitted the buildings going up elsewhere in north Oxford in the 1860s, even if it seemed out of step with the stone of the older colleges. It also suited the uncompromising and provocative new foundation as it confronted the symbolism of modernity represented by the Museum.

Keble's site linked the older part of the University with the developments taking place in north Oxford in the late nineteenth century. The new University Museum, and the Parks, acquired by the University in the same period, were directly opposite. A layer of about six metres of gravel underlay the soil on the site itself, and the paths in Liddon quad had to be raised, enabling the creation of a sunken quad which, albeit of grass, recalled Tom Quad at Christ Church, with which the new College had such strong connections; indeed, Pusey himself paid £800 to complete the gateway. The effect of such an arrangement was that when the Chapel was built in 1873–6, its great height was enhanced even more.

Below: The Chapel from the University Parks

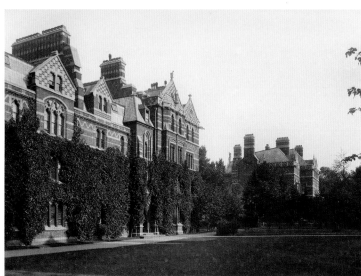

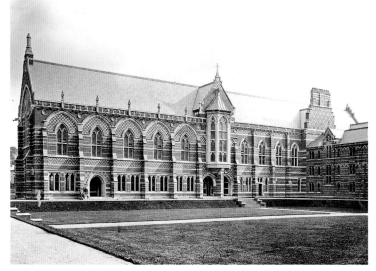

Photographs of Keble College by Henry Taunt (1842–1922)

Top left and right: *Pusey quad, 1870 and 1880*
Centre, left: *Parks Road frontage, with railings, 1880;* right: *Pusey quad, covered in creepers, 1907*
Bottom, left: *Keble College from the University Museum, 1870;* right: *Liddon quad with Hall and Library, 1880*

Early photographs still convey something of the original brightness as well as the mass of Butterfield's buildings. Even the temporary hall and chapel were built on a substantial scale, and occupied most of what would become the south side of Liddon quad. They also show how stark and uncompromising Butterfield's designs could be, without any softening from gardens or beds at the foot of the walls. It is clear that, within a short period, climbers were planted to modify this impression, and the many of the exterior walls were heavily covered in climbers for many decades. Butterfield had not intended or desired such an effect, but so persistent was this approach that it is only recently that a decision was made to remove the remaining coverage. Internally as well as externally, Butterfield's coherent vision extended even to small details. Patterns, tiles, friezes and brickwork in the Chapel, Hall, Library, Senior Common Room and Lodgings echo the external decorative themes and make a strong statement of unity. Panelling, as in the study and dining room of the Lodgings, and the crenellated tops of doors and shelving bays express a sense of dignified self-worth.

Left: *Liddon quad under construction*

Below right: *Creepers on the gateway*

Below: *The west end of the Chapel from the Arco roof*

Nothing about Butterfield's designs was symmetrical, yet the repetition or variation of colour and pattern in all parts of the College from the Hall to the Lodgings gives a powerful sense of unity to the whole. The higher the part of the building, the greater elaboration in the external patterning, some of which can indeed be seen only from the external gallery on the roof of the Chapel, or the roof terrace of the Arco building. Every element was designed or deliberately intended by Butterfield, including the ironmongery, the furniture, the library shelving and the floor tiling.

Opposite page:
Butterfield details

Right: *The Warden's garden*

Below: *Butterfield corridor before and after restoration*

The rectory-like design of the Lodgings is clear, and its built-in sideboard in the dining room is very typical. Butterfield also equipped the Lodgings with a small chapel for family prayers, marked on his plans as an oratory. This was typical of Tractarian houses of the period; Tyntesfield also had a substantial oratory before the new chapel was created, and when the Talbots moved in in 1877, the small oratory in the Lodgings and the house itself were blessed by the bishop in a 'beautiful little service'. The building is distinguished from many late Victorian houses by the elegance of the main rooms, with tall windows, especially on the garden side, with their narrow balconies and elegant ornamental ironwork. The oratory is now a cloakroom and the internal layout has been altered, not always happily. The small garden on the west side, reached by an iron stair from the downstairs sitting room, was known to early Wardens' children as 'the Pit'; it was paved only by Eric Symes Abbott, when it was probably also laid out with low box hedges as today, and seems to have been planted with roses by the 1980s. It is now overlooked on one side by the ABK buildings and on the other by a lecture room, but has been replanted in recent years by Caroline Brett, mainly in white and pink, with a magnolia grandiflora planted in 2006 to mark Averil Cameron's award of a DBE.

Butterfield's original panelling, shelves and sideboard designed for the Lodgings remain, but elsewhere only a few items of his furniture have survived. Much of the rest, as well as the 'oaks' or external doors of the student rooms, was sold off or otherwise disposed of, just at the point when consciousness of the aesthetic qualities of Keble's architecture was rising in the fellowship. Of the disposal of the 'oaks' in 1961, the College *Record* stated that 'they evidently no longer served the purposes intended'. It went on to say that their removal made the corridors lighter and 'deprived the undergraduates of at least one of the means of creating noises in the night'. A restoration of the Butterfield rooms in Liddon quad has recently begun, which respects the original designs for the rooms and corridors, and even the appearance of the 'oaks'.

Butterfield conceived the College as an entity, with a very clear hierarchy overall. The verticality of the Chapel set it above the horizontally designed Hall and Library, which in turn are more complex than the residential buildings.

However, Butterfield's design was built in stages and not fully completed. When the Warden's Lodgings were built in 1876–7 a 'gap' was left between them and the east range of Pusey quad which has remained unfilled. It gives a view onto Parks Road and the University Museum and provides the opportunity for grass and planting, as well as for an essential and increasingly well disguised headquarters for the gardens and grounds team. Thoughts of filling in this area have recurred at various times but been rejected. The clock tower block, with rooms for College servants, was added in 1875, the Chapel finished in 1876 and the Hall and Library in 1878. The north range of Liddon quad was still incomplete until 1957, when the Besse building was added, designed by Knapp Fisher and Rayson and built by Benfield and Loxley with the help of a gift from Antonin Besse, which provided a new staircase, L6, and continued the range up to the then fellows' garden. However plausible and useful such imitation, Butterfield would hardly be allowed in today's heritage environment.

Above: *Arcading in the Chapel*

Right: *Hoggarth sketch of student room (see also page 106)*

As the College grew, so alterations and additions were made. As early as 1881, 'a sum not exceeding £30' was placed at the Warden's disposal for a junior common room. Later changes included the enlargement, in 1958, of the senior common room smoking room, and its redecoration by Leslie Franks. This was made possible through the benefaction of Lord Quickswood, after whom it is named. It is described by Douglas Price as Palladian, and as being rather like a 'flash west end hotel'. Also in 1958 there was a restoration of the interior of the Chapel in accordance with the arrangement in a watercolour given by John Betjeman. The drab green-grey curtains were removed and replaced by red-brown ones. The brickwork of the west end was made visible, as was the arcading either side of the altar, and the memorial tablets could now be read without having to 'creep behind a curtain with a torch'. It was daringly agreed in 1959 to 'provide a ladies powder closet if a suitable site could be found'. In 1965, an extension to the SCR was designed by Alan Stubbs and an SCR dining room created in mock-Butterfield style. The interior had an unsuitable powder-blue ceiling, though it was later to be transformed into the stylish de Breyne Room. A total of £45,000 was needed for this project, and the appeal brochure explained that, in order to make space, the whole of the back of the College would be tidied up and modernized, and the 'cloaca maxima' swept away.

Butterfield's Furniture

In 1869 it was agreed that each undergraduate would need '1 table; three chairs to match; 1 elbow or folding chair; 1 bookcase with cupboards at the side; 1 carpet; blinds; 1 stump-iron bedstead with a straw palliasse mattress, a quilt, wool bolster and pillow; 1 washstand; 5 pieces of crockery; a goblet and a tumbler; 1 looking-glass; 1 chest of drawers; 1 water can; 1 bath; fire-irons, guard, fender, and coal scuttle'. However the treasurer of the Keble Memorial Fund, writing in March 1870, expressed concern that there would not be enough money to furnish the rooms which were being built. About this time the Bursar, Colonel Legge, obtained a quotation from Druce and Co. of Baker St, London for furnishing 50 sitting rooms at £10.19s.6d each and bedrooms at £8.12s each, the latter to include a washstand with five accessories, a straw palliasse and a horsehair mattress. Every article was guaranteed to be of a 'good, serviceable and useful description'. In November, William Butterfield's accounts with Parnells included the production of specimen furniture for a bedroom and sitting room at £15.2s.6d, and would-be undergraduates in 1870  were informed that the College would supply for their sitting room a table, 2 chairs, 1 elbow chair, a bookcase with cupboards (at £5.15s.), a carpet, a blind, a fender and set of fire-irons, a hearth-brush and a coal scuttle. For the bedroom the College would supply a bed and bedding, a washstand with glass and crockery, a looking-glass, a chair, a chest of drawers, a water-can and a bath. The undergraduate himself would need to supply sheets, towels, pillow-cases, laundry bag, candles and soap.

Much of this early furniture was discarded or sold off cheap, not least in the 1960s and 1970s. Photographs (see page 106) of a study dating from 1902 show some sound typical late Victorian study furniture of a mass-produced nature, notably the captain's desk chair and a small desk with turned legs. One piece of modest residential furniture which remains is a dresser, which probably housed small amounts of crockery and glass in its base and books above. The lower part is animated by the inset, open bay in the centre. The shelves above ascend in pronounced steps and levels of diminishing depth, catering economically for different sizes of books, between very stout uprights. This gradation is completed by a moulding at the top of the uprights, which combines with one that runs full width to roll into the face of the wall. This has to be by Butterfield.

David Yandell

The College Gardens

Very little remains in the College archives about the history of the gardens, and there are no indications on Butterfield's plans of planting or garden designs. The exception is the paths on Liddon quad with its sunken lawn, of which Lavinia Talbot wrote excitedly in 1871 that the new grass was beginning to grow and had even been mown for the first time. The sunken lawn is usually explained by the fact that the site was originally a gravel pit, and Butterfield had to bring in soil to make up the terraces. However, it is worth noting that the country house he designed, Milton Ernest Hall in Bedfordshire, also had three sunken lawns, as well as a lime avenue. A letter written by Butterfield in May 1873 conveys his belief in the importance of gardens in providing the right setting for the buildings, and suggesting that he himself should decide on these matters. It was agreed that £200 be spent on laying out the garden on the west side of the College, but no further correspondence of Butterfield on the subject has been found, nor does Paul Thompson's biography of Butterfield cover gardens.

Contrary to Butterfield's known wishes, creepers soon covered many of the walls, but there seems to have been no other planting where the walls joined the quads for some time. The paths were originally of earth; the corner between Liddon quad and the fellows' garden (also known in early days as the tutors' garden and later, for many years, as the dons' garden) was also merely of earth and was home to an outhouse, described as 'decrepit' in 1923. Iron gates designed by F.C. Eden (Keble 1882), architect to the College, who also designed the war memorial chapel, were installed in 1926. The present gates date from 1959 and were the gift of the Reverend Hiram Kennedy Douglass (1921) of Alabama. However, the great copper beech in Pusey quad outside the Lodgings has been there since the foundation of the College, and recalls the copper beeches at John Keble's home at Fairford, where he also served his curacy. The removal of unsightly bicycles by the library, at the corner of Liddon quad, directly opposite the Lodge, has restored the view to the Chapel.

A few of the references to garden matters in the archives deserve mention, for instance the proposed removal in 1921 of the telescope hut, and in 1929 of pigsties and the telephone hut. Lime trees on the north side of the dons' garden were pollarded in 1922 and the catalpa tree treated with the help of the forestry department. Herbaceous beds in Liddon quad are mentioned in 1922 and bulbs and rose trees for the dons' garden in the following year. By the 1960s Mr V.L. Griffiths was honorary curator of the fellows' garden and this position was confirmed

Far left: *The fellows' garden, 1947*

Left: *The opening of Newman quad and the Sloane Robinson Building, 2002*

Right: *Magnolia in Hayward quad*

Below: *1967 planting in the fellows' garden*

for the centenary preparations and the visit of Princess Margaret. Plans exist from 1967 onwards, which resulted in the creation of a Victorian rose garden in the fellows' garden and beds of 'Victorian' begonias, pelargoniums and fuchsias in front of the row of limes. Other Victorian plants included hostas and ferns. There had been plans for a double herbaceous border with a grass path down the centre, but only a single border was planted. The apple tree in Pusey quad, important for the Apple Tree Club, was replanted in 1979. On the west side of the fellows' garden along Blackhall Road stands a row of five large London plane trees, leading in the 1970s to the ABK buildings, and now to the Sloane Robinson Building of 2002. The fellows' garden disappeared with the building of the Arco and Sloane Robinson buildings in 1995 and 2002, and was re-landscaped, again with a sunken lawn, and named Newman quad when the latter building opened. The current planting has evolved from plans drawn up by John Phibbs and Sarah Ewbank, and further developed by Stephen Heyes (garden master from 2003–7) and Caroline Brett, who was appointed college gardener in 2003. Caroline maintains the gardens with the help of Steve Beasley, who has worked for the College since 1965.

With thanks to Caroline Brett

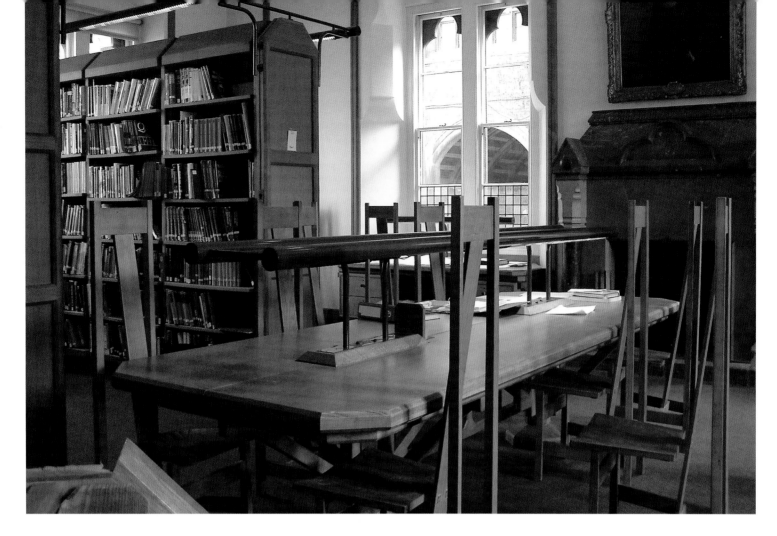

Above: *The lower Library*

Left: *The hall in the Warden's Lodgings*

Ahrends, Burton and Koralek were employed in the 1970s, not only for the de Breyne and Hayward quads which were finished and formally opened in 1977, but also for the elegant design of the lower reading room of the Library and its stair to the upper level, completed in 1981. They also relocated the Bursary and JCR to ground-floor space in Pusey quad. The idea of building along Blackhall and Museum Roads was not new, and with the prospect of the end of the 99-year leases originally granted by St John's, Keble opened negotiations for acquisition in 1958; in order to purchase the freehold of the houses on Blackhall Road, the College raised £55,000 by means of a mortgage of £20,000 from St John's at 6 per cent and a loan of £35,000 from Barclays. In 1968 the houses on Blackhall and Museum Roads were demolished, and the Keble curtilage had increased to an area of 4.5 acres. As early as 1963 a plan was produced by Alan Stubbs for the fellows' garden, and a more ambitious master plan was put forward in 1967 by Casson Conder. ABK had designed a theological college at Chichester in 1964 and had recently completed Templeton College at Kennington. The choice of this practice for Keble was a bold one, favoured by the younger fellows and supported by Dennis Nineham as Warden; the selection committee comprised Spencer Barrett, Adrian Darby, James Griffin, Christopher Stead, Roy Harris and

Dennis Shaw, and three practices were shortlisted, the others being James Stirling and Denys Lasdun.

The ABK buildings (the De Breyne and Hayward quads) also incorporated a new circular College bar with a roof garden, and an adjoining middle common room. Built in two phases in 1972 and 1977, they face the Butterfield buildings with cascading expanses of glass, but present a massive, fortress-like exterior with slit-like apertures onto Museum and Blackhall Roads, as well as directly overlooking the College car park and, beyond its wall, the walled garden of the Warden's Lodgings. Their material is brick; not red brick, but a warm buff, sympathetic to the stone and brick of nearby buildings, and combined with large areas of glass on the internal elevations. They house both tutors' rooms and graduates, and their footprint is narrow and sinuous, curling at one end into a circular, internal quad curving round a plane tree, with, at the other, a tail which ended, originally, in a fellow's flat. A glass-canopied walkway runs the whole length of the building, which is built in a Stamford-stone, yellowish brick, which echoes both the brick of Butterfield's buildings and the prevailing colour of local stone. Despite the shortcoming, by current standards, of its expanses of single-glazed windows, the quality of this design was recognized by the early award of Grade II* listing, just as the College was

The College bar and the ABK building

embarking on a comprehensive internal refurbishment in 2001–2. Extra showers were put in where possible and all the rooms renovated with close attention to period detail, retaining the original built-in furniture by John Makepeace or replacing with exact copies. Subsequently the bar was also enlarged to provide a social space, with the creation of a new and well-equipped MCR suite in Pusey quad.

The very successful remodelling of the senior common room complex dates from the 1980s. A young architect called Peter Inskip, who had worked at Cambridge, created the present Quickswood Room and Writing Room by reopening the Butterfield passage between them. He acquired an original Butterfield fireplace from the house the architect had built for his sister, and installed it in the Writing Room. Both rooms were papered with designs dating from the 1880s. The present entrance hall to the senior common room was created, and a pantry made out of a storage room. In the old senior common room itself, a carefully chosen colour scheme for the soft furnishings complemented the original French 1870s wallpaper, and the de Breyne Room, where senior members still have lunch, was redecorated in a strikingly dignified, yet modern style, with a rich, bright red wallcovering, which forms a perfect setting for the red-framed Butterfield watercolour designs for the Chapel mosaics which hang there. Inskip worked closely with Larry Siedentop, fellow in politics from 1973, who also found and chose furniture and pictures. The result is a strikingly impressive suite of rooms,

restored and remodelled from a highly unpromising existing arrangement, which are entirely in keeping with Butterfield's style for the College.

Larry Siedentop also restored the ground floor of the Warden's Lodgings in 1989, lifting many layers of linoleum from the entrance hall floor and of wallpaper from the walls, and revealing Butterfield's floor tiles and his original Pompeian red and green stencilled designs for the walls. In 1959 a kitchen had already been carved out of the grand downstairs drawing room, replacing the original basement

94

Top: *The Quickswood Room*

Above: *The Senior Common Room*

Above right: *The de Breyne Room*

Below right: *The bike racks on Blackhall Road. Compare the former fellows' garden, page 90, bottom left*

servants' hall and kitchen, but again, original Butterfield doors were now discovered and installed, providing a far more elegant solution to what had been a merely utilitarian arrangement. Internal rearrangements on the upper floors of the Lodgings remain to be restored more sensitively to the architect's original intention. The space on the top floor was made into fellows' accommodation, rented out at £200 per year, in 1957, and the basement, converted to teaching space at about the same time, now houses computing facilities and a seminar room decorated in an unexpectedly hotel style.

The final phase of building on the original site of the College resulted in two buildings designed by Rick Mather Associates. The first, completed in 1995, is the Arco building, named in honour of the then Atlantic Richfield Oil Corporation, the source of the major donation. The second, which complements the first from the other side of the fellows' garden, is the Sloane Robinson Building, named in honour of George Robinson (1975), founder with his partner Hugh Sloane of the investment management firm of Sloane Robinson LLP.

The fellows' garden was no more, and was now landscaped and renamed Newman quad. In a typically innovative stroke the many bicycles, which used to be piled in untidy heaps at the entrance to Liddon quad from the lodge, have been relegated to new and ingeniously hidden bike racks beneath the plane trees on the Blackhall Road side. There is no further room for development within the curtilage, except in the 'gap', and as David Yandell, the College's conservation architect, has written, 'the College has managed by the appointment of three brilliant architects almost to have completely developed its island site in three contrasting but entirely united ways'. Both the Mather buildings are in red brick cladding, carefully matched to the Butterfield originals, and with a subtle patterning which acknowledges his decorative manner. The Arco building provides 93 study bedrooms, arranged in flats with kitchen/living rooms, its corridors following the Butterfield precedent rather than the ABK staircases. On the north

boundary, the eaves' line and roof pitch is aligned with the Butterfield range nearby, but an extra storey can be seen from the south side, providing the kind of variation also characteristic of Butterfield. Both buildings are clad on all four façades with narrow handmade red bricks, laid in contrasting bond patterns and of a special size, but without polychromy. Interiors use a greenish grey slate, with white walls and stainless steel, and a dramatic rooflit stairwell gives an impression of modernity and light, leading at the top level to an attractive roof room and a large roof terrace, with extraordinary views directly onto the most decorated upper parts of the Butterfield buildings.

Both the Arco and the Sloane Robinson buildings are energy-efficient to a high degree, with heavily insulated cavity walls and triple-glazed windows. In the Arco building, much of the heating is passively supplied by the body-heat of the occupants, and the small heaters in individual rooms need to be used only rarely. Both buildings are heated and cooled in the main by a heat exchanger on the low-pressure ventilation system. The Arco building has concrete floors supported on the inner block walls, and a creative use has been made of the lower levels, while the Sloane Robinson Building, which sits on deep piles, uses an innovative system whereby pipes for heating and cooling pass through the piles themselves. In addition to 20 study bedrooms and a series of seminar rooms, the latter includes a flexible and technically advanced studio theatre and a recital room, as well as a beautiful common room with spectacular views across the

new sunken lawn of Newman quad to the Butterfield elevations on the west range of Liddon quad. This room is used in term as a café which can be used by any member of the College and has become a favourite space where undergraduates can write their essays and pursue their social networking on the internet.

Far left: *The Hall*

Left: *The Hall, with the Watts painting in place*

If the Chapel is the architectural glory of the College, the Hall is perhaps the place most remembered by students. Hundreds of meals are still served there every day, and dinner, which is served every night in term except Saturday, is simply referred to as 'hall'. In maintaining this tradition, the College is also maintaining the desire of the founders that undergraduates should gather together for communal meals. The Hall plays a very important role in making possible the interdisciplinary conversations and meetings which are distinctive about Oxford college life, and which graduates in particular say how much they value. Keble is proud of the fact that it has the longest college hall in Oxford – deliberately longer than Christ Church, which it resembles in some ways, just as Liddon quad resembles Tom Quad. As in the Chapel, the walls are divided into three zones, oak panelling, banded stone and then polychrome brick. The west window was designed by Alexander Gibbs, who also designed the mosaics and stained glass in the Chapel. The trussed ceiling is stencilled in a rather delicate repeating pattern, which was revealed again below decades of dirt when it was cleaned and restored in 2003–4. The minstrels' gallery is nowadays used by the choir for carols at Christmas, and, by a recently invented tradition, for sung grace before dinner on

Below: *Cleaning the Hall ceiling, 2003*

Below left: *Detail of decoration*

Above: *Dinner at Keble*

Sundays. The blazing fires in the massive fireplace are often mentioned in memoirs by former students, and the tradition has been revived recently, for instance for the traditional Christmas lunch each year, when staff are served by the Warden and fellows. The floor of the hall is laid in diagonal patterns using coloured encaustic tiles, some of which have become very worn, and certain areas have been repaired in the past in an unfortunate manner. The restoration of these parts of the floor is due to begin in 2008–9, and would have begun sooner, had it not been for the difficulty of obtaining tiles sufficiently similar to the original tiles used by Butterfield.

Harsh fluorescent lighting was introduced into the Hall and Library in 1948–9, but this was eventually replaced by more suitable table lights. 'Loudspeakers' were introduced in 1959, and for the first time a speech could be heard. From 1975, thanks to the agency of Douglas Price, the hall housed a huge painting by G.F. Watts, 'A story from Boccaccio', painted in 1844, on long loan from the Tate Gallery. The picture, which is 30 feet long, shows a naked Philomena being chased by a wounded suitor and mad dogs. It was presented to the Tate Gallery by the Cosmopolitan Club in 1903, but the Tate has not found space to hang it. Watts may have seemed a suitable artist

for Keble, but the relevance of its message of the permanent cycle of frustrated love was one that Wardens seated at High Table found hard to explain. It was returned to the Tate in 2003, when the Hall ceiling and upper levels were cleaned. It leaves what many people regard as an uncompromisingly bare wall, but if so it is a bareness that was clearly the intention of Butterfield.

With rising aspirations and changing expectations, the College has had to balance practical need with the challenge of making 19th-century buildings work. The Porters' Lodge, hub of any Oxford college, has been remodelled more than once, most recently in 1999 but most notably by Spencer Barrett in 1962–3, when the conversion into a new post room of the former resident porter's sitting room meant that the JCR could be cleared of letter racks. The block leading from the Porters' Lodge on the east side of Pusey quad has become the home of the administrative offices of the College. Some undergraduates successful in the room ballot count are still able to live in rooms in the clock tower, built with dormitories housing the College servants, but this also now houses necessary offices. The old bathrooms there had been made into student accommodation in 1966, and this was regarded as a choice place to live.

The Keble Organ

Above: *The organ case and Micklethwaite's tribune*

Below: *Keble organ stops*

The original organ in the Chapel was a three-manual instrument by William Hill and was installed at ground level below the present organ loft. The simple organ case, consisting of four flats of decorated pipes, held in place by a wooden framework with gothic gables and pinnacles, dates from Butterfield's time, though he himself never mentions it in surviving materials and was little interested in organs in his churches. It seems unlikely that Butterfield himself stencilled the display pipes, with French mouths in typical Hill style, which are still in situ. In 1892, when the present side chapel was created, the organ was raised by Henry Willis and Sons, who had taken over its tuning in 1884, and the façade was probably altered to fit the new arrangement.

In 1904 the organ was enlarged and rebuilt with pneumatic action by H.S. Vincent and Co. of Sunderland. Originally a four-manual scheme, the result was a reduced version at a cost of £300. In 1908, after problems had arisen with the pneumatic action (using rubber tubes), and the hand-blowing arrangements, the care of the organ was transferred to Messrs Gray and Davison, and an electric motor installed in 1909. In 1914 Messrs J. Binns were called in, but no action taken. By 1923 the purchase of an existing four-manual organ was considered, but in 1924–6 the Keble organ was rebuilt by Rushworth and Draper to the specification of Dr Henry Ley, former organ scholar and at the time organist at Christ Church. A committee was formed, consisting of the Warden, Dr B.J. Kidd, the Sub-Warden, Mr W.H.V. Reade, the Bursar, Lt-Col. O.R.E. Milman and 'Crab' Owen, and a fund established. During 1925 a piano had to be used, as the organ had broken down completely, and the rebuilding was not finished until the beginning of Hilary Term,

1926. The organ was cleaned in 1937 and estimates obtained for three further stops, but these were not installed. After the war the College was rewired to 230 volts, alternating current, and this caused difficulty with the electric fan. The organ was cleaned in 1951, but further problems led to more work being done by Rushworth and Draper in 1961, with some changes to the stops; the contra fagotto was the gift of Parkes. This was followed by yet more work by J.W. Walker and Sons in 1976.

While David Parkes wrote in admiring terms of the organ in the 1960s, it was argued in 1986 that little remained of historic value, and in 1992 that the organ had never been very distinguished, and had been compromised over the years by successive and incomplete changes. But Keble and its organ attracted many extremely distinguished organ scholars. A recording exists of music from Keble, directed by Jeremy Filsell (1982) and with Simon Over (1984) as organist, which preserves its characteristic sound in 1985.

By the 1980s the organ was falling into a state of serious disrepair. An appeal was launched, with the College agreeing to put in £100,000 towards the cost of a replacement. Four proposals were considered, from Roger Pulham, Woodbridge, Peter Collins, Redbourn, J.W. Walker and Sons Ltd, and Kenneth Jones Pipe Organs Ltd of Bray, County Wicklow. A new three-manual pipe organ of 43 stops with a new case was commissioned in 1987 from Kenneth Jones Pipe Organs Ltd, at a cost of £214,500. This would have incorporated some existing pipes into a new instrument designed for a wider repertoire, the organ still being sited on the gallery and the organist at the side of the base of the organ. 'Poor case design' and 'unfavourable siting' added to the view that neither repair nor rebuilding of the existing organ would any longer be practical ways forward. But with delays, Jones's price continued to rise, reaching more than £300,000.

The Jones design also provoked hostile comment from the Victorian Society. The College had been warned of the likely reaction; the existing case, it was argued, had little merit as an organ case but considerable historical value as a work by Butterfield, which justified its preservation. The agreement of donors was sought in 1991 for a new chamber organ, but this proved too large, and had to be returned in 1992, at which point the present Copeman Hart electronic organ was acquired. Most of the existing pipework was sadly removed at this time, in part to allow the installation of large speakers in the organ gallery. No further capital expenditure was to be made on the organ for at least ten years, although it was affirmed that the College's aim remained to install a new pipe organ.

Right: *New chairs in the Library*

Below: *Library, detail*

One of the changes has been the much greater need for security. Thus, while all College members now have key and swipe-card access at all times, the physical security of the College has had to be greatly increased with the aid of electronic devices and CCTV cameras. During the 1990s, doors were installed at the foot of the previously open staircases giving access to the corridors of rooms, which by then had been converted into 'en suite' with an eye to attracting more conference business. The servery into the Hall was altered with the aim of making this very small space more practical, but bringing food for several hundred people from the kitchens through this confined area into the main hall remains a minor miracle. Gravel was laid on the main paths, not wholly successfully, but a great improvement over the previous tarmac (itself a major step forward when it was laid in 1949) in terms of colour, and ramps introduced for disabled access. A steady change has also taken place in the general awareness of the require-ment for conservation and stewardship of the historic buildings. In 2001 a new set of 60 chairs was commissioned from Luke Hughes (son of William Hughes, history 1935) for the Library, and old members invited to contribute, with individual chairs named; the design was named 'Butterfield' by the maker, and the response was so lively

Right: *St Michael*

Below: *Brickwork, detail*

Opposite page:
Butterfield steps

that more were commissioned to replace the existing chairs in the side chapel. New garden benches were soon acquired on the same principle, and in 2002 the lower level of the Library was again remodelled to provide more archival space, better facilities for housing the manuscripts and rare books, some modest facilities for visiting scholars and readers, and at last an office for the Librarian. It is an indication of its higher appreciation of historical and conservation issues that the College took on a professional archivist in 2004, and indeed that has proved invaluable in making this book possible.

There is much to be done. The maintenance of the Butterfield buildings in particular is expensive. By the 1950s the external stonework, especially the gargoyles, was showing signs of crumbling, and in 1961 a gargoyle on the Lodgings was replaced, the first since the 1870s. In 1958 the College hoped to obtain a grant of £25,000 from the Oxford Historic Buildings Appeal, and when this was turned down on the grounds that Keble was not an historic building, it came as a great shock; Douglas Price wrote at the time that he thought the trustees had 'behaved despicably'. A memorandum from the College was supported by Sir Kenneth Clark, Sir Albert Richardson and the then Vice-Chancellor, and the committee was further lobbied, but the College only received £8,000. While the praise which the College's buildings had received from such prominent people contributed to their being listed Grade 1, this accolade makes their maintenance and restoration even more expensive, since it must be done in accordance with the most rigorous principles and methods. The exterior frontage along Parks Road (which now carries very heavy traffic) has lost its brightness and is particularly in need of cleaning. Extensive work on the stonework and roof of the Chapel has taken place over a long period, but a further comprehensive programme of necessary work has been identified, including the repair and restoration of the stained glass windows and ironwork. Tiles and stonework are often worn, not only in the Hall but elsewhere too.

The College's Conservation Statement of 2005 identifies a programme for the 'reversal of degeneration' and notes that 'every change needs to be carefully considered'. Keble has not always adopted such principles in the past when introducing changes, but the juxtaposition it has achieved between its magnificent Butterfield buildings, and its bold commissioning of spectacular and elegant new buildings and careful landscaping and planting, makes it one of the most memorable and striking of all Oxford colleges.

5 STUDENT LIFE BEFORE THE SECOND WORLD WAR

Keble emerged from the shadow of the 1914–18 war as a bruised institution. Numbers were up in the immediate post-war years, but this was an emotionally scarred generation. The buildings had been battered about by occupation by cadets, and there were still pigsties in the gardens: they were soon joined by 'hutments', temporary accommodation for the overflowing numbers. Keble was still looked down on by the rest of the University: writing to Warden Kidd in 1920, William Hatchett Jackson, the science tutor, claimed that his best pupils had suppressed the identity of their college to secure preferment. Moreover, the College's economical principles were imperilled by the effects of wartime inflation, which left the Council with no alternative but to increase fees to £50 per term, but that covered tuition, accommodation, and (in line with the founders' vision) all meals.

Student routines were dominated by the rhythms of the communal life including Chapel and meals. Students would be awakened between 7 and 7.30 a.m. in time for ablutions before Chapel, which was compulsory three times per week in addition to one of the Sunday services. Whereas in other colleges it was customary for undergraduates to take breakfast and lunch in their own rooms, in Keble everyone was expected to turn up for the communal meals in Hall, with the opportunity to opt out of only two per week. Lectures were scheduled for mornings; the hours between 2 p.m. and 5 p.m. were largely reserved for sport or for recreation, ending with tea in the JCR, though most appear

to have returned to their studies, working for a couple of hours before dinner.

In line with the principles of the founders, Keble undergraduates were expected to live economically. Undergraduate expenditure continued to be monitored by the Council. They were not supposed to spend more than £7.10s.0d. per term on their battels (covering incidental expenses like JCR teas, buttery purchases, beer in Hall, meat at lunch, extra baths and club dinners), and the exceeders were listed at every meeting of the Finance Committee and reported to the Council.

Above: *Keble freshmen, 1919*

Right: *The Library*

Rooms were sparsely furnished, comprising a sitter with a table, two chairs, and built-in bookcases, and a bedder with bed, washstand and chest of drawers, though there was no longer any prohibition on undergraduates bringing their own cushions! Students gradually improved the amenities, Edward Garfitt recalling how he acquired an old Minty chair with corduroy cushions on a wooden frame with moveable back and a wicker chair by means of second hand purchases from those going down. But conditions remained pretty spartan. The wattage of the electric bulbs was deliberately limited, and the light switches prevented the simultaneous lighting of the sitting room and the bedroom. According to Hilary Barnes, the windows did not fit well and were painted a peculiar brown known as 'Bursar's blood'.

Dominating the undergraduate psyche until the late 1950s, when more bathrooms were provided, was the washstand, on which stood the chamber pot (stamped with the College crest) and a bowl for ablutions, for which the scout would bring a pint of hot water each morning. The main lavatory block was located between the old JCR and the Clock Tower. There were just eight baths for the whole College, and they were all located on the upper floors of the Clock Tower; each morning, bathrobed figures swinging their wash bags would be seen scuttling across the quads.

Above: *Design for buttery window satirising domestic arrangements, from the JCR cartoon album*

Above: *Hoggarth sketch of room in Pusey quad*

Above left and left: *Interiors of student rooms, 1902*

Keble Plays

Above: *Keble Plays, 1924*

Frown Not Upon our Latest Innovation
If where High Table was, is now a stage
(Prologue by the Crab to the Keble plays, 1924)

From 1924, a highlight of the Keble year was the plays put on in the College Hall during Eights Week (two evening performances and a matinee). 'The Crab' (A.S. Owen) was a key moving force, acting as treasurer; the young Russell Meiggs acted in the plays, and the costumes were made by Mrs Kidd and Miss Hall. The music was provided by the organ scholars and the programme covers designed by resident artists. The first performances in 1924 were of two short pieces by Lord Dunsany, *The Lost Silk Hat* (a comedy) and *A Night at an Inn*, and a piece by Anatole France, *The Comedy of a Man who Married a Dumb Wife*. In later years the plays included pieces by Calderon, Pirandello, Gogol, O'Neill, Congreve, Fielding, Shaw, Mrs Inchbald, and Hardy; Shakespeare was not to be performed until 1947.

The Keble players, who otherwise remained entirely amateur, were fortunate in being able to draw each year upon the advice of the actor Leslie Banks (1890–1952), who had never finished his Classics degree at Keble, but whose thespian proclivities had been encouraged by the Crab. By the early 1920s he had established a reputation in the West End; he was later to appear in films, including leading roles in *Goodbye Mr Chips* (1938) and appearances in Hitchcock films like *The Man who Knew Too Much* (1934) and *Jamaica Inn* (1939). Banks recalled arriving in College 'in the middle of the night to see that superb Heath Robinsonian monument to the science department, the original switchboard, being erected amid a welter of tankards and sandwich crusts'. The Crab was everywhere prominent, assuming the role of the leading lady in her absence during dress rehearsals, growing 'infinitely coy and feminine, and demurely pointing a provocative boot, declaim[ing] her lines in a high flirtatious falsetto'. The after-production suppers were the occasion for more bonhomie, with Russell Meiggs treating the assembled company to 'brilliant frenzied mock Italian speeches … an orgy of mad, almost schizophrenic histrionics'.

Above: *Leslie Banks, adviser to the Keble plays*

Left: *The Mock Doctor, 1925*

107

The baths were available between the hours of 7 and 9 a.m., and again between 3.30 and 5 p.m.; one bath per week was free, others were charged at 6d. per time, though sporty types were encouraged to compound at the rate of 10s. per term. Baths were drawn by an attendant, but the fact that the faucets were operated by a spanner in the attendant's custody was sufficient, in Douglas Price's words, to deter bathers from 'sybaritic wallowing'. Sportsmen often had to be content with a cold shower.

Keble was a pretty cold and dank place in those years. The walls of the Hall staircase dripped with condensation. Each undergraduate had an allowance of coal (5 cwt. per term), but it does not seem to have been sufficient to provide comfort all day long. In hard winters, like 1929–30, the water in the bowls in the washstands would freeze over. One of the attractions of the Hall breakfast was the blazing fire. The cold in student rooms seems to have driven them to the JCR (in the interwar period located in the area now occupied by the Lower Library) which had a fire, though the leather armchairs closest to it were reserved for the 'seniors', and the JCR was closed between 9.30 a.m. and 12.30 p.m. An alternative was the Reading Room (the original JCR of 1870), the so-called 'Alpine Room' in the gateway over the Porters' Lodge, heated by a gas fire, but competition for seats was fierce.

Food was more than adequate, but menus uninteresting. Interwar breakfasts were hearty affairs (porridge, bacon and egg or fish, and toast; students would supply their own labelled jars of marmalade), but lunch consisted always of bread and cheese, which could be supplemented for an extra charge of 2s. by some meat; dinners were usually the classic meat and two veg. Beer but not wine was available at lunch and dinner. For those requiring afternoon refuelling, afternoon tea, prepared by Mrs Butler with her classic anchovy and honeyed toast,

was available in the JCR. For those wanting to picnic, hampers were available from the Steward at 5s. per head, with wine extra at 3s. per bottle. There were supposedly no cooking facilities in rooms or along the corridors, but undergraduates improvised, hanging sausages over the fires in their rooms; the toasting fork was an essential piece of equipment.

The disciplinary regime was strict. The main gate was shut at 9.15 p.m., but the College remained accessible by the wicket gate until 11 p.m. Thereafter, latecomers would be fined. Nor were those living out likely to be easier off. Oxford landladies ran strict houses and reported infractions to the Dean. The limits on leisure time, and the close regulation of many aspects of their lives, inevitably produced a reaction in the form of episodes of indiscipline and ragging, to some degree tolerated by the College authorities. Bump suppers were one obvious occasion for such licensed misrule. After the Torpids bump supper of 1930, the 'unpopular men' were debagged; a bonfire of wooden latrine seats was set up in Liddon quad; the bill for damages came to £200. Keble students also participated in the often riotous shenanigans pitting town against gown in the bonfire celebrations on 5 November, that were so regularly an occasion for proctorial heartache.

Above: *Interior of the Chapel, 1921*

The Morning Read: a gallery of Keble types from the 1890s

KEBLE
HUNDRED YARDS HANDICAP

Above: *The Chapel run: getting to Chapel on time*

Right: *Leaving Chapel: no need to hurry*

ledgers however suggests that the level remained constant.

The religious regime found many enthusiastic adherents. Harold Coney coming up on the eve of the armistice in 1918 quickly found a group of like-minded young men, the 'quartette' as he dubbed them. On their second day after dinner they had cocoa together 'prior to going to the preparation for the Holy Communion on the morrow'. Warden Lock was very good at 'pointing out what a great band of fellowship the eucharist was, the common cup alone drawing us nearer to one another, and emphasizing the beauty of beginning our college course by means of such a bond. It seems as though I have been at Oxford for years and that the quartette, for which I see a great future, … seems to have been from the cradle'. Coney records

Perhaps disorders were more limited at Keble than in other colleges. An Anglican ethos continued to pervade all Oxford colleges in the interwar period, but it was probably more marked at Keble, where candidates for admission still had to present the Warden with a copy of their baptismal certificate. Many of its intake were the sons of clergymen, and many were destined for ordination. Chapel attendance was compulsory three mornings per week (reduced to two for those living out), on saints' days and at one of the Sunday services. In the rush to make it in time, undergraduates would turn up with their surplices covering their pyjamas. Absentees would be marked by P.W. Auger, the superintendant of scouts, who sat in the gallery at the west end with the register, his task eased by the fact that undergraduates had designated seats. The delinquents would appear before the Warden on Monday morning, the so-called Monday Club, at which Kidd would deliver a homily on the theme of 'the Devil's got you, and if your sinful life continues, you will be well down the primrose path'. By the early 1930s compulsory attendance was a live issue, with the JCR making representations against it in 1933; it is striking that the pressure came from the scholars, for most of whom Keble had not been their first choice of college. Comparison of Chapel attendances in 1913 and 1938 monitored in the collection (student report)

regular meetings of the quartette, which seems to have evolved into a study group, 'a little society amongst ourselves with power to introduce suitable members to encourage study and expression of religious subjects'. Also revived at this time, with the Warden's encouragement, was the Guild of All Saints, the College branch of the Oxford University Church Union, 'to encourage the formation of habits of religious observance and to endeavour to bring a definitely Christian observance to bear on College life and conduct'. For undergraduates like these, the cycle of Chapel worship was supplemented by trips to churches like St Barnabas in Jericho or the Cowley Fathers.

Keble's founders had been determined that the College should be more than a theological college, and that whatever its religious purposes, it should offer a rounded community. As Winnington-Ingram, old boy and now Bishop of London, put it at the jubilee celebrations in 1920, 'it is not merely a theological college, but a real college, where plenty of all sorts were turned out.

109

Although he loved to see so many priests and bishops, they were equally proud of their laymen'. A narrow clericism was muted by figures like 'Crab' Owen, who would advise those intending a career in the church to read history. Hilary Barnes, who was such a person, recalls that the result was that he was exposed to various non- (if not anti-) clerical influences, and his parents were to blame Owen for their son's loss of vocation while at Oxford.

Vital to the maintenance of the regulated community were the College servants. Many spent the bulk of their working lives at Keble, and developed formidable levels of knowledge about the community, dons and students alike. Among them was Percival William Auger (1876–1965), who joined the College on leaving school at 14, beginning as an indoor messenger on 4s. per week with board and lodging; in 1891 he became a boy scout (i.e. assistant to one of the leading scouts) and in 1893 he was promoted to staircase scout, now at £15 per year with board and lodging and 3s.3d. per week beer money. In 1903 he became superintendant of scouts, a position he held until his retirement in 1953. F.W.M. Colborn (known as 'Tom' by all, the name given him by his First World War comrades), joined as a temporary under-scout in 1919, working under David Tailboys, who holds the record for the longest service. He moved to the buttery in 1921 and took charge of Hall in 1942, succeeding Mr A. Evans. Men like these developed a formidable knowledge of the College and its members. They could often be relied upon to deal with the foibles of the young with tact. Of Jimmy Dance, a scout from 1911 to 1957, Roger Milton (1929) said that 'he could, without going beyond the bounds of propriety, exercise a caustic wit at the expense of any member of his staircase who stepped out of line with inconsiderate demands or more than usually irresponsible ragging'.

College Servants

Joseph Cooper on the College servants, 1931
There were three porters, and as I struck up an immediate friendship with them which remained throughout my three years at Oxford, I feel I must include their names. They were known as Baker, the head porter, who was an army serjeant-major type; Jack, who often liked to break into a song and tap-dance routine; and Day who was wizened and gentle. They were never known by any other names. All three had a sense of humour and responded to mine. The Porters' Lodge also had the College telephone exchange in it and I don't think it would be an exaggeration to call the Lodge the nerve centre of the College. If the Warden or a don wanted to speak to one of the undergraduates, he would immediately contact the Porters' Lodge by telephone; the porters had a very simple way of getting hold of people – they would stand outside the Lodge facing the main quadrangle and would shout the name they wanted. They didn't have to shout very loudly because the acoustics of the quadrangle were as clear as a Greek open-air theatre – as I was presently to discover when I started playing the piano in my room.

I went to find my scout…. He was immediately friendly. I enjoyed his company. He liked to gossip about the old times, including the fact that when Douglas Fox had been an undergraduate he had been a scout then. He told me about the buttery …. You could get almost anything you wanted, from personal items like soap or toothpaste, to fattening items like buns and bars of chocolate. Mrs Butler ran the buttery, a charming lady with a friendly smile, and everybody loved her.

Then there was the lady who cleaned the steps and the landing outside the rooms in my particular block, who rejoiced in the name of Mrs Luckett. She loved undergraduates who joked with her and she didn't mind a bit if you made up limericks about her name.

Late 1950s
Tom Colborn remembered
When not officiating in Hall he could be seen in progress from the ample cellars beneath the Bursary, attired in a green baize apron and carrying an enormous butler's basket full of bottles thought to represent the Bursar's daily consumption of vintage port. Tom was assisted in his labours by Raymond [Tanner], with the physical appearance of a stoker on a Lowestoft trawler, whose duties appeared to encompass virtually every aspect of the College's domestic needs from the replenishment of the boiler and the washing of dishes to the conveying of messages on a dilapidated bicycle around Oxford.

F.W.M. ('Tom') Colborn (1896–1983)

Long-serving servants and staff

David Tailboys	Scout, Assistant Butteryman, JCR Scout	1875–1943	68 years
Percival William Auger	Messenger, Scout, Superintendant of Scouts	1890–1953	63 years
John Ivings	Scout, Servant to the Tutors, SCR Butler	1892–1946	54 years
John Mimms	Scout, Assistant Butteryman, Butteryman, Chapel Verger	1876–1930	54 years
J.E. Thurgood	Carpenter	1907–1960	53 years
Albert Treadwell	Scout	1899–1950	51 years
James Warrell	Under Butler, Common Room Man, Chapel Attendant	1871–1921	50 years
A.F. Grundy	Electrician	1915–1965	50 years
F.W.M. ('Tom') Colborn	Scout, Buttery Staff, Hall Steward	1919–1967	48 years
Alfred W. Green	Junior Clerk, Chief Clerk	1884–1932	48 years
Charles Bourne	Bursary Clerk, Domestic Bursar	1921–1969	48 years
James T. Wakelin	Clerk	1878–1924	46 years
C.J. Berry	Scout, Chapel Scout	1910–1956	46 years
J.B. (Jimmy) Dance	Servants' Hall Man, Assistant Butteryman, Scout	1911–1957	46 years
Jack Nurser	Messenger, Scout, Junior Porter, Head Porter	1909–1954	45 years
Ernest Day	'Shoe Cleaner and Under Porter', Porter	1905–1949	44 years
T.E. Jackman	Buttery staff, Scout	1922–1966	44 years
H.W. Leonard	Scout	1920–1964	44 years
Norman Wilson	Bursary Clerk	1927–1971	44 years
Reuben Barson	Shoe Black	1879–1921	42 years
R.H. Lee	Cook	1929–1971	42 years
C.H. Arnatt	Cook	1913–1953	40 years

Of the current members of staff, the longest serving is Steve Beasley, Assistant Gardener, who joined the College in 1965.

Above: *Steve Beasley*

Right: *The Head Porter, 1902*

Essential to the maintenance of order and providing crucial lines of communication within College was the head porter; for many years (1928–51) Keble Lodge was ruled over by Mr Albert Baker; 6ft 3ins tall and ex-army, he emphatically fitted the part. Baker was celebrated for the combination of firmness and tact with which he dealt with all with whom he came into contact. The length of service meant that sections of the staff built up extraordinarily close relations with the undergraduates and dons. In the Lodge, Baker served alongside other College stalwarts like Jack Nurser (who succeeded him as Head Porter, and whose father had been Warden Talbot's butler) and Ernest Day.

The domestic side of College was very labour intensive. The scouts' day began between 6.30 and 6.45 a.m., when the round of wake-up calls commenced; from 9 a.m. they would be occupied in making beds and slopping out; after that they would serve lunch; afternoons might be free, but from 6 p.m. they would be collecting dirty crockery from the rooms; at 7 p.m. they would be on duty in Hall again to serve dinner; they would end work between 8 and 8.30 p.m. The coal fires meant there was an incredible amount of dust and soot; each vacation scouts would have to black lead the fireplaces and sand the fire irons. Shoes were collected daily on a shoe trolley and cleaned by Charlie Reeves, the bathroom attendant. It was hard work, but the College was a paternalistic employer, and the staff enjoyed annual outings (in 1924 they took charabancs to the Wye Valley) and a Christmas party, with entertainments for their children.

By 1913 the domestic establishment of the College comprised 56 persons; by the summer term of 1921 this had increased to 63: the Hall had 11, the kitchens 12, the Lodge four, there were 15 scouts for the students and three tutors' servants; there were three men who mixed boot-cleaning, bicycle repairs and attending the baths; an electrician and carpenter comprised what would now be the maintenance department; the entire administrative load seems to have been borne by the four clerks under the Steward. The staff was overwhelmingly male: there were just seven women and only three of the 17 scouts were women. There were College characters among the female staff, like Mrs E.A. Butler, 'a bright, bird-like woman', who came to the College in 1924 as seamstress, and was responsible for making the surplices which undergraduates had to wear in Chapel; she later came to preside over the College shop below the Clock Tower, and retired in 1953. Almost all the scouts were employed for only 39 weeks of the year. The staffing levels of 1921 were regarded as too high, and economies were proposed which would reduce numbers to the pre-war level. It might be worth noting for comparison's sake that in 2008, the staff serving three times as many students and five times as many tutors, in well over double the housing stock and with many more public spaces to tend (bar,

theatre, café and seminar rooms) comprised 90, (of whom 31 were part-time). The balance between the domestic and administrative sides has shifted: today 12 are employed in administration, another two in the Conference Office, and four in the Development Office, while the kitchens employ ten, the Hall three, and housekeeping 30, of which 22 are part time; the SCR establishment, with three, is the same as in 1921; the Lodge now employs seven, of which two are part-timers, and the maintenance team has expanded to six.

The strict regulation of leisure time and the lack of developed mass media meant that undergraduate sociability tended to revolve around societies and sports, though many found solace in games of cards. Edward Garfitt (1932) recalls his importunate neighbours combing the corridors to rake up a fourth at bridge. For those seeking to cultivate their minds, there were several College-based societies catering for a variety of groups. Soon after the First World War, for example, there was a vigorous Debating Society, a Theological Society (founded in 1919), a Musical Society, an Essay Club, a play-reading group (the Mummers) and, briefly, no less than two history societies. Tenmantale, the history society, founded in 1881–2 by D.J. Medley and others, enjoyed a continuous existence, with brief interruptions in 1902–5 and during the wars, until the early 1980s. Like most of the societies, Tenmantale began with an elective membership (not more than fourteen ordinary members elected from among those reading for the Final Honour School, and all the history tutors and lecturers), but later expanded. Members were expected to deliver papers when called upon. There was a regular dinner, and a Christmas party with charades (typical examples from the 1930s include 'Clarence drowned in a butt of malmsey', 'the Battle of Hastings', and 'Charles in the oak') and other horseplay.

The Morning Read: more from the daily routines of Keble life

Above: *The kitchens, 1933*

Below: *Selection of inter-war menu cards*

Also venerable, active from 1873 but, unusually, open to all members of the College, was the Debating Society, which provided training slopes for would-be Union debaters. Its heyday was perhaps in the 1890s, when its luminaries included the later Archbishop of York and College Council member, Cyril Foster Garbett (1895), who was president of the Oxford Union in 1898. One of the debates of 1894, when 108 members of College had been present to debate the motion on the present government that 'since its incapacity = its tenacity ∴ it ought to resign', was long remembered. The Essay Club held its 900th meeting in Michaelmas term 1934, at which we are told 'Mr [Edmund] Blunden made some excellent acid remarks on the Novelist vs. the Essayist, and Professor [J.R.R.] Tolkein read magnificently from Beowulf'. Other groups were more ephemeral. The Mars Hill Society, in which 'the aim of each member must be to tell or hear some new thing' functioned between 1926 and 1930. Also active in this period were the Monoclists, a society formed for 'the purpose of increasing and extending the popularity of the wearing of the monocle'.

113

Organ Scholars in the Early Twentieth Century

Keble enjoyed a long line of distinguished organ scholars. The talents of Henry Ley (1887–1962), organ scholar from 1906, were so remarkable that he was appointed organist at Christ Church Cathedral in 1909, before he had taken any degrees. His virtuosity at the organ was still more remarkable in view of the fact that he suffered from the disability of a club foot. 'He looked like Pickwick, but was much more like Puck' remarked an Eton pupil, for Ley was ever genial.

Among Ley's pupils were a number of distinguished Keble organ scholars, including Douglas Fox (1893–1978), organ scholar in 1912, whose right arm had to be amputated above the elbow when he was seriously wounded in action.

Sir Thomas Armstrong (1898–1994), who had sung solo for Mendelssohn's 'Hear my Prayer' during the lying-in-state of King Edward VII in 1910, was elected to the scholarship in 1916 but had to defer until 1919 because of military service. After a career which took him to Manchester Cathedral, St Peter's Eaton Square (the local church of Lord Halifax, the prominent member of the Keble College Council), Exeter Cathedral and Christ Church, Oxford, he became principal of the Royal Academy of Music (1955–68). Another Ley pupil was Ralph Downes (1904–93), organ scholar from 1925. Of humble background, he had played the organ in cinemas. At Keble he was active in directing the orchestra for the plays. His later career was highly distinguished. According to the *Oxford Dictionary of National Biography*, he was 'the guiding light to transforming people's attitudes to the organ in mid-twentieth-century Britain', a task he accomplished through his work on the organ for the Royal Festival Hall. Influenced by the American reform movement of the 1930s, he was a leading advocate of electric rather than mechanical actions on the keyboard.

Joseph Cooper (1912–2001) was perhaps a less conventional figure. He became organ scholar in 1931, combining the academic study of music with a passion for dance music. 'Sleepy', one of his compositions

Above: *Henry Ley*

Left: *Ralph Downes*

for the Oxford University Dramatic Society, was overheard by the actress Fay Compton in rehearsal, and she asked if she could use it in the West End. Cooper agreed, provided that it appeared under his own name, to avoid giving offence to the Keble establishment. He enjoyed teasing 'Crab' Owen, who prided himself on being able to identify the organ voluntary. On one occasion he chose the tune 'Today, I feel so happy', which he improvised in the style of a Bach fugue. 'If I am not mistaken that was a very good example of early Bach', was the Crab's response. Cooper developed a career as a pianist, but was increasingly drawn into broadcasting, chairing the musical quiz *Call the Tune* and it's television spin-off *Face the Music*, which made him a household name.

This line of distinguished organ scholars was maintained by others later, including Meredith Davies (1922–2005), whose tenure was interrupted by wartime service. He was later heavily involved with the Three Choirs Festival, and became one of the foremost interpreters of the operas of Benjamin Britten, conducting the first performance of *War Requiem*.

Some groups cultivated a deliberate exclusivity. The XIII Club, active from 1894, seems to have met for discussion and cards; despite its own protestations to the contrary, it was dominated by the sporty types. In the 1930s the De Coverly Club was the focal point for real or aspiring country gentlemen with the obligatory hacking jacket. They were notorious for their rum punches, the preparation of which would signal the start of a 'bender' or 'binge'. The elective nature of many of the clubs could generate a cliquey atmosphere. It is striking that in 1933 a group of eight freshmen formed the Druids, a rival play-reading group to the Mummers. Within two years they claimed to be Keble's largest society. 'This flourishing growth', they asserted, 'has been brought about by keeping to our original idea in founding a society to be free from all graft and to be open to all interested parties in all years,

Right: *Erecting a lighting rig for a play in Hall, 1933*

'The President was congratulated upon his faultless attire. Clothes do not make the man' (21 February 1921). It is to our eyes a rather tedious humour, but it was through such encounters that reputation within the College community was calibrated, and 'character' formed.

Undergraduate reputations were also secured in sports. Garfitt recalls that achieving College colours was a major achievement, entitling one to 'wear a special flannel scarf and to have the magic initials KCRFC embroidered in white silk under the brass-wire college crest on one's blazer'. Probably about half the College were active in sports in 1920; in the 1930s about a third seem to have been playing first team sports.

especially to those of the first year to whom far too many Keble societies are closed'.

All these societies had in common the valorization of wit and repartee. Debates, for example, were always preceded by so-called 'private business', during which the members sparred with each other. A few of the more transparent examples from the Debating Society in years after the Great War will suffice to give the flavour, but the minutes teem with carefully documented examples. 'The President was asked to request Mr Armstrong [Tommy Armstrong, the organ scholar] to name the particular member of the choir against whom his animosity was directed when, on a recent occasion in Chapel, a commotion took place in the organ loft. Mr Armstrong was shocked that the incident should attract attention; a tumult in the organ loft was quite a normal occurrence he thought' (3 November 1919). 'Mr Gay drew the attention of the House to the efficient working of the College cold storage department; freshmen, was the pinpoint of his remarks, were being daily converted into frozen meat' (3 November 1919). 'Mr Wrenford asked whether or no it would be possible to arrange a debate with a ladies' college. The President replied that having tried and failed to arrange this he had fixed the nearest approach to it by arranging a debate with Worcester College, near Oxford (2 February 1920). 'Mr Clough was asked if the ladies of St Hilda's approved of his moustache. He replied that they had all steadily set their faces against it' (24 January 1921).

Keble's musical and cultural life between the wars was geared towards the plays and the Eights Week concert. The Musical Society put on one concert in Hall in Eights Week. Liddon quad, with a marquee in the middle for refreshments, was festooned with hundreds of tea lights in glass jars for the occasion, and a red carpet covered the steps up to Hall. The concert was organized by the organ scholar, who would sometimes perform piano solos. An ad hoc choir consisting of the Chapel choir afforced by dons and north Oxford ladies provided the singing. Professional musicians from London's Queen's Hall Orchestra were engaged at nominal fees through the good offices of their leader, Charles Woodhouse. That the College was able to mobilize such talent speaks highly of the quality of the organ scholars between the wars. The plays were performed in Hall each year from 1924. The concerts and plays were highlights of the social calendar, as undergraduates invited members of their families. The organ scholar Joseph Cooper recalled how his cousin Doris stole the show with an enormous hat festooned with osprey feathers.

The Morning Read: more Keble types

Among the tutors, 'Crab' Owen and Billy Reade were key sponsors. Owen was treasurer of the Keble plays; Reade's sister played the viola, and one of his close personal friends was the famous oboist Leon Goossens, who came to play in the Eights Week concerts. The wife of the Bursar, Colonel Milman, was a crucial mediator with the 'north Oxford ladies'. Though Warden Kidd was not particularly musical he seems to have taken a close interest in the choir, Joseph Cooper recalling how the list of names he was handed at the beginning of term was in the Warden's own hand.

Keble was rather introverted. Many undergraduates formed their friendships almost exclusively within its walls, and there were complaints in the mid 1930s that 'no Keble speeches are nowadays to be found in the Union: we are not the dominant force in any one political club or in fact in any University club'. The tendency to look down on Keble as second rate was still very pronounced. But to that sense of inferiority as a limiting factor on wider sociability were added the relative poverty of many students, who simply could not afford many out-of-college activities, and the University's strict regulation of access to leisure facilities. There were various cafés and restaurants to which undergraduates gravitated for a treat. The George opposite the New Theatre provided an upstairs posh restaurant and a downstairs grill popular at lunch times, while Stuarts in the Cornmarket offered Viennese-style coffee. Afternoon tea with cream-filled brandy snaps, to the accompaniment of a violinist and cellist at the Cadena Café in the Cornmarket, was a particular favourite. But undergraduates were not allowed to use the pubs, and a considerable amount of ingenuity went into evading the Proctors (the 'progs' as they were called), and their officers (the bulldogs). Pubs close to College, like The Pheasant on the corner of Keble Road and St Giles, were vulnerable to their attentions, but punting expeditions ending at The Victoria Arms in Marston were likely to be immune. The Royal Oak was preferred to the nearby Lamb and Flag because the bulldogs had more than one approach route to the latter. There were various cultural distractions out of College. In 1924 Basil Drennan wrote home negatively to his mother about a performance of *The Marriage of Figaro* by the Old Vic Opera – 'very badly both as regards production, acting, and singing' – but he was enthusiastic about the new film by Fritz Lang, *Die Nibelungen*, 'the most artistic and beautiful which has yet been produced'.

Above and right:
Cornmarket in the 1920s

Opportunities for ranging further afield were limited by the fact that in the 1930s only about four Keble undergraduates seem to have owned motor cars, which were subject to strict control by the Proctors. Only senior undergraduates were allowed cars, which could only be parked in designated garages; they had to bear distinctive green lamps on their radiators; and they could only be used between the hours of 1 p.m. and 9 p.m. It was possible to visit London by train (rail fare about 7s. in the 1930s), and Lyons Corner House in Piccadilly was a favoured destination, but it was necessary to be back by midnight to avoid fines. The 10.30 p.m. departure from Paddington, arriving in the nick of time at 11.45 p.m., became known as the 'Flying Fornicator'.

Women were outnumbered by men in a ratio of ten to one in interwar Oxford, so even had the regulations and conventions for sociability been more relaxed, there would have been limited opportunities for the sexes to mingle. Hilary Barnes (1917) described undergraduates living in what he called 'Islamic seclusion'. In his words: 'I never saw any females in College except briefly at the time of the Eights Week concert. In my last year I did form a rather tenuous friendship with a young history graduate at St Hugh's called Jane Harvey. I contrived this with the greatest care and difficulty, for I was very shy. It never got further than morning coffee and a rare tea party'. Women had been made full members of the University in 1920, but they were barred from full membership of the Union until 1963. Indeed a motion at Keble's Debating Society in favour of the admission of women to the Union in 1919 was lost by 43 votes to 48. Opportunities for entertaining women within College were limited. Female guests had to be chaperoned, and were required to leave the premises by 6.30 p.m. Within Keble, the Cow Club played some makeshift hockey, lacrosse and netball against women's colleges, but seems to have been primarily a drinking society. During the interwar period the women's colleges began to host evening dances, but they ended promptly at 11.30 p.m. with the singing of the National Anthem, and they were alcohol-free events. The Labour Club was apparently one of the few University societies where the sexes mingled with relative freedom, and for that reason its 'hops', held in a hall at the end of Walton Street, proved popular.

Eights Week provided opportunities for the mingling of the sexes, though usually with members of one's own family as guests, on the College barge. Other colleges held balls in Commemoration Week at the end of Trinity term, but Keble was not to do so until 1939. Perhaps in a conscious effort to distance itself from the frivolities of other colleges, the highlights of the Keble summer social calendar remained the musical concert and the College play.

We might sum up this picture of undergraduate sociability in the interwar years by looking at one term in the life of Douglas Price, who came up from King Edward VI School, Stratford-on-Avon, in 1933 to read Modern History under the young reformation historian A.G. Dickens and the medievalist E.A. Jolliffe, and whose diary runs in continuous sequence from Easter Monday 1935. Price was a hard-working student, attending eight lectures in the first week of term, dividing his reading time between the Radcliffe Camera (or 'Radder' as the 1930s slang would have it) and the Union library, and always anxious for feedback (he felt Dickens tended to lecture him, and found Jolliffe more encouraging). He was not sporty, although he rowed in the second boat in his first year, before dropping out having failed the 'swimming test'. But in other respects his leisure pursuits were probably typical of those of relatively limited means. He hosted friends to tea, but they were usually members of his Keble set, and he very rarely visited other colleges; women are hardly ever mentioned. In Trinity term, 1935, he attended four meetings of The Druids for play readings (one of them

on the river), two meetings of Tenmantale, and a meeting of the University Archaeological Society. He watched a University cricket match in the Parks, attended the Eights Week races three times, and went punting at least four times. He made several visits to the Ashmolean and did brass rubbing at New College on four occasions. He went to the cinema seven times – he was ecstatic about Basil Dean's *Lorna Doone*, 'truly a film in a hundred' (he went twice, and immediately started on the book) – and the theatre three times, to the comic opera *Merrie England*, a musical comedy *Leave it to Love*, and a revue *1001 Marvels*. And there was, of course, the Eights Week Concert with the Keble Choral Society and Woodhouse's string orchestra, as well as some fine piano playing by the organ scholar, Laurence Gerrish.

He had his own wireless, listening to football matches and the Derby (for which the JCR ran its customary sweepstake), and Henry Hall's *Guest Night*. The highlight

of the term was the Royal Jubilee, celebrated on 6 May. Keble's official decoration was a crown in electric bulbs with the letters GR in the middle, displayed over the gateway, but the rugby team ensured that it was supplemented by a string of rugby shirts in red, white and blue, across Parks Road. After chapel at 8 a.m., with the national anthem, Price went on a long punting expedition with his friend Ross Stone, decorating his boat with the Keble arms. At dinner in Hall, the Warden proposed the toast of 'The King'. After Hall he listened to the King's speech on the wireless ('most moving'), and then went out to view the illuminations and mingle among the crowds in The High: 'the dense masses of people were such as I have never seen before … I have been aroused from comparative apathy to a degree of enthusiasm for the King of which I never knew I was capable'.

Keble was not very political. Typical was Russell Clarke (1937) who claims to have joined the Oxford University Liberal Club 'probably because it held very good sherry parties'. The instinctive conservatism of the College was evident at the time of the General Strike, when a group of Keble students acted as strike-breakers by keeping the buses and trams running in Hull. As the international situation deteriorated in the 1930s, they began to show signs of higher levels of political interest. Reg Prideaux and Cliff Baylis were founding members of the Oxford University Next Five Years Group, which sought to build a consensus on an agenda of progressive social and economic reform, anticipating many postwar developments.

Left: *Traffic congestion in the High Street on the occasion of the Silver Jubilee, 1935*

Below: *Keble strike-breakers head for Hull, 1926*

From Barge to Boat House

Before the building of the boathouses from the later 1950s, it was customary for members of Oxford colleges and their guests to watch the races from their respective college barges. The Keble barge, one of the last, was built by Salter Bros in 1898–9; the contract price was £850 but additional items beyond the original specification brought the cost up to £936.8s.6d. The barge was elaborately decorated in art nouveau style, the bill for carving coming to £77. From the stern arose a sea satyr, apparently supporting the overhang of the upper poop deck. A richly carved cartouche bore the Keble College arms.

By the 1950s the barge was in bad condition, leaking badly, and all the woodwork above the waterline decayed. As restoration seemed impracticable, the College reluctantly decided that it had to be abandoned, but the question of its disposal proved highly problematic. The Thames Conservancy would not allow the barge to be sunk; and the offer by Davey, the college chef, to place the barge in a stretch of meadow he owned just above Iffley Lock, met with opposition from the planners as the meadow was in the green belt. Davidge, one suspects pulling a fast one, negotiated a compromise with the planners whereby the barge might temporarily be taken out of the river 'for inspection of its bottom'. The next obstacle was to secure permission from the Thames Conservancy for the raising of the river level sufficient to flood Davey's meadow. Faced with the prospect of more bureaucratic delays, Davey took matters into his own hands, digging a trench through his meadow to the dimensions of the barge;

Above: *The Keble barge, 1912.*

Left: *Boat crew being ferried from the barge, 1930*

the river level was then allowed to rise through an 'accidental' delay in adjusting the flood gates, and water flowed into the excavation; the barge was now hurriedly released and propelled downstream under the power of a tractor. As *The Record* put it, 'the waters retreated and the barge was safely on its Ararat'.

For a few years the College made use of a second hand barge purchased from Magdalen College for £500. Keble's position was somewhat romantic; all the other Colleges were now building boathouses, and the Keble barge was looking increasingly anomalous. The risk that all the best sites for boathouses would be snapped up was a real one, so in 1961 the College finally decided to build its own boathouse in conjunction with Jesus College. The architect was Z.W. Nirrenski and it was opened in 1964. Its design plays with nautical themes, the front representing the bridge of a ship, the windows to the side shaped like portholes, and the water tank on the roof being made to resemble a funnel.

Peter Osmund, writing home in 1933, expresses his admiration for G.H.R. Dent of the Everyman publishing family, a leading light in The Druids, who is 'by profession a materialist & a communist but really extraordinarily grand'; that is the only sign of any communism in interwar Keble, and this kind of banter is hardly convincing evidence. At the other end of the spectrum of responses,

three members of College were followers of the controversial evangelist F.D. Buchman, whose Oxford Group became Moral Re-Armament in 1938.

The College ideal was (and is) a community. How far were these ideals realized? Colleges were intensely hierarchical organizations: the gradations between year groups, and between scholars, exhibitioners and commoners, marked out by where they sat in Hall and in Chapel, or even by the leather armchairs reserved for seniors in the JCR. Another line of division was that based on schooling. Although these differences were perhaps less marked in Keble than in some other colleges, they were present. 'Grammar and county school boys', we are told, 'were usually acceptable provided they broadly adhered to similar behaviour and speech patterns, or whose sporting prowess could not be ignored; otherwise they were classified as oicks or yobbos'. Or as another put it, 'there was no animosity: we knew each other but we did not mix'.

Undergraduates in the interwar period did not necessarily feel close to the dons: 'they seemed to be a race apart'. For some who were reading subjects not offered by Keble tutors, which until the early 1930s included law, the practice of 'farming them out' to external tutors had the effect of weakening the bonds of identity. Keble's lack of its own scientific laboratories meant that the handful of students reading science subjects had to be dispatched to Queen's. Douglas Henchley (1930), reading engineering, was sent off for tutorials to Mr Hume-Rothery at the top of Headington Hill.

Relations between dons and undergraduates varied according to individuals. Lock as Warden was a ubiquitous and approachable presence. Coney records meeting him immediately on arrival, talking to him at breakfast the following day (suggesting that breakfasts and lunches brought dons and undergraduates together at that date), hearing inspiring addresses and sermons over his first term, going to tea with him, and being taken on a long two-hour walk in which the Warden talked of the architecture and history of the College, as well as complimenting him on his academic progress. But Lock's successor, Kidd, seems to have been much more aloof. There are numerous references to his ceremonious presence in Chapel, many fewer to his relations with undergraduates. 'His vital dominating personality hid his soul from most observers', recalled one contemporary. There were painful tea parties in the Lodgings at which 10–15 students practised the art of balancing tea plates while making small talk with Kidd, his wife and her companion, Miss Hall 'the Concubine' (Conc for short). Mrs Kidd and Miss Hall were, however, involved in making the costumes for the Keble plays, and it was said that the Warden's wife was willing to admit late-comers through the Lodgings after hours, in defiance of the regulations.

Above left: *Warden Kidd, 1933*

Above: *Warden Kidd with Mrs Kidd and Miss Hall ('the Concubine'), 1920s*

The Morning Read: the Keble day continues

~ c/Ου Πόλις στήσειε τοΰδε Χ̀ρὴ κλύειν.

NIM-READE — — — —
— A MIGHTY — — HUNTER —

ANCIENT BAS-RELIEF: DISCOVERED AT KIBUL
IN THE PROVINCE OF NORTH-OKKET.
DEC. 1912, by H.R.Higgs.

Above: 'The Crab'
(A.S. Owen), tutor in classics

Right: 'Billy' Reade, tutor in
philosophy

Then, as now, some dons were more accessible than others. In the interwar years the 'Crab' (A.S. Owen) and 'Billy' Reade stand out. Both were sponsors of the Keble plays. Owen hosted undergraduates to tea (prepared by his doting sisters) in his north Oxford house; he would invite groups to his sparsely furnished Cotswold cottage at Bourton-on-the-Water, or to his estate at Pembrokeshire (where undergraduates might alarmingly find themselves asked to address the tenants' dinner); all trips entailed the attendant risks of the Crab's highly erratic handling of his Morris motor vehicle. Famed for his facility with limericks, he was the sort of man around whom College folklore gathered. 'He is reputed to be omniscient', explained Basil Drennan, 'It is said that the Day of Judgement will be notable, amongst other things, for a dispute between the Crab and the Recording Angel over the date of certain occurrences'. Also among the more approachable was Leonard Rice-Oxley, remembered by generations of undergraduates for the ever-open sherry bottle. In the interwar years, R-O's parties were notorious for the

performance of mock Elizabethan melodramas, where objects (for example, wet gloves with the fingers stuffed to signify dead men's hands, grapes for their eyes, and so forth) were handed round to the audience sitting in the dark, and games of strip poker, where the forfeits were so strictly enforced that all the participants would be naked by the end.

The meetings of the societies provided opportunities for licensed misrule between dons and undergraduates. Price recalls the hilarious appearance of A.G. Dickens, 'normally so dignified a don', at the Tenmantale Christmas party in 1935, 'with his nose reddened, artificial eyebrows, a beret, dressing gown &c, reciting a very funny prologue' to one of R-O's Elizabethan playlets. The formalities were of course reasserted once the evening was over. And one wonders how far into the student body the hospitality of men like the Crab and R-O extended. The Crab, for example, may have directed his attentions predominantly at the more 'handsome' undergraduates, and eyebrows were certainly raised at the young man who accompanied him on holiday to Algeria.

Keble Sport Between the Wars

The new intakes of freshmen in the years after 1918 were not slow to take up competitive sports, although club captains constantly moaned about the lack of eager and talented bodies, as well as the weather. The 1919 tennis season was interrupted by a snow-storm at the start of Trinity term, although the courts which had been planned and financed before the war were finally completed. At this time roughly 100 Keble students were active in sports – allowing the College to put out two teams in rugby, football and tennis. In time, rugby managed a third XV too. There were plenty of matches to play. In 1920 the football team played 25 matches, while the rugger team won 21 of its 23 fixtures in 1929. In 1923 the XV lost only once, racking up 306 points and conceding only 57, though this was still not good enough to defeat University in the semi-final. So popular was rugby in the College, that Keble could field two teams on the same day. In fact other sports, notably football and hockey, complained that rugby attracted all the best men. Although in the early 1930s well over a third of the student body was active in first-team sports, by 1935/6 football had to abandon its second XI for want of players. By the end of the 1930s, even rugby was struggling to find enough for a second XV. The introduction of new league competitions in the 1930s added another layer of collegiate sport; football began in division one, but rugby could only make division two in its league.

Above: *Keble Hockey Club, 1931–2*

Below: *Keble rugby, 1926*

> *Games were played not only against college teams, but also against the City Police, the University Press, the Post Office, the Church Army Press, St Edward's School, and Morris Motors.*

There were rival pursuits – the golf club revived in the 1930s, and 19 students entered the college competition – and clubs were organized for fives, billiards and table tennis. In the mid 1930s the De Coverley Club was formed to encourage field sports, horse riding and natural history. Members rode from Stanton St John and played 'mounted rugger'. In 1930 the 'Crab' donated a rugby fives court which was located in the fellows' garden and survived until demolished in 1975 as part of the ABK building project.

One sport that did flourish in the 1930s was cricket; up to 40 people played in the College, almost a quarter of all undergraduates at the time. The first XI was unbeaten for several years, notable for its strong batting line-up. Brian Belle (who also won a football blue) and R.W.G. Mitchell made the University side, along with F.C. de Saram. Belle played 26 times for Essex 1935–7, scoring 776 runs, including 63 in a famous victory against Yorkshire. When he died in 2007, he was the last survivor of that feted 1935 side. Games were played not only against college teams, but also against the City Police, the University Press, the Post Office, the Church Army Press, St Edward's School, and Morris Motors (whose radiator works stood adjacent to the College's sports field). The Keble Vagabonds cricket team played against various Cotswold villages and toured Sussex each September.

Right: *2nd VIII in Eights Week, 1929*

Below: *2nd VIII in Eights Week, 1936*

There were far fewer internationals than there had been before the War, when games such as football and rugby gave more scope for amateurs. Arguably the most interesting Keble sportsman of the era was Frederick Cecil de Saram, also known as Derrick de Saram (1912–83). Hailing from a wealthy aristocratic Sri Lankan family, he came to Oxford in 1931 but found himself shunned by the University cricket authorities. After winning a tennis blue he finally broke into the cricket side and won blues in 1934 and 1935. In his first season he scored 1000 runs, the only amateur to do so on debut. Against the Australian tourists, who included Bradman, O'Reilly and leg-spinner Clarrie Grimmett, he scored 128 of Oxford's 216 runs. De Saram later captained Ceylon (as it then was), but was gaoled in 1961 for his part in the unsuccessful coup against the Bandaranaike government.

Alisdair Rogers

ACADEMIC LIFE SINCE 1918

As one of the larger and more poorly resourced colleges, for a long time Keble struggled to attract applicants of calibre. With 175 undergraduate members in 1904, it was ranked third in terms of size behind Christ Church (199) and New College (179). In the interwar years the College had an average of 187 undergraduates and 20 BAs on the books. Sustaining numbers of this scale while maintaining academic quality was a real challenge. In the 1930s an average of 85 men a year were applying for 56 places, a ratio of 1.5 applicants to each place. As was said in 1937, this was 'a small margin from which to choose a number of capable men sufficient to keep the College full. But we have just done it'. Of the 130 candidates for classical scholarships in the group of colleges of which Keble was a member, only 35 had placed Keble anywhere among their choices. The intake in the mid 1930s comprised 52 per cent public schools, 42 per cent state and 6 per cent other university colleges or private tuition. Six per cent of the undergraduate body came from overseas, mainly from the empire and dominions. That Keble still tended to attract men of modest means is clear from the numbers of sons of clergy who were admitted, no fewer than 37.5 per cent in the 1930s. Nearly half of those admitted (46 per cent) were proposing to seek ordination. One quarter of the intake was admitted on reduced fees, reflecting their straitened financial circumstances. As the report to Council put it in 1936: 'It is significant to note the change that is taking place in the class from which the clergy of the near future

are being drawn. They are the sons of poor men, and will be themselves poor men: at a time when benefices will be poorer, and the marriage of the clergy a problem of increasing difficulty'.

Above: *Leonard Rice-Oxley, tutor in English, with undergraduates in the fellows' garden*

Above: *Spencer Barrett, tutor in classics*

an increased revenue from endowments'. But the 1930s were not a good time for fundraising.

The gloom persisted after the Second World War. There was another surge in student numbers, as the College recruited demobilized members of the forces, and as those who had taken foreshortened wartime degrees came to complete their education. Undergraduate numbers peaked at 322 in 1950, but the College was pessimistic about future expansion, responding to enquiries from the University with the observation that 'we ... doubt whether the number of those intellectually and financially equipped for an Oxford education will show a substantial and permanent increase over the pre-war figure once the present abnormal rush subsides'.

Keble continued to have difficulty in attracting top-flight candidates. 'The general standard of candidates was mediocre', reported Jolliffe and Price of candidates for history scholarships in 1953; in the following year 'the standard of performance ... was disappointing, perhaps the most disappointing since the war'. The reports on individual candidates hardly provide ringing endorsements of scholarly potential. Basil Mitchell and Spencer Barrett were only able to fill two of their available five classical scholarship places in 1952, and wrote of one of the successful ones: 'X is not frankly a strong candidate but he was on balance the best of the candidates available to us; he is a pleasant and cultivated person whose work throughout maintained a reasonable level, and who showed some sense of style. He is said by his school to have shown marked improvement in the last few months'. Some of the fellows were in any case pursuing agendas unlikely to ensure the admission of the best candidates. Douglas Price noted wearily, after a meeting on entrance candidates in March 1958, that 'as usual there was precious little attention paid to the marks so far as theology and law were concerned. I particularly objected to Davidge's admitting one X whose sole qualification was his rowing – a complete moron otherwise'. Davidge's distinctive admissions policies are clear from the fact that, whereas only eight Etonians were admitted before in the eight years before 1959, thereafter until 1965 there were an average of six a year.

Scholarship examinations were conducted on a group basis, Keble being grouped with Balliol, Magdalen, St Johns, Wadham, and Pembroke. Basil Mitchell, recalling his experience of the system, explained that Balliol always had more good applicants than they could find places for, while Magdalen and St Johns were self-sufficient, their awards matching their supply of able applicants.

The College's difficulty in attracting applicants in part reflected the difficult economic circumstances for middling and poorer families in the interwar years, and the lack of state support for tertiary education, but it was also at risk of losing its niche as the college for persons seeking to live economically. The increase in fees after the Great War meant that the College's competitive advantage was lost. Living costs and tuition at Keble were now no cheaper (and in some cases more expensive) than those at other colleges, so that the College had no special claim to be providing for persons otherwise 'debarred from University education' (one of the original Charter objectives). This contributed to the general lowering of Keble's reputation. A report to Council in 1933 rather depressingly noted that 'in the schools, it is widely believed that a member of Keble does not quite get the real life of Oxford, and there is some reason to fear that this feeling is tending to grow stronger'. The College was caught in a catch-22 situation: 'The only way to increase and improve the supply of candidates for admission to the College is to lower the fees, and this is impossible without

Above: *'Where I quaintly proved ...': sitting the examination*

Right: *Donald MacKinnon, tutor in philosophy*

The result was that Wadham, Pembroke, and Keble competed for the best of the Balliol surplus. 'In this unequal struggle', recalls Mitchell, 'we had only one weapon. A scholarship trumped an exhibition, and either trumped the offer of a place. So if Wadham –and it usually was Wadham – had any able candidate they could not find awards for and would like to give a place to, we could secure him by offering him an award. It would sometimes not be until the final meeting that all the decisions were sorted out'. It was a complicated system, but one which might reward those dons like Spencer Barrett who, not trusting the judgement of his colleagues at other colleges, would re-mark the students' work, willing to put in the extra effort.

What was the quality of teaching? Student recollections of their dons tend, of course, to focus on their eccentricities. The historian John Bromley is remembered as 'an inspiring teacher, though his habit in tutorials of letting long paper spills used to light his pipe burn down to his fingers, while he discussed an abstruse point, created such a tension and expectancy as to obliterate any recollection of what he was saying'. Of Donald MacKinnon the stories abound: one student recalls having his first tutorial in the garden, and MacKinnon leaping from his chair to try to catch a squirrel; another tells us that 'if he was not lying on his back he was standing on a table fiddling with the light fitting or wandering about the room apparently poking his teeth with a safety razor blade'.

It is rather difficult from stories such as these to plumb the quality of the education on offer. Brian Bosworth (1961–5) recalls that Oxford tutorials in the 1960s were 'often tired affairs in which an overworked tutor nodded through the essay reading and then delivered a prepared harangue with little or no relation to what had preceded'. Brian Fieldhouse, writing of the previous decade, recalls that 'there was little conception of development in the weekly work we were doing, nor of preparation for an examination'. Douglas Price's diaries reveal that he might be giving as many as twenty hours per week tutorials in the 1950s and 60s, on top of University lectures and classes. Basil Mitchell recalls that 'if I was to limit my teaching to fourteen or fifteen hours a week, I must take them in pairs'. It is hard to believe that this volume of teaching was delivered with quite the level of engagement with individual undergraduates that the tutorial ideal might lead one to expect: there are strikingly few references in Price's diaries to the marking of essays. Tutorial teaching could be unrewarding. Price regularly expresses his frustration.

Dons' Styles

Malcolm Parkes

What characterized Malcolm's teaching was the respect he gave to the ideas of his pupils, the eagerness with which he investigated their hypotheses, however apparently jejune (though the investigation might begin with a long pull on the pipe and an exasperated 'Oh Gawd'). Malcolm has a remarkable gift for opening up an idea with a few well chosen embellishments, so that you went away with your head reeling with ideas newly fermented (and lungs newly kippered), a sense that you had been given a glimpse of and a map towards a broader intellectual landscape, a list of things to be brooded on, and an awareness that all the subject still hadn't been fully explored even after perhaps three hours' discussion. His consequent and recurrent late arrivals on High Table (his gown increasingly green and tattered as the years passed) were the subject of occasional undergraduate betting syndicates and frequent Beckettian expectation.
Vincent Gillespie in The Record, *1997*

Spencer Barrett

As an undergraduate from Christ Church … I first set eyes on [him] in the Pusey Room in 1959.… He made an immediate impression. It seemed that in some respects I had not been taught Greek correctly at school: the letter sigma should be written always as a half-moon; where we had been told to write iota under the previous letter (subscript), it should be on the line (adscript); zeta should be pronounced sd, not ds (hence Hippolytus' mother was, in Greek, an Amasdon, not an Amadson). None of this, as I recall, was explained but conveyed with an air of such calm authority that one could not doubt its correctness. As the course proceeded there was always something to marvel at: the emendation made by John Milton, 'a scholar who was also a poet', or the poor editor who was usually mentioned for ill but just once saw the truth when everybody else, including Wilamowitz, got it wrong. Above all there was the insistence on precision and rigour of argument.
Adrian Hollis in The Record, *2002*

> ## None of this, as I recall, was explained but conveyed with an air of such calm authority that one could not doubt its correctness.
>
> *– Adrian Hollis on Spencer Barrett*

Denis Meakins

Denis firmly believed that it was not essential to pick the absolute alpha quality candidates at interview, but those with whom he could interact well and who would benefit from a well organized and taught tutorial regime once they arrived. His meticulous organization of work and attention to detail converted thirds into seconds and seconds into firsts. His downgrading of the traditional Oxford essay, the expansion of tutorial groups into four and his use of the whiteboard during tutorials were, in Oxford terms, innovative, yet they catered more accurately for the needs of the subject.
Mike Mingos in The Record, *1993*

Paul Hayes

He was a tutorial Stakhanovite: he regularly taught 25 to 30 hours a week. Besides undergraduate tutorials, there were the Foreign Service course, the Hong Kong course, and the Special Diplomas.… It was not ones and twos I would meet coming out of Paul's rooms, but fives and tens. The total number of pupils Paul taught in a week must have been staggering. Some pupils found him overbearing, but others found him exemplary. He once said to me that one of his greatest satisfactions was to show confidence in pupils and see them become capable of achievements that previously they had not believed possible.
James Griffin in The Record, *1996*

Jim Harris

A master of synoptic compression, he expounded the most perplexing areas of the English law of property and trusts and the concepts of jurisprudence with a rigid and penetrating clarity.
Ed Peel in The Record, *2004*

Here he is on the history finalists of 1959: 'the majority of the men have simply no academic guts. They have drifted through their time here expecting to be taught rather than to teach themselves. I have never had so lazy a crew' [they ended up with eight seconds, four thirds, and two fourths]. But to be fair, Price was a reflective teacher, and often expresses frustration with his own lacklustre performances and lack of preparation. And Bosworth, whose testimony has just been quoted, nevertheless makes an exception for Spencer Barrett, 'the most prodigious verbal memory for Greek literature I ever expect to encounter', while there are various affirmations of the qualities of Mitchell as a tutor. Mitchell himself explains that 'one was never taught how to conduct a tutorial... All I had to go on was my own experience at the receiving end with Woozley and Hampshire, I remember how I had prospered less with Woozley's purely critical approach than with Hampshire's taking a clear line himself and thus presenting me with one possible way of organizing the material'.

Vere Davidge, on the other hand, did little to conceal his lack of intellectual credentials, but he had an eye for talent, and recruited effective 'week-enders' like Leolin Price, who came up to do the law teaching. Some tutors clearly found the tutorial grind too much. Jolliffe lost his cutting edge after his Latin American sojourn on behalf of the British Council during the second world war: his 'air of utter weariness I attributed at the time to the boredom of my essays', recalls one undergraduate. Jolliffe eventually took early retirement to Portugal. G.D. Parkes, who, it should be remembered, carried one of the heavier administrative loads in College and was responsible for all the scientists as well as the musicians, reportedly regularly fell asleep during tutorials. Over-teaching by Oxford dons was to be one of the criticisms of the Franks Report (1967), to which Keble's Governing Body would respond with the observation that 'such a reduction was not practicable at the present time'.

The gradual rise in academic standards between the 1950s and 1980s is well attested in the documentary record, as the College moved out of the lower reaches of the Norrington Table. It was due to a number of factors: effective leadership and strategic planning by successive Wardens and Senior Tutors; tighter regulation of tutorial teaching, particularly out-of-college tuition; the expansion in the size of the fellowship; the increasing diversification of courses offered and the changing balance between arts and science undergraduates in the student body; increasing outreach work into the schools; a vigorous building programme, which increased the volume of accommod-

The Norrington Table

The Norrington Table is the brainchild of Sir Arthur Norrington, President of Trinity College (1954–70) and Vice-Chancellor (1960–2). It attempts to compare the academic performance of colleges by awarding five points for a first, three for an upper second, two for a lower second, and one for a third. Scores are expressed as a percentage of the total possible score. Tutors tend to decry it when the College's position is poor (the weightings are contestable, the gap between top and bottom not that great, and results are subject to wide variation from year to year), and for a while the University authorities failed to cooperate in its production. But when the College's position rises, it is celebrated, as in *The Brick* article 'Reasons to be Cheerful' of Michaelmas 1999. The graph shows Keble's position from the inception of the table in 1964 until 2007: from a near rock bottom position in the 1960s, Keble had pulled itself up steadily to average around 21st position in the mid 1970s, and 13th in the mid 1980s; a series of good years (1987–91) saw the College average at around 10th. Since then its position has faltered, and although there were good years in the later 1990s (the best year was 1998 when Keble was sixth), the early 21st century saw the College slipping back to an average position around 17th.

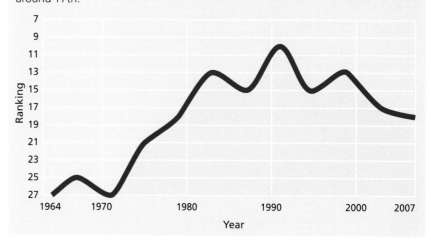

ation on offer and hence attracted more applicants; and the gradual (but by no means complete) integration of graduates into the intellectual life of the College. But although the broad outlines of the narrative are clear enough, the responsibility for change is contested. Some see Eric Symes Abbott's charismatic Wardenship as putting Keble on the map, eclipsing its reputation for second-raters; others place more emphasis on the steady guidance, patience, and reforming vision of Eric Stone, 'an expansionist and an optimist', and Senior Tutor from 1965 to 1976; others still would delay the decisive changes until the 1970s, and put the success down to Nineham's Wardenship, working in alliance with new recruits, particularly in subjects like PPE; there is perhaps a general reluctance (given the Governing Body's later difficulties with him) to recognize the contribution of Christopher Ball's Wardenship to the tightening of teaching standards and a more aggressive profile on admissions. It was, in fact, only under Ball that the hard work of the preceding decades really came to fruition.

The fact that there is disagreement reflects in part different understandings of what constitutes success: some would be horrified by the notion that bringing a lot of oarsmen into the College in the later 1950s (the product of an alliance between Davidge and Abbott) could contribute to its academic success, but Abbott tried to ensure that Davidge recruited his rowers additional to his normal quota, and regarded the sporting success as a key element in getting the College noticed. Douglas Price, no especial admirer of Davidge, nevertheless claimed that he recognized the necessity for the College to diversify its subject base. The truth is that the process of improving standards was evolutionary, the product of the interaction of a variety of forces within the College, and working in conjunction with often favourable outside forces, the role of which is sometimes underestimated in our internal narratives of institutional change.

One of the key positions in levering change within the College was that of Senior Tutor, an office which was effectively established in 1946, though it was first styled Tutorial Secretary, and the higher status title did not follow until 1954. The primary responsibility of the new officer was 'to arrange the external tuition of men reading in schools for which the College does not provide, as for example modern languages and geography, to get reports from external tutors, and to see that these are entered in the Collections Book; also to keep in touch with fellows who are arranging external tuition'. The Tutorial Secretary was also to deal with University examination entries and with all correspondence with the University authorities about tuition. He was also responsible for writing up the minutes of College meetings. The first incumbent was the bluff Yorkshireman, George D. Parkes, a chemistry don and tutor at Keble since 1924, who acted from 1946 until 1965. But by comparison with today's ever lengthening paper trails, Parkes' touch was decidedly light. Here is his standard formula in letters of appointment to out-of-college tutors (in this case to Dr George Bishop): 'The terms of the appointment are that you should take charge of the organisation of the teaching of the men of this College reading physics, ultimately to my approval.

Far left: *Eric Stone, tutor in history*

Left: *G.D. Parkes, tutor in chemistry*

Vere Davidge (1901–81)

Cecil Vere Davidge, educated at Abingdon School and Pembroke College, Oxford, had achieved a second in Jurisprudence in 1923, and took the bar in 1927, while also acting as a leader writer for *The Times*. His association with Keble began in 1927 with his appointment as college lecturer, which was followed by the tutorial fellowship in 1933. During the war he worked in the Treasury and Cabinet Office, the breadth of his experience making him a natural choice for the Bursarship of Keble, which he held from 1948 until his retirement in 1968.

Davidge would not have been embarrassed by his reputation as an anomaly; indeed he declared his intention of founding a 'society for the perpetuation of anomalies'. He combined the duties of Estates and Domestic Bursar with the life of a country gentleman on an estate at Little Houghton, near Northampton, where he would hunt regularly with the Oakley. He relied on the imperturbable Bursary clerk, Charlie Bourne, for the smooth running of the finances.

He eschewed 'intellectual' values; his published output was minimal (an obscure article in the *Law Quarterly Review*); he claimed not to read books, and the stories of his interviewing for undergraduates focus on his probing of their aptitude for sport rather than their commitment to academe. Davidge was in many ways a caricature of himself. Doubtless there were elements of the self-fashioned man of effortless superiority; doubtless, too, the reputation owes much to the selective memory of undergraduates.

One of Davidge's passions was rowing: he himself had rowed for Pembroke, and as a member of a trial eight, he was entitled to wear the pink cap of the Leanders; his son, Christopher, had stroked the Oxford crew in two memorable races against Cambridge, and became a rowing celebrity.

Davidge ensured that Keble became famed, not to say notorious, for its hospitality. The Bursar cared deeply about his food and drink, recruiting one of the best chefs in Oxford and laying down prodigious quantities of port. In Common Room Davidge would gather his cronies at one end of the table and protract proceedings into the early hours, engaging in a peculiar badinage which some found offensive, but he knew when he had gone too far. Basil Mitchell recorded the elaborate lengths he took to apologize to a distinguished psychiatrist who had been subjected to a stream of silly jokes about 'shrinks' and 'trick cyclists'. His response to any of his guests suggesting that they were unfit to drive home was a supportive arm on the shoulder and a worthless assurance that he knew all the chief constables between Oxford and the guest's home county.

Davidge had been heavily involved in the drafting of the 1952 Statutes, which provided for a retirement age for fellows of 67, but

made an exception in the case of a fellow serving as Bursar, who might be extended to age 70. As Davidge's 67th birthday approached, relations in the Governing Body became tense. Davidge made no secret of his desire to carry on to mastermind the centenary celebration in 1970, but some of the newer appointments regarded his behaviour as bullying; contemporaries like Douglas Price found his High Table antics increasingly irksome, and there was a clear need for modernization in the Bursary. So it was decided not to extend his tenure, and to split the Bursarship between the 'estates' and 'domestic' roles. Davidge was seriously peeved, but eventually solaced with the award of an Honorary Fellowship, an unprecedented act for a serving fellow.

Davidge clearly enjoyed winding his colleagues up, and never more so than in his gift of his portrait. Arrayed in hunting pink, port glass in hand, he defiantly asserts the values of a bygone age. It was fitting that he should have died while hunting in 1981.

This really means in effect that any doubtful matters should be referred to me. I should hope that you would run the thing in your own way, as Mr Keeley has done for so many years.' Parkes was succeeded as Senior Tutor by the historian Eric Stone (1965–76), whom many credit with the energy and tact to drive through crucial changes.

Harry Carpenter had warned the fellows in 1948 that the present student numbers were not sustainable without some expansion in the size of the fellowship, but slender resources meant that opportunities were limited. The Besse benefaction was used to support not only the extension of the Chapel wing, but also to establish a fellowship in French. The first holder was Denys Potts, an expert on eighteenth-century French literature elected in 1952. But the College was still woefully unprovided with science fellows, G.D. Parkes continuing to undertake the organization of all teaching for men reading science subjects. It was only with the appointment of Dennis Shaw in 1957 that the forwards march of Keble science truly began. And whereas most colleges had two philosophy dons, one for Greats and one for PPE, Keble limped along with one. In areas where there were no tutorial fellows, the College appointed lecturers: among them was Michael Foot, politics lecturer from 1952 to 1959, later the historian of the SOE, a man who in spite of politics which put him at odds with the conservatives on Governing Body (he wrote a letter to *The New York Times* at the height of the Suez Crisis which Price thought worthy of censure)

identified fully with the College, and in 1953 took a party of Keble undergraduates to help repair the shore defences damaged in the disastrous East Anglian floods of that year. In 1960 the College still had only 13 fellows: three of them were historians and there were only two scientists.

How were fellows appointed? In the early years the Warden had been given a very large role in the hiring of academic staff; this was an area in which the Council did not interfere. With the new Statutes of 1952, Governing Body gained the control over appointments, and it is a power it took seriously. One might take the election of a new history fellow in 1959 as an example of the process. In the Long Vacation of that year John Bromley announced his intention of taking a chair at Southampton, much to the disgust of Price who thought Southampton very inferior. Advertisements were placed in the Oxford and Cambridge journals of record, and letters sent to the registrars of other universities; testimonials were taken up from a number of possible candidates, albeit, according to Price, in a rather dilatory fashion. More important than this were the informal consultations and lobbying: Price records conversations about the fellowship with John Owen, tutor at Lincoln, and with Hugh Trevor-Roper, recently appointed Regius Professor. There were no interviews. The serious candidates were dined separately over several weeks in the course of term: Price thought this a crucial element of the process (an English appointment was under way at the same time, the one that eventually went to John Carey), and he was annoyed with his colleagues for their relative lack of interest. Price's comments on the candidates might be taken as suggesting that conversational prowess at dinner was a more important element in the decision than scholarship. Of one candidate from Durham he wrote 'good academic record – but very heavy going from a social point of view. Eric Stone's description of him as an "eiderdown" is not inappropriate'. Of Maurice Cowling,

the founder of the Peterhouse school of historians, he wrote, 'though only 32 he looked nearer 50; and he had a disagreeable bloated, rather surly look'. The election of Alec Campbell, the eventually successful Americanist, was nearly derailed by Bromley's 'obstructionist' tactics at the College meeting: of Bromley's favoured candidate, Price writes, 'as unsuitable as one would expect, second class degree, one-track research line, and a complete bore'.

One of the major changes in the College between the late 1950s and 1980 was the expansion and diversification of the fellowship. Table 1 below shows the date at which subjects acquired their first tutorial fellows.

Several of these new subjects soon acquired additional fellows, so by 1980 there were two University Lecturers, a professorial fellow, and a Junior Research Fellow in engineering, two University Lecturers in physics, and another two in chemistry. Other established subjects also benefited from a reinforcement of provision. Law received injections of fresh blood and academic rigour with appointment of David Williams (1963–7) and Peter North (1965–76), later vice-chancellors of Cambridge and Oxford respectively. By 1980 PPE was supported by two philosophers, two economists, and a politics tutor. Throughout the 1960s Keble history, still the largest honour school in College, was run by the triumvirate of Douglas Price, Eric Stone and Alec Campbell. It was not to be downsized to a two-tutor establishment until Price's retirement in 1982. The Governing Body was, as a result, much larger in 1970 than 1950. In 1950 there had been eleven fellows of whom only one was a scientist; by 1980 there were 35 fellows, of whom eleven were scientists. This expansion was not painless. By the late 1960s Warden Farrer felt the College was selling out to 'industrial interests', that it would be turned over 'to engineering and business management with a little commercial Spanish'. Farrer hoped that the 'non-Sci Fellows, who are still a plain majority, will rally round the Ark of the Covenant and lay down a line to hold Nat Sci to 33 per cent'. Other conservatives like Douglas Price fretted that expansion resulted in a fellowship that was disengaged from College life. This was Keble's own playing out of C.P. Snow's 'two cultures'.

The conventional understanding is that as teaching fellows were appointed, so the College could expand in size. In fact, somewhat counter-intuitively, the period of maximal growth in undergraduate numbers in percentage terms was in the mid 1950s, when there was hardly any increase in tutorial provision. Between 1955 and 1960 the

Table 1. Subjects acquiring tutorial fellows for first time 1950–2000

Subject	Name	Year
French	Denys Potts	1952
Geography	Gordon Smith	1957 (formerly College Lecturer, 1952–7)
Physics	Dennis Shaw	1957 (formerly College Lecturer, 1956–7)
Mathematics	Eric Phillips	1962 (formerly College Lecturer, 1953–62)
Engineering	Raoul Franklin	1963
German	Richard Green	1964 (formerly College Lecturer, 1960–4)
Physiology	Robert Kay	1965 (formerly College Lecturer, 1964–5)
Politics	Paul Hayes	1965 (formerly College Lecturer, 1964–5)
Philology	Roy Harris	1967
Music	John Caldwell	1975 (formerly Research Fellow, 1969–75)
Biochemistry	Ian Walker	1975 (formerly Research Fellow, 1969–75)
Zoology	Stephen Kearsey	1985
Computation	Stephen Cameron	1989 (formerly Research Fellow, 1986–9)
Japanese	Brian Powell	1989
Archaeology	John Bennet	1998
Management	Geoff Jones	1998

student body increased in size by 27 per cent: whereas 85 students were being admitted per annum between 1950 and 1954, between 1955 and 1959 the number was 113 per annum, reflecting the phasing out of National Service. Teaching resources must have been very pressed at this time. The greatest increase in the size of the fellowship took place between 1965 and 1970, enabling a 'catch up' in tutorial resources at a time of relative stability in undergraduate numbers. Undergraduate numbers increased by 10 per cent in the 1970s, were fairly stable in the 1980s, and increased markedly again in the early 1990s (12 per cent increase, 1990–5), another period of strain on tutorial provision.

As numbers grew, so the balance between arts and science subjects changed. Already by 1970, according to the centrally collected data, 32 per cent of Keble undergraduates were reading science subjects, rising to 39 per cent in 1980 and 43 per cent in 1990, a level which has been sustained.

Left: *University Challenge, dons vs students, 1975*

Table 2. Balance between arts and science undergraduates at Keble, 1970–2005

Year	U/g Arts	U/g Science	U/g Total
1970	232	108	340
1975	243	135	378
1980	240	154	394
1985	229	166	395
1990	231	173	404
1995	267	178	445
2000	258	183	441
2005	250	192	442

The new tutorial appointments also probably did much to invigorate the quality of teaching. Tim Faithfull recalls the PPE team of his years (1964–7): Adrian Darby managed to 'convey his sense of the enigmatic nature of much economic theory and analysis'; Basil Mitchell was 'engaging, able to explain, stimulate, and guide in dealing with complex ideas'; Paul Hayes was good on exam technique; while James Griffin injected 'a new dimension of outlook and style'. Among the scientists Alan Corney (Research Fellow from 1966, Tutorial Fellow from 1969) and Denis Meakins (Tutorial Fellow from 1965) brought rigorous (some might say terrifying) organization to Physics and Chemistry respectively. 'Redo and resubmit' was Corney's response to substandard work. The commitment to academic standards was evident also in

increasing quality control. Christopher Ball developed a reputation for taking a hard line with subjects that were performing below par; the College was perhaps the first to introduce a form of tutorial feedback, interestingly confidential to the Warden at its inception in 1987, which demonstrates just how controversial it was felt to be.

Keble had always suffered from its second-rate status in the eyes of the rest of the University, but from the 1970s it was in a more expansionist, outward-looking mood, much more aggressive in fund-raising, determined on new buildings, responsive to the changing climate of the University. It also benefitted from more favourable publicity, including a BBC film by John Betjeman in 1968, an article in the *Daily Telegraph* supplement in 1974, and a victory in ITV's *University Challenge* competition against Hull in 1975, which was followed by a dons versus students match, which put Denys Potts, Paul Hayes, Douglas Price and Raoul Franklin before the British public.

Publicity was important to another dimension of the College's activities, and that is its profile in undergraduate admissions. As the Governing Body expanded and the profile of the College shifted, so too did the efforts made to attract high quality candidates. In the post-war years very little effort went into outreach work into schools. Recruitment depended on the networks of Keble men in established teaching posts in the secondary sector. When, in 1952, it was decided to hold a couple of headmasters' dinners, separate events were held for public schools and grammar schools in order to 'promote the social ease of each function'. The priority was seen as recruitment from public schools ('it is our connection with these schools which most needs strengthening at present') because it was felt that in this type of school that the College's reputation was low, and that there was a need to attract better quality scholarship applicants from them.

Reports on Students: What the Tutors Said

The nightmare before the viva

From 1874 to 1948 the reports on all Keble undergraduates were entered into folio ledgers, with one page per student, subdivided into sections for each term of his residence. Chapel attendance was also recorded for each term. It was hidden behind these books that students remember the Warden conducting 'collections' in Hall.

W.P. Herringham
Leading doctor, and later honorary fellow

Walter Lock wrote, 'regular but with great appearance of inattention, lounging &c; perhaps more appearance than reality, as his paper is good'. Later he remarked 'rough but something of the diamond I think'. Herringham's Oxford career was chequered: his Chapel attendance was 'most irregular', and in Easter 1875 he was rusticated on the authority of the Bursar for a few weeks, for going out of College after the gates were closed.

W.P. Herringham

Arthur Foley Winnington-Ingram
Later Bishop of London and honorary fellow

On his arrival in 1878, J.R. Illingworth wrote 'I like what I know of him. Hope he will not be spoiled'. A few terms later his record remained spotless, A.T. Lyttelton quipping that 'we shall have to ostracize him if he does not develop a vice'.

C.F. Garbett
President of the Union, later Archbishop of York and honorary fellow

D.J. Medley wrote in Michaelmas 1895: 'he keeps his imaginative and his practical roles too far apart. If only he could use the one to illumine the other, he might do some excellent work'.

F.M. Stenton
Later a distinguished Anglo-Saxon historian, and honorary fellow

Billy Reade, his tutor, wrote in Michaelmas 1899 that he was 'a rather weird person with some wits.... Volunteering may be good for him'. G. Baskerville wrote of a later term that he 'works hard, but … is (I regret to have to say) deplorably conceited…. A very hard worker but cannot be induced to see how serious are his limitations'.

Thomas Armstrong
Organ scholar and later honorary fellow

E.L. Woodward, his history tutor, remarked in 1920: 'I hope his history is not robbing his music as his music is robbing his history'. Billy Reade was more supportive: 'His first duty here is to music and he performs it admirably'.

Peter Pears

Peter Pears
Singer

On his arrival in 1928, 'Crab' Owen remarked, 'A very attractive man: I hope we shall be able to keep him'. Pears left after a year.

Chad Varah
Founder of the Samaritans and honorary fellow

George Parkes wrote in Michaelmas 1931 that he was 'absolutely lacking in self control when it comes to matters of expenditure on tobacco and similar matters'.

Joseph Cooper
Organ scholar and later pianist and presenter of Face the Music

'His teachers in music do not speak well of his work. He still has much to do if he is to get a degree in three years'.

Michael Goodliffe
Actor

Geoffrey Dickens, the historian, wrote in Michaelmas 1934, 'painstaking but dull'.

Patrick Shovelton
Later prominent civil servant

Spencer Barrett wrote in Trinity, 1939: 'Unable I'm afraid to realise that a wood is composed of trees and unless he can acquire the habit of getting to grips with details is in very real danger. Sometimes good, sometimes atrocious. Sense of style is good but there is a limit to the multitude of sins it can cover'.

By the later 1960s, however, there was a growing awareness of the need for greater proactivity, and in 1972 the post of Tutor for Admissions was created: the first incumbent was Richard Green. Eric Stone as Senior Tutor had always taken a strong interest in secondary education, and encouraged the College's admission of PGCE students, as well as developing (with the help of Dennis Shaw) the schoolteacher fellow scheme, funded from 1971 by British Petroleum with a grant of £10,000. This scheme enabled teachers to spend a term in Oxford on their research projects. In 1977 and 1978 the College hosted school-teacher conferences. By the early 1980s Keble was much more aggressive on the admissions front. In 1982 the College held an open day ('an experiment'), and produced an admissions brochure for the first time. By the later 1980s open days were attracting 250 sixth-formers, it is an indication of the changing scale of the admissions operation that by 2000, 700 were attending this event.

Keble was also more willing to strike an independent line on admissions. In 1982 the Governing Body, steered by Philip Capper as Tutor for Admissions, and very much with Christopher Ball's encouragement, agreed to the so-called 'Keble scheme' in which the College proposed to make open (as opposed to conditional) offers. The announcement had the effect of bouncing the collegiate University into a more general effort at reform, and the Keble scheme was put on hold as the Dover Committee (on which Keble's Warden, Christopher Ball sat) deliberated. Ball was keen on widening access before it became politically fashionable, and began the scheme by which current undergraduates visited schools as doubtless more effective ambassadors than the academics. In the mid 1980s, 60 per cent of the entry offers went to state school candidates, just 37.5 per cent to candidates from the independent sector, interestingly, roughly the same proportions as in 2006–7 after several years more sustained access work by the collegiate University. In 1984, 1986 and again in 1987, Keble had more first-choice applicants than any other College; it found itself increasingly in the unusual position of being able to 'export' its surplus, as many as 33 candidates in 1987. The forward momentum was maintained into the 1990s. For five years from 1994 to 1998, Keble attracted the highest number of applicants for undergraduate courses of any college (a position from which it has subsequently slipped back). Increasing numbers of applicants meant increasing competition for places, in 1968–72 the ratio of applicants to places was 1.52, in 1984–8, it was 3.20, and in 1994–8, 3.83.

"...a brilliant gaudy red"

"Five times I've searched.....the list from..."

Above: *Scrutinising the class list*

The surge in applications in the 1980s was surely a major factor in improving standards.

Table 3, which charts the performance of Keble finalists from the 1890s to the present, actually underestimates the low level of achievement in the earlier period, because it excludes those reading for the pass school, which were as many as 14 a year in the 1890s and early years of the 20th century. By the 1930s the numbers reading for the pass school had dropped to about six per year, and there had

Table 3. Performance of Keble finalists (degree classifications)

	I	II	III	IV	Fail
1892–6	4%	21%	43%	20%	12%
1932–6	6%	46%	41%	7%	NA
1952–6	5%	44%	43%	7%	NA
1972–6	8%	74%	18%	0%	NA
1982–6	14%	76%	10%	0%	NA

	I	II.1	II.2	III	Pass
1992–6	15%	65%	17%	3%	<1%
2002–6	21%	67%	10%	1%	<1%

Above: *A finalist celebrates*

It does not look as though the decision to go co-educational had much to do with raising levels of performance, for the gender gap was initially very pronounced, as the table makes clear. The gap has narrowed over time, and while the lower second class is becoming a male preserve, women still have difficulties securing firsts. The reasons for that are, needless-to-say, quite complex, but it is interesting that, in recent years, some subjects, which have historically been heavily male-dominated in Keble, like geography and chemistry, have become more feminized.

Table 4. Performance of Keble finalists by gender

	I	II.1	II.2	III
1986–90				
Males	22%	55%	19%	4%
Females	7.5%	51%	38%	2.5%
2003–07				
Males	22%	66%	10%	1%
Females	16%	78%	6%	0%

Another variable is the arts-science split. A closer examination of the results at the time when the College began its growth in science is instructive.

Table 5. Percentage of those graduating gaining a first or second class degree

		1957–61	1962–6
Arts	Keble	47.0%	56.6%
	University	62.1%	67.6%
Science	Keble	58.7%	63.6%
	University	64.3%	72.2%

The performance of Keble men in the 1960s still lagged behind the University average; but as Keble scientists outperformed their arts contemporaries, a shift in the balance of the student population would contribute to a raising of overall standards. But it is perhaps among the Keble arts undergraduates that the most marked improvements were registered in the 1960s, an indication of the depth of the trough from which they were being dragged! The contribution of Keble science to improving performance is still clearer if we move to a period in which

been some reduction in the number of fourth class degrees, but the proportion of firsts had only inched forwards. The men of the 1950s appear to have performed little better than their forbears in the 1930s. It was a situation which depressed the fellows, Douglas Price noting in 1958 that the lack of firsts means that schools 'will only send us their inferior products and a vicious spiral of academic deterioration will result'.

It took a lot of slog to raise standards. The determination to make a difference was evident in the Governing Body's resolution in 1980, that henceforth, no-one would be admitted who, in the opinion of their tutors, was not capable of getting at least a second class degree: a comment which is as revealing about the previously prevailing standards as it is about the progress being made. Shortly thereafter the College abandoned the notion of a fixed academic establishment, and decreed that henceforth, whenever vacancies occurred, the new post would have to be justified 'de novo' in competition with the claims of other subjects. The first casualty was history, which was shrunk from a three-fellow to a two-fellow subject on Douglas Price's retirement in 1982, to make way for a new post in civil engineering. From 1982 onwards Alan Corney, one of the physics tutors, maintained the so-called 'Corney table', which compared the performance of Keble finalists against the University averages for that subject. It became a powerful shaming tool in Governing Body discourse. By the later 1980s, the efforts were paying off. Just as applications were surging forwards, so the College broke through on the Norrington Table, holding the position of ninth for two years in a row in 1987 and 1988. Keble was judged the top science college in Oxford by *The Independent* in 1987.

Above: *Dr Ian Archer with University of Georgia students on field trip at Long Melford Hall*

the College had pulled itself up the Norrington Table, and compare the performance of Keble students with their peers in the University in selected arts and science subjects. By the early 1990s, Keble arts students were performing respectably, with 82 per cent gaining upper seconds or above, compared with a university average of 75 per cent. The scientists, however, outstripped University performance by some margin, with 83 per cent gaining at least an upper second compared to the University average of 70 per cent.

Table 6. Finals performance in selected arts (history, English, and modern Languages) and science (chemistry, physics, mathematics) subjects: Keble students compared with University, 1990–4

		I	II.1	II.2	III
Arts	Keble	14.5%	67.5%	14.5%	3%
	University	16%	59%	22%	3%
Science	Keble	31%	52%	15%	2%
	University	23%	47%	22%	8%

Top and above: *Students at work*

Another variable much discussed in the College's academic performance has been sports. Christopher Ball was fond of tabulating the combined numbers of sporting blues with the number of firsts as a sign of the College's virility, and it is notable that the period of greatest academic success in the late 1980s coincided with a period of sporting vitality. Others, remembering Davidge's oarsmen, saw the College's 'sporty' reputation as an obstacle to raising academic standards. Davidge was not alone in his interest in sport. Dennis Shaw had coached the third VIII as a young don; Paul Hayes was a fanatic for cricket and hockey; the law tutor Ed Peel played rugby for the College in his early years. Paul Hayes, though he would have loathed the comparison, became as notorious for the promotion of sport as Davidge had been, and the whole question of the relationship between academic standards and sport became regrettably entangled in the rather separate issue of the 'Dip. Socs' in the early 1990s.

The Special Diploma in Social Studies was a postgraduate course recognized by the University but understood as an access course, available to those who might have followed less conventional career paths and wanted a bridge into further study. Although many of the students studied at institutions that were not formally part of the University, Paul Hayes noted that there was no reason why the course could not be studied in a college. He steadily increased the numbers on the course at Keble, so that they peaked at 21 in 1994; the quota was then cut to 12 at a Governing Body meeting, which rendered him apoplectic. To critics who claimed the College was being packed with rugby, cricket and hockey blues, and that this was having a detrimental impact on its image, Hayes would respond with a fierce defence of the rigour of the course and its financial benefit to the College. And to be fair to him, many of his critics failed to see that many of the students were indeed highly capable, as well as among the more sociable members of the MCR community. But he never really got the point about perceptions. At the height of the controversy, the student newspaper *Rear End* ran a brilliant spoof, alleging that students were being admitted on other than sporting criteria. In a wonderful parody of the SCR discourse on admissions, an 'SCR insider' was reported as claiming that 'if we have two applicants of equal sporting prowess, then academic ability will be one of the criteria we use for choosing between them, but it can't be allowed to take precedence'.

So, what is the truth about the relationship between sporting excellence and academic performance? We have analysed the academic results of the full blue sportsmen and women during the 1980s, as the College pushed its way up the Norrington Table.

Above: *Hockey Club, 1973–4 with Imran Khan (back row, third from right) and Paul Hayes (front row, far left)*

Table 7. Academic performance of full blue sportsmen and women, 1980–90

	I	II	III	Pass
Male full blues	5	22	2	3
Female full blues	1	11	0	1
Total	6	33	2	4
Percentage	13%	73%	4%	9%
Overall results (1982–6)	14%	76%	10%	NA

Comparison with the overall performance of the student body is rendered difficult by the fact that the published lists do not record pass degrees, but it is pretty clear that by this date it would be wrong-headed to assert that sport impeded academic success, as the students involved do not seem to have performed in a very markedly different way from the non sportspersons. There may have been more pass degrees but there were fewer thirds, and the proportion of firsts is not out of line with overall performance. There were another five blues among the postgraduate body in the 1980s, only one of them, Mark Crawley, a Dip. Soc.; this would shift in the 1990s as the course took off, and the issue became controversial.

QUICK LUNCH CO.
FAST AFTERNOON TEAS ALSO PROVIDED

THE AMERICAN INVASION.
What the Rhodes' Scholars might have brought about.

Above: *Early prejudices about Americans in Oxford: cartoon by Hoggarth*

Table 8. Student numbers, 1950–2005

Year	Undergraduate	Postgraduate	Total	Fellows (including Research Fellows and Professors)
1950	272	6	278	9
1955	265	27	292	12
1960	344	28	372	13
1965	346	32	378	20
1970	358	72	430	35
1975	378	95	473	34
1980	394	79	473	35
1985	395	75	470	37
1990	404	96	500	41
1995	451	127	578	39
2000	458	157	595	39
2005	448	174	622	51

The other major shift in the College's academic profile since the Second World War has been the rising profile of postgraduate students. In 1954–5 there had been a sprinkling of colonial service and Diploma in Education candidates; ten years later the intake was more varied, including six men reading for doctorates or the B.Litt. and nine men reading for diplomas (including now six for the Diploma in Education). There was a marked surge in postgraduate recruitment in the later 1960s, and again in the 1990s. Whereas postgraduates accounted for 7.5 per cent of total Keble students in 1960, they were 17 per cent in 1970, 17 per cent in 1980, 19 per cent in 1990, and 26 per cent in 2000.

The effect of increasing postgraduate numbers is a marked internationalization of the student body, the effects of which are visible in the maps of student origins. Whereas in the 1920s, 12 per cent of students were non-UK in origin, many admittedly the children of colonial officials, in the 1950s the proportion had shrunk to just 6 per cent, though there were a handful of Africans like Jehoash Mayanja-Nkangi, a PPE-ist of 1954 who went on to be a minister in the Obote government and founded the Ugandan Conservative (monarchist) Party in 1979, and Francis Wellington Addo-Ashong, who came on a Ghanaian scholarship to study forestry in 1955. In 2007, the proportion of non-UK students was 27 per cent (of which 8 per cent were EU, and the remainder overseas). Even the undergraduate body is becoming more varied in terms of student origins: in 2007 2.5 per cent of undergraduates were EU and 6.5 per cent overseas. There have been steady flows from the elite schools of Singapore and Hong Kong, and in recent years from China, to the benefit of subjects like computer science. The international character of the student body has been fertilized also by various associate student schemes with North American institutions: from 1987 until 2004 students from the Centre for Medieval and Renaissance Studies, founded by John Feneley and his wife, shared Keble social and sporting facilities; since 1994 a stream of students from the University of Georgia has enjoyed similar privileges. A very successful student exchange scheme with Dartmouth College was established by Tim Jenkinson in 1996, and it was soon followed by an association with Washington University at St Louis.

The needs of postgraduate students only slowly asserted themselves on the Governing Body agenda. There was no middle common room until 1964, when rooms on the Chapel wing, formerly a fellows' set, were allocated to the fledgling community. Graduate needs became more clearly articulated with the appointment of a Tutor for Graduates in 1970.

Where the students came from

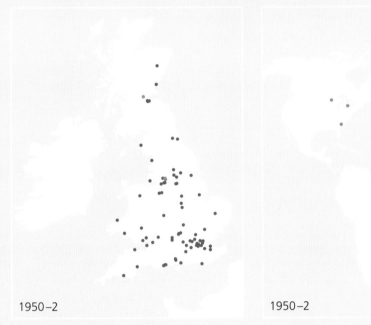

1950–2

1950–2

2007

2007

Key

- undergraduates
- graduates

141

Left: *James Griffin,
fellow in philosophy*

Below: *MCR garden party,
centenary celebrations, 1970*

The post was first held by Stephen Wall, and from 1973 by the young philosophy tutor James Griffin, who was both a powerful advocate as well as a source of hospitality and support. The MCR moved to the space adjacent to the college bar with the opening of the ABK buildings in 1977, but it was never a very satisfactory space, and it became increasingly cramped as the College expanded graduate numbers in the 1990s.

In increasing its numbers the College was responding to University pressures, as taught-course graduate numbers mushroomed. Keble was one of the first colleges to admit graduates taking the newly instituted MBA course at the Saïd Business School. Its long-standing strength in law meant that it also had a notable intake of lawyers reading for the one-year BCL and M.Jur. Many of the graduates were on one-year masters' courses, some of them self-contained and attracting high fees to their departments (though not to the College), although others served as a required preliminary for entrance to the D. Phil.

The expansion initially took place without much in the way of increased resources, and by the later 1990s some members of the Governing Body commented with unease that graduates had become the College's milch cow, supplying fees in return for facilities of questionable value. In 1980 a review of graduate provision noted the need for more accommodation, but undergraduate needs remained paramount, and even in the 1990s, the opening of the Arco building did little to increase the number of rooms for the graduate community, many of whom lived in houses outwith the curtilage. There were modest interventions like the establishment of a separate graduate academic fund in 1986 to assist with research expenses.

The key to attracting graduates lies inevitably in money, and here the College has only been partially successful. As early as 1949, two postgraduate awards of £50 per annum each were offered. In 1969 the College again offered two postgraduate awards at £100 each, with the right to dine on High Table twice per week. This marked the beginning of the support of the Keble Association for graduate studies, but there were still only three such scholarships ten years later. Although the Association has withdrawn from supporting graduate scholarships, the de Breyne and Sloane Robinson awards have more than filled the gap. The re-jigging of some of the trust funds for ordinands has also resulted in helpful support for theology postgraduates.

Graduates have moved steadily up the agenda of the collegiate University as part of the programme of what is

now called 'embedding' graduate studies. In the global university world of the 1990s and beyond, with its heavy emphasis on research, graduate students are seen as evidence of research excellence and of the competitive standing of the institution, and although Oxford is not yet able to compete with ivy league universities in the US in terms of the funding it can offer to graduates, redressing this situation is now recognized as a central objective.

Keble has responded to this changing environment in a number of ways. Funding for graduate scholarships is, as we have seen, a key goal. Graduates have been concentrated at a point closer to College with the acquisition of the Acland Hospital site and the sale of the outlying houses where many of the graduates previously lived. At the same time, the remodelling of the bar meant that the MCR could move out of its cramped quarters to the suite of three rooms it now occupies adjacent to the JCR in Pusey quad. The bedding down of a new admissions process has enabled the College

The Library

Within a year of opening in 1878 the Library had received 8,000 volumes, including John Keble's own library, as well as a large number of books presented by Earl Beauchamp. The important manuscripts are described elsewhere, but the College also possesses 99 incunabula (pre-1500 printed books), many of which came in the Brooke and Liddon collections. In 1902 Reverend Henry T. Morgan bequeathed to the College his Port Royal collection of 300 volumes, possibly the largest single private collection of Jansenist literature in the country.

The Library: above, 1933; left, today

The Library was initially for the use of tutors only, but Geoffrey Baskerville, Fellow Librarian from 1906, managed to build up a working collection for undergraduate use, and books were being lent after 1913. A room in the gateway (the JCR from 1870 to 1878) over the Lodge operated as an undergraduate reading room. By the 1950s student demand was such that the Governing Body was being petitioned for extensions to the opening hours. From 1957 the Library was to close at 10 p.m.; an experiment with 24-hour opening was abandoned in 1986, and the undergraduates had to wait another seven years for the opportunity to bring their essay crises to fruition in the Library.

The allocation for expenditure on books was raised to £400 in 1958, but there was a significant increment in 1966, when it was raised from £450 to £2,360 per annum in one bound. The absorption of the collection in the reading room in the entrance gateway, and increasing pressure of space necessitated the building of a book stack in 1966 to achieve a marked increase in 'research' postgraduates, designs by Alan Stubbs, and the extension of the Library into the ground floor rooms by the conversion of the former JCR and Memorial Room to designs by ABK, opened in 1981. In the sixties many books were still catalogued in ledgers: it was Spencer Barrett, with his characteristic attention to detail, who devised the indexing scheme, which produced the card index. The Library catalogue was computerized between 1993 and 1995. Another indication of the Library's raised profile was the appointment of Jean Robinson as assistant librarian to support the work of the fellow librarian in 1968.

In 1978 the library contained some 30,000 volumes, by 2007 the figure was about 53,000. Although the data are unlikely to be strictly comparable, it was estimated that, in 1967–8, 2,720 volumes per term were being borrowed; in 1977–8, 4,500 volumes per term; and in 2006–7, 3,242 volumes per term (excluding renewals). These figures reflect changes in undergraduate working practices: increasing amounts of material are available online, and students probably work more often in their rooms, or in the social space of Café Keble.

to achieve a marked increase in 'research' postgraduates, that is students working for doctorates, rather than students on one year courses. In 1996 Averil Cameron initiated the graduate discussion evenings in the Lodgings, in which graduates explained their research to an academically mixed audience. This has been followed by initiatives like the Keble Social Sciences Group (2005), the brainchild of Jamie Edelman and Howard Smith, fellows in law and economics respectively, which brings graduates and academics together to hear papers by distinguished visitors. The postgraduate community also benefits from the increased number of research fellows. Fellows have been encouraged to take seriously their roles as college advisers to graduate students, while the routine of graduate collections, already well established in the 1990s, has enabled the College to assist in 'trouble-shooting' for problem cases.

A further distinct trend is for professorial fellows to attract graduates to the College in their own fields: this is exemplified by the students of Mike Brady in information engineering, Jonathan Zittrain in internet governance and Barry Cunliffe and his successor Chris Gosden in archaeology. It has also been true of Averil Cameron in Byzantine studies, and of other fellows such as Ole Paulsen in neuroscience and Stephen Cameron in computer science. These changes have not been without their tensions: as resources shift towards graduates and to some extent away from undergraduate tutorials, the older college patterns have to be modified in the face of the desire on the part of many fellows to spend more time on graduate teaching and supervision. Another area where more work needs to be done is fostering interaction between graduates and undergraduates, which is patchy, the undergraduate body sometimes treating the graduates as an alien species, though some integration has occurred through College subject societies, particularly in theology, medicine, and history.

The character of the fellowship has changed markedly. As research and graduates have become more important, so the composition of the fellowship has shifted with more professorial and research fellows relative to tutorial fellows. In 2007 the fellowship comprised the Warden, Bursar, Senior Tutor, Chaplain, 31 tutorial fellows, 10 professorial fellows and 14 research fellows. In 1950 there had been just one professorial fellow and no research fellows, and in 1980 there had been 30 tutorial fellows, three professorial fellows, and two research fellows. Internationalization among the fellowship is even more marked than among the student body. By 2007, of 51 fellows, no fewer than 19 were non-UK in origin. There were five US-born fellows, three Australians, two Germans, two Greeks, one Austrian, one Norwegian, one Dane, one Italian, one Canadian, one Indian, and one South Korean. The gender balance is, however, less impressive. Although Keble is one of a minority of colleges to have a female head of house, only six of the 44 Governing Body members in 2007 were women. There has been some change from the early 1990s, when the 'hard men', as they were dubbed by Averil Cameron on her arrival, would loudly hold forth with their views (not to say prejudices) on the issues of the day and the failings of their colleagues, both over morning coffee in the SCR and again at the lunch table, where they tended to sit together. The arrival in recent years of many younger colleagues has undoubtedly had the effect of encouraging a more liberal atmosphere, but the gender balance remains problematic.

The College has sought to foster the careers of beginning academics through research fellowships. Here, as in other areas, it has been stymied by the relative lack of resources compared to some other colleges, but research fellowships have long been a priority. Rolls Royce funded a Junior Research Fellow in engineering from 1978, and the E.P. Abraham Research Fund a JRF in medical or chemical sciences from 1980, but in both cases there was no full endowment. In 1980 the Governing Body determined on three fully endowed JRFs as a fund-raising objective. The Keble Association offered support, and David Eastwood (at the time of writing the chief executive of HEFCE) became the first holder of its fellowship in 1983; a further donation of £20,000 from Douglas Price for an arts JRF followed in the next year. The Centre for Medieval and Renaissance Studies likewise funded a research fellowship in history for a few years. None of these arrangements had any permanency, although briefly in the mid 1980s the College did fulfil its ambition of three functioning research fellowships (EPA, Rolls Royce, and Keble Association). In 1998 Tim Jenkinson as Senior Tutor came up with the Research Fellow and Tutor scheme, which takes advantage of the desire of the growing number of post-doctoral researchers to gain a college affiliation in return for meeting

IT Provision

Above: *The ubiquitous laptop*

Computerization of the bursary began under Adrian Darby in 1979, but its impact on other sectors of the College was delayed until the mid 1980s. In 1984 the fellows' secretary acquired a word processor, and the first word-processed minutes appeared in that year. At the same time, a committee on computer provision for junior members agreed to acquire a single machine (a BBC computer) costing £800. Over the ensuing years computer provision expanded considerably, but the College got by with part-time IT support from graduate assistants until 1996, when Steve Kersley was appointed to a full-time position; he acquired an assistant in 1998. Networking the College site had already started with the Arco building, but by 1998 nearly every room had ethernet connection. It was then that the College decided, in the face of reluctance from the JCR (who pointed out that there were only 24 College terminals, perhaps missing the point about the implications of ethernetting) to make email the default mode of communication. In 1996–7 there were 34 students with computers on the network, by 2002 the figure was around 300; at the time of writing, with the Acland site wired in, there are 500. In addition to this there are about 150 computers belonging to staff and fellows. The network has been steadily upgraded, and the fibre-optic network that joins the buildings together now operates at 1 gigabyte per second. Wireless access is available in the Café, Library and MCR and is shortly to become more widespread. It is estimated that the College regularly sends and receives over 200 gigabytes in internet traffic per day.

Steve Kersley

some of the tutorial needs. In 2007 there were seven such posts. They are supplemented by British Academy post-doctoral fellowships – there were three in 2007 – which have transformed the research profile in the humanities in the College in recent years. Another recent initiative designed to enrich the intellectual vitality of the College is the scheme for college associations for postdoctoral staff who would otherwise have no college connection.

All these changes have brought about a marked shift in the nature of the academic's role. The traditional model of the Oxford don was the bachelor resident in College, and thoroughly identifying with it. Examples from the interwar years were 'Crab' Owen and Billy Reade. After the war the ideal was epitomised by Douglas Price, but with the marriage of Christopher Stead in 1958, Price became the only bachelor don, a matter over which he fretted, remarking how difficult it would now be to find a suitable man to be Dean. Price increasingly self-fashioned himself as the defender of traditional College ideals against the 'five-day-week non residents' (1957). In 1969 he complained about the disastrous consequences of the expansion in the fellowship: 'they have neither the willingness nor the ability to play their part in the government of the college, they ignore their social obligations, relations with the junior members have steadily deteriorated as the dons have hidden behind committees'.

Above: *Douglas Price*

Above and left: *Schools picnic with Basil Mitchell, Peter Cuff and others, early 1960*

The problem with his model was that he published very little, working for years on the Elizabethan volume of *English Historical Documents*, which remained uncompleted at his death. For all that he presented himself as the lone bastion of traditional values, the research of others also suffered because of their dedication to College: G.D. Parkes and Eric Stone likewise directed their energies into the office of Senior Tutor, and produced little. There is a worrying tendency in the years before 1970 for Keble's most productive fellows to have been those who escaped, men like Russell Meiggs, Donald MacKinnon, A.G. Dickens and John Carey.

As University funding has rewarded research over teaching, and as departmental pressures have mounted, first in the sciences, but increasingly in the other disciplines too, fellows have found it difficult to juggle their conflicting responsibilities. In the early 21st century, departments have responded by buying out College teaching, sometimes to the apparent detriment of tutorial relationships. The College has responded to the pressures on fellows' time by a growing 'professionalization' (though the word is resisted in Governing Body discourse) of its leading officers. Adrian Darby was the last Bursar to be a workaday fellow; since his departure in 1984, Bursars have been full time. In 2003, recognizing the increasing difficulty of finding fellows to serve the office of Senior Tutor and acknowledging the increasing complexity of the job as the audit culture infiltrated the academy, the College amalgamated the offices of Tutor for Graduates, Tutor for Admissions and Senior Tutor into a full time post. The first incumbent was Sonia Mazey (2003–7), formerly a politics fellow at Hertford College, whose light touch reassured the sceptics who feared creeping 'managerialism'. The implications for governance cannot yet be determined, but there are risks as the fellows now have less collective experience of the key offices.

An element of Price's pessimism about the processes of change was the way in which they eroded the traditional social bonds between tutors and students. He regularly drove undergraduates out to country pubs, and hosted parties after club dinners in his rooms. In common with other dons he organized Schools picnics, in 1957–8 hiring boats on the Thames, the precursors of Schools dinners. But his lament about the decline of hospitality may miss the point that it has changed in character, becoming more formalized, and less inclined to selectivity in its beneficiaries.

By the later 1960s the practice of offering a formal Schools dinner had become widespread, but it was only in 1972 that the College agreed to fund these rather than fellows having to fork out from their own pockets. The 'time of troubles' in the late 1960s and 70s made relations more strained, the older generation finding it difficult to come to terms with the changing mores of the young. A variety of experiments were tried including joint SCR/JCR lunches in the early 1970s, to bring the two groups closer together. There has perhaps been a retreat in the valorization of sport in social occasions: bump suppers were replaced by the entertainment of winning teams on High Table in 1973, and then in 1993 by a Sports Lunch for victorious teams. The fellows are perhaps rather keener on the celebration of academic success in the cycle of

Above: *Sonia Mazey, first full-time Senior Tutor*

scholars' dinners. The multiple pressures on today's academics mean that relations between academic staff and students are potentially more distant, but the scale of the change should not be exaggerated. Although Price bemoaned the demise of the bachelor don, nine Keble fellows and the Warden still live in; they still provide a nucleus of College-based sociability, and many more fellows (and sometimes their partners) mix with students in fairly relaxed social settings through drama, music, and Chapel. There is also a regular cycle of formal College events bringing academics and students together: the separate freshers' dinners for undergraduates and graduates in the noughth week of Michaelmas term (as part of the expanded freshers' week), the freshers' parents lunch instituted in 1997, the St Mark's Day Dinner, instituted in 1982 through the generosity of Mrs Patricia Mills and in recent years a much enhanced occasion, the garden party, begun in 1980 at the suggestion of the Keble Association and from 1987 designated as being for second years and their parents, and the 'big bang' graduations, of which Keble was a pioneer in 1998. Sociability has been channelled into more 'formal' events, but it surely remains the case that Oxford students continue to enjoy a far higher level of access to academic staff than would be the case almost anywhere else in the world.

Right: *MBA students at matriculation, 2007*

Below: *Ralph Hanna as Dean of Degrees leads the graduands to the degree ceremony*

7 STUDENT LIFE SINCE THE SECOND WORLD WAR

On 24 May 1950 Keble celebrated its first Eights Week bump supper for 45 years. The first VIII had secured five bumps, climbing from Division III into Division II and finishing in 23rd place, while the third VIII (a 'Schools' eight) secured six bumps. The first VIII took their place of honour on High Table, and invited four dons to sit with them, the Warden, Davidge (Bursar), Hugh Jones and Price (Dean), all facing into Hall; the other dons were relegated to low tables. High Table was decorated with the barge flag, rudders, and the rowing cap and posy traditionally worn by the cox. The VIII's oars stood against the wall behind High Table. There were speeches from the Warden, who gave the loyal toast and proposed the health of the College, to which the JCR President responded with a toast to the Boat Club; the Captain of Boats replied, and the Secretary proposed the guests, on whose behalf a man from St Edmund Hall responded, a representative from each of the boats Keble had bumped having been invited. The diners then retired to the celebrations in the quad, where the boat was burned, and men rode bicycles through the midst of the inferno. It was by the standards of bump suppers a relatively orderly occasion. An attempt to raid Wadham was foiled; there were some illicit fireworks made out of rifle ammunition, but the bill for damages (including breakages in Hall) only came to £42, and Douglas Price who, as Dean, feared that his room would receive 'mischievous attention', thought he had got off lightly with just a beer barrel dumped in his

bath. It was an evening where the community came together: 'here a don may forget his station and put himself on a footing with the undergraduates on an occasion like last night without any permanent loss of dignity or reputation', he noted the following day. 'Today I was being 'sir' called in a perfectly natural, respectful way by young men who last night were putting their arms on my shoulder and addressing me as Doug'.

Above: *Above: Bump supper, 1950*

Right: *Students at work in Café Keble (the Douglas Price Room)*

warmer is very doubtful. Some very limited food preparation facilities became available in the scouts' cubby holes. Rewiring also eased the work of the domestic staff, for it meant that labour-saving devices like vacuum cleaners could, for the first time, be used in undergraduate rooms. The kitchens acquired their first dish-washing machine in 1955 at a cost of £700.

The fellows were, however, very slow to encourage those facilities which undergraduates were coming to regard as essential. There was a brief experiment with a 'beer loft' in 1952, located in the old changing rooms in the Clock Tower, but the opening hours were very restricted (6.30 to 7.15 p.m. four nights a week, with an additional hour 8 to 9 p.m. on Tuesdays and Fridays) and it was not until May 1958 that the College acquired a beer cellar (a former coal cellar in Pusey quad), much to the annoyance of the more conservative dons: Douglas Price bemoaned the 'vulgar celebrations' at its opening, 'the College seems ever more ready to facilitate time-wasting than to encourage effort'. Hours were still strictly limited and the consumption of spirits was banned. In the early 1960s we are told that it was presided over by a man 'of such incompetence and slowness that there was little chance of over indulgence'. Nor was it easy to broaden one's horizons by contact with the outside world. There was only one payphone for the entire College in the early 1960s; a request for a TV set in the JCR was refused in 1960; it was not until 1963 that one was acquired as a reward for the College's team doing so well in the *University Challenge* competition (unbeaten in three successive rounds).

Musical and dramatic activity revived, though they were perhaps not quite so central to the Keble ethos as they

Dinners such as these allowed the College's members to forget the essential shabbiness and austerity that surrounded them. The College's buildings were showing real signs of age with pieces of masonry falling off; there had been few improvements in amenities, with men still expected to use the lavatories, the 'cloaca maxima', at the back of Hall. Austerity continued for several years after the war. Rationing reduced Wednesday lunch to a thin soup, an apple and bread; the jellied slice of fatty meat regularly served up became known as Bursar's beef; the notorious cabbage in undergraduate folklore was rumoured to come from Davidge's own farm; students would rush from College lunch to one of the British restaurants on either the Plain or at Gloucester Green where boiled cod and mashed potato could be had for 1s.

Things were beginning to change, but slowly. One effect of the wartime occupation by the female secretaries was that a few more baths had been provided, but it was not until the years between 1958 and 1963 that every staircase was equipped with a bathroom. The College had been comprehensively rewired after the war, at a cost of just over £10,000, and electric fires replaced coal fires in undergraduate rooms, a change rendered more urgent by the post-war fuel shortages. The site of upwards of 150 Keble chimneys simultaneously sending smoke heavenwards was no more, but whether rooms were any

Keble and the Oxford Union

C.F. Garbett

Since its foundation in 1870, Keble, though one of the larger colleges, has supplied just 10 Union Presidents, lagging far behind Balliol (79), New (42) and Christ Church (38), but roughly on a par with Lincoln (10), Brasenose (9), Jesus (8) and Wadham (8). The College's own Debating Society may have provided a substitute, and there were complaints in the interwar period that Keble undergraduates were too introverted.

Keble Presidents of the Union

Hilary 1887	C.A.H. Green, later Archbishop of Wales
Easter 1898	C.F. Garbett, later Archbishop of York
Michaelmas 1942	Sir James Cameron Tudor, later politician in Barbados
Trinity 1943	Courtenay Blackmore, later head of administration at Lloyds
Hilary 1953	Bryan Magee, philosopher, opera writer and broadcaster
Hilary 1954	Tyrrell Burgess, educational journalist and author
Michaelmas 1955	Desmond Watkins, spent most of his career with British Petroleum
Michaelmas 1960	Robert Rowland, later BBC TV Producer, programme Editor (*Panorama*, *Money Programme*) and Head of BBC Open University Productions
Hilary 1978	Nicholas O'Shaughnessy, later academic, and currently Professor of Marketing at Brunel
Trinity 1994	Peter Gowers, currently Chief Executive, Intercontinental Hotels Group Asia-Pacific

had been before the war. The Keble plays now drew upon the services of Michael Goodliffe, old member and now a distinguished actor, who had been a prisoner of war in Germany. The plays initially continued in Hall, with all the dining tables assembled on the dais and covered with ex-blackout, thick woollen curtains, and a vast canvas sheet to serve as a stage, but the performances were uneven: the 1950 play *Too Good to Be True* was untidily curtained and there was no music, only a clumsily amplified gramophone; only one third of the hall space was used for seating. After a while the Hall was declared unsafe for these performances, and by the late 1950s Keble plays were being performed sometimes in the College gardens, and sometimes at the Clarendon Press Institute in Walton Street. In the Long Vacation of 1956 the players took *King Lear* on tour to

Germany, after rehearsing for three weeks in the village of Buxhall, Suffolk. The cast lists of some of the productions of the 1950s and 1960s read rather impressively. A production of *A Midsummer Night's Dream* in the Fellows' Garden in 1965, for which the assistant stage manager was Aung Sang Suu Kyi, the Burmese dissident and Nobel Peace prize winner, saw Geoffrey Nice, later prosecutor in the International Court at The Hague, as Don Pedro, Ivor Roberts, former diplomat and future President of Trinity College, Oxford, as Borachio, and Humphrey Carpenter (author and broadcaster) as Dogberry. Carpenter, who had grown up in the Warden's Lodgings, composed the incidental music for several of the dramatic productions, and is also remembered for playing 'I'm forever blowing bubbles' at the 1967 bump supper.

The Dean's Black Book: Discipline in the 1950s

Douglas Price acted as Dean from 1950 to 1962, with responsibility for discipline over the junior members. It was a demanding role: the Dean was responsible, among other things, for managing the permissions for parties, guests in College, gate-hour extensions, the registration of electrical appliances and motor cars, and the organization of degree days. From 1958 the role was split between a Senior and Junior Dean, the latter a junior fellow, rather than, as now, a graduate student. Maintaining discipline meant being on duty during term time, sometimes lying in wait for those attempting to climb in. On one occasion in 1961, when one of the night porters was suspected of pilfering the fellows' port, Price lay in wait in the smoking-room cupboard, and apprehended the hapless member of staff, who was dismissed the following day.

Price recorded the disciplinary infractions of junior members in the 'black book', which is carried on by the current deans. His meticulous record-keeping enables us to chart the pattern of student discipline during his tenure. In the 26 terms from Trinity 1950 to Michaelmas 1958 inclusive, 332 acts of discipline are recorded, plus three collective sanctions on disorderly clubs. Fifteen (5 per cent) junior members were fined for sumptuary offences, such as sitting at the scholars' table in a commoner's gown, or appearing at dinner with a scarf rather than a tie. Thirty-six (11 per cent) were fined for noise-related offences, usually playing radios or pianos after hours, but also 'blowing a bugle and causing a general disturbance'. There were various miscellaneous offences, 'reading grace in hall in an Italianate and improper manner', 'failing to accept the Dean's compliments when making a slide in the quadrangle'. But the largest category of offences (43 per cent) related to the tight regulations on hours and the entertainment of guests: 76 were fined amounts between £1 and £2 for climbing in; another 28 were sanctioned for being out of college after hours, and 23 for failing to secure the necessary consents for leave of

David Paton, the 22-year-old undergraduate sent down by Keble College, being given the "last rites" before leaving Oxford.
His "mock funeral" was held yesterday in the garden of his lodgings, in the shadow of Keble Chapel. From his "bier" he recited an improvised epitaph on his Oxford career: "Ashes to ashes, dust to dust, if the Proctors don't get you the S.C.R. must."
Later "mourners" were dispersed at the station when the Senior Proctor, Mr. B. G. Mitchell, arrived on the platform.

OXFORD MOCK FUNERAL IS BROKEN UP

FIRST SINCE WAR

DAILY TELEGRAPH REPORTER

Oxford's first mock funeral for an undergraduate since the war was dispersed by proctors and "bulldogs" yesterday afternoon. The undergraduate was David Paton, 22.

Paton, who has been reading politics, philosophy and economics at Keble, claims he has been sent down for burning the bedding of the dean of his college, Mr. Francis Price. The burning took place on bump supper night, yesterday week.

Keble had celebrated the victories of their boat in the torpid races. Paton said yesterday that he left the college dinner early and 'found the door to the dean's house locked. He climbed through a window and passed the dean's bedding out to friends.

The bedding was placed on the bonfire on which the college boat was burning. The dean, says Paton, saw it being destroyed without knowing the sheets and blankets were his own.

DEAN'S DENIAL

But Mr. Price says: "It is quite untrue that Paton is being sent down on account of his responsibility for the damage in my room. The college meeting considered his whole record at Oxford, and as far as I am concerned, this particular incident had nothing to do with the decision."

Paton says other people were involved in the incident. He is thinking of getting a job which offers "adventure and initiative".

He has recently been fined twice by the university authorities, once for rolling a barrel of beer into the maternity ward of the Radcliffe Infirmary at 2 a.m. and once "when a friend threw stones out of my window while I was holding a party. They accused me of holding a stone-throwing party."

At his Oxford lodgings yesterday he lay in state," draped in Union Jacks and a 10s 6d wreath. Friends, for whom drinks were supplied, paid tribute round the bier while Paton declaimed his own "epitaph."

STATION RENDEZVOUS

In an attempt to avoid the proctors Paton and his friends left separately for the station. They reassembled there in the left-luggage department, but the proctors had followed them.

As Paton was being wheeled to the train on a trolley the undergraduate who was pushing it, Eric Nobbs, of Keble, was seized by a "bulldog." He was taken out of the station and the handkerchief he was using as a mask was pulled from his face.

A small group remained to see Paton off with shouts and a blast from a hunting horn. Then a proctor and two "bulldogs" walked on to the platform and took the name of another undergraduate as the "mourners" dispersed.

Paton travelled to London. He will stay for a few days before returning to his landowner father's house at Grandholm, Aberdeen.

absence or overstaying the licensed periods. Eighteen students (including Bryan Magee) were fined for offences relating to the entertainment of guests, usually having women in their rooms after hours. The next largest category of offenders, 104 in all (31 per cent) were guilty of breaches of order of varying degrees of severity (removal of Belisha beacon globes, over-boisterous behaviour at sconces in hall, 'being in a bed in the middle of the quad during the College ball [and] suspected of being in an incident with fire hoses', throwing china out of a window), though usually aggravated by drunkenness. Others displayed considerable ingenuity in their pranks: one man was fined the double damage charge 'for entering the Clock Tower loft, interfering with the mechanism of the clock … and lowering himself by a rope down the face of the Clock Tower to chalk a JCR election slogan on the wall'.

Club and sports dinners were often a testing time for the Dean. The 1957 bump supper at the conclusion of Torpids ended in the wrecking of several dons' rooms (Price's own bedding was burned along with the boat), and what was described as 'hooliganism' outside College. Bump suppers were banned for an unspecified period, and five men were fined £10 each, while a ringleader was sent down. His friends then organized a mock funeral, for which the undergraduate concerned composed his own epitaph, 'Ashes to ashes, dust to dust; if the proctors don't get you, the SCR will'. The party was intercepted at the railway station by the University's bulldogs led by Basil Mitchell, then Senior Proctor.

The disciplinary authorities did not always prevail: one member was summoned before the Proctors for attempting to climb out of College after a bump supper, and for abusing a Pro-Proctor in Welsh from the roof of the bicycle shed. In the event the charges were dropped as the Proctors were unable to prove that the words spoken in Welsh were of an abusive character.

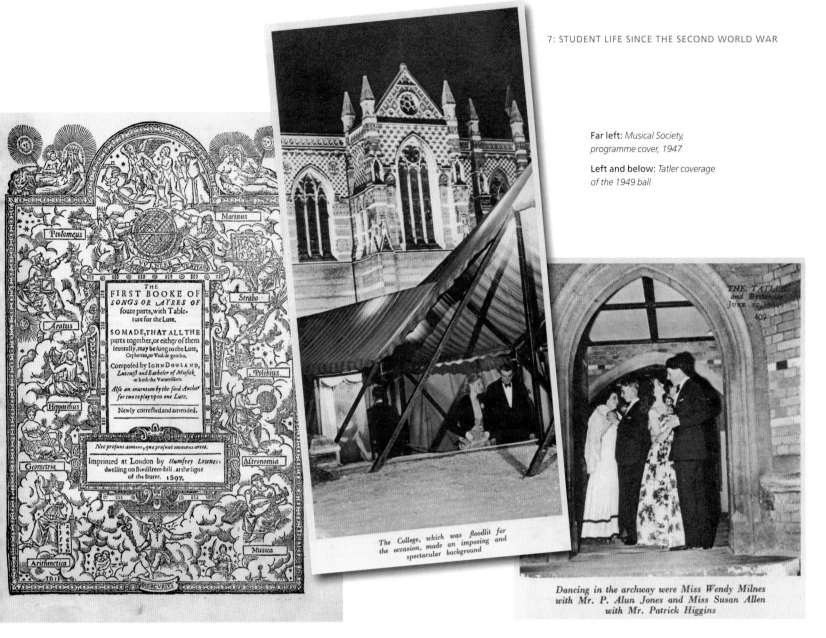

Far left: *Musical Society, programme cover, 1947*

Left and below: *Tatler coverage of the 1949 ball*

The College, which was floodlit for the occasion, made an imposing and spectacular background

Dancing in the archway were Miss Wendy Milnes with Mr. P. Alun Jones and Miss Susan Allen with Mr. Patrick Higgins

The traditional Eights Week concert was replaced by a summer dance from 1947 onwards, but musical life remained vigorous and professional performers continued to be drawn upon from London. A concert programme of 1947 elaborately reproduces the title page of John Dowland's *First Book of Ayres*; the soloist was the soprano Cicely Arnold. By the late 1950s the Musical Society was putting on termly concerts. In 1958, for example, the Robert Masters Quartet performed in Hall in February; in May the Italianate Opera Company performed works by Purcell, Pergolesi and Dibdin; and in November the College was host to the Camden Trio, with Lady Barbirolli on the oboe. Some of these concerts were real crowd-pullers: the 1957 Summer Concert of madrigals and lute songs with the Deller Consort had 400 people packed into the Dining Hall. In March 1964 there was a memorable performance of the *St Matthew Passion* in Chapel, with Peter Pears returning to the College as the Evangelist.

Many of the College societies revived after the war, and from 1947 the Memorial Room, converted from the former lecture room beneath the Library, provided a new venue for club dining. Although the clubs remained vigorous in the years up to 1965, thereafter the fortunes of many faltered. The Debating Society, for example, resumed its activities very soon after the war. 150 were present at the dinner debate at the Randolph Hotel in October 1946, when Richard Crossman and Richard Law MPs were among those debating the balance between the United States and the Soviet Union. The organizers could still rely on being able to mobilize some distinguished talent. Russell Clarke (1949) recalls that, as President in 1951, he pitted Lord David Cecil against Fr. Donald Nicholson, vicar of St Barnabas, to debate the proposition that 'enthusiasm is a bad thing'. Keble debaters took part in competitions with teams from other institutions of higher education, including Liverpool and Bristol Universities, and Wye College.

Dancing 9 p.m. to 4 a.m.
Two Bands, Three Floors
Lavish Boar's Head Buffet
Midnight Cabaret
Fully Licensed Bars
Hotdogs at Dawn
Double Tickets only 55/-

from

DAVID PENWARDEN — KEBLE

KEBLE COLLEGE SUMMER BALL

Chappie d'Amato and his Orchestra

May 27, 1955

Above left: Summer ball, 1949

Left: Beer mats for the summer ball, 1955, organized by David Penwarden

But there were increasing complaints about lack of attendance at College debates and at speaker meetings, and the Society seems to have wound up in 1965. The XIII Club resumed its dinners, though its members were shorn of their glorious waistcoats; it was subject to periodic censure from the Dean, and carried on into the early 1960s. The Wills Club replaced the Essay Club as the College's literary society, and it could host memorable speaker meetings like that given by David Wilson in 1957; it retained its customary 'odes' and wagers, but declined rapidly after 1961, becoming a dining and drinking club consisting of 'the most feeble intellects in the college', according to one jaundiced observer, and it disappears from the College annals in the mid 1960s. Of the original core societies only Tenmantale survived into the late 1960s and beyond, and there were complaints about poor attendance even there. It shifted from being a self-selecting club to an open society in 1967, much to the chagrin of its leading sponsor Douglas Price, who felt that its 'character' had been destroyed.

There were, however, some newly formed societies like the Mitre Club, set up in 1946 in a back room of the Eagle and Child pub, for prospective parsons, churchwardens, and church organists. From 1950 until his retirement the club enjoyed the patronage of the history fellow Douglas Price. It retained rituals of a very traditional kind. At the end of the annual dinner, the incoming President would be chaired around the quad, and members retired to Price's rooms for the after dinner entertainments, which continued into the early hours (Price regularly recalls going to bed at 4 a.m.): these included charades, games of rugby fives in the court in the garden, 'a species of rugger' in the quad, bicycle races, and on at least one occasion, a fencing match.

In an effort to escape the shadow of post war austerity, the first summer dance was held in 1947, the College requiring a security of £100 from the organizers, and it seems to have been an annual event thereafter. Tickets were 45s; the College was floodlit, and a marquee erected. These were sufficiently 'society' occasions to attract the attention of national magazines like *The Tatler*. There was dancing from 9 p.m. to 4 a.m. and a midnight cabaret. Through the late 1950s a regular feature was music by Nat Temple, a household name through his numerous radio appearances. The dancing was still dominated by ballroom dances, waltzes, foxtrots and quick-steps, with a dash of Latin American. By the mid 1960s, the musical fare had changed: Marianne Faithfull, Chris Farlowe and the calypsoist, Lance Percival, featured; at the 1968 ball the chart-topping Tremeloes and Jethro Tull, who were just releasing their first album, were the performers. Balls became unfashionable in Keble in the 1970s, but were revived from 1980.

Student Pranks

Mrs Kidd, the Warden's wife, on being complimented on the apple tree in her garden, remarked that it so rarely bore fruit. The following morning she awoke to find it adorned with chamber pots.

Early in the Second World War, undergraduates stamped out in fresh snow in 20- foot-high lettering the word 'Carp' in celebration of the Warden; as the snow receded the lettering remained clearly visible in the grass, necessitating investigations by air reconnaissance as to whether this was some recondite signal to the Luftwaffe.

In the years after the second war there were numerous rags directed at Wadham. In 1952 Keble men painted 'Floreat Keble' on the Wadham barge; Wadham seized Keble's barge flag in reprisal.

During the building of the Besse building (1955–8) the surplus of bricks proved too tempting, and undergraduates attempted to brick up the entrance to Chapel. Unfortunately one of the perpetrators was severely concussed when his delicate construction collapsed, and had to secure an *ægrotat* for his examinations.

In a variant prank in 1965, undergraduates sought to block the entrance to the senior common room with cement bags during one of Davidge's lengthy desserts. Two of the perpetrators were promptly rusticated.

On 4 June 1962 'some of the men let loose a pig' in Douglas Price's rooms. 'This I was prepared to make light of as a characteristic

Left: *St Michael with new accoutrements*

Below: *A rag, 1959*

undergraduate prank, but I was much annoyed by their telling the yellow press'. The story appeared in *The Daily Mail*.

In 1964 a red Mini belonging to a French lecturer was transported through the fellows' garden, and then parked half-way up the Hall staircase.

On 12 February 1968 members of the College awoke to find an effigy of Vere Davidge, proudly sporting an OUBC sweater and clutching a port bottle, suspended from one of the gargoyles on the Library.

Some may be apocryphal. Did a theologian really awake one morning to find himself still in bed in the middle of Liddon, *en plein air*, surrounded by the entire contents of his room?

Above and above left:
Keble VIII victorious, 1959

Undergraduate life in the 1950s still seems to have revolved around speaker meetings, though University societies seem to have been displacing the College as the focus for student activity. David Milne kept a detailed diary through the Michaelmas term of 1955. He attended meetings of the Labour Club and the Liberal Club, as well as the Spectator Club, a literary group, and Crime a Challenge, a penal reform society. In that first term he heard, among others, Malcolm Muggeridge, Hugh Dalton, Herbert Morrison, Hugh Gaitskell, Harold Wilson, Peter Thorneycroft, Frank Swinnerton and Phyllis Bentley. He attended a Union debate on capital punishment, organised that term by his fellow-Kebleite and Union President, Desmond Watkins, and heard Billy Graham at St Aldate's. Milne was active in playing hockey for the College, made occasional visits to the cinema, and saw Ram Gopal and his Indian dancers at the Playhouse. Only once did he go dancing in the Union cellars, notorious as the 'Black Hole of Calcutta'.

Milne was also an active Methodist, a Wesley Memorial regular, and participant in religious study groups. The 1952 Statutes envisaged that undergraduates should be members of the Church of England, with the Warden having the discretion to make exceptions. In 1945 Carpenter had relaxed the Chapel rule to compel attendance at a service on Sunday only, and any compulsion had disappeared by 1949. Surplices had been abandoned in the war for lack of material and did not come back; students now had to wear gowns to Chapel. Attendances in the immediate post war years could still be high, but dropped through the 1950s (only the Warden, five fellows, and 37 students were present for the founders and benefactors'

service in 1957). But the College continued to attract a higher proportion of the religiously minded young. Keble reputedly enjoyed the largest membership of OICCU in the late 1950s. Warden Farrer's book of fresher photographs from the early 1960s is annotated in his hand with information on their religious affiliations; to judge from the 1962 freshmen, most (72 of 102) declared themselves still members of the Church of England, although of these, eight were lapsed or non-communicant, and six unconfirmed; in addition to the Anglicans there was a sprinkling of nonconformists (six methodists, three presbyterians, one congregationalist and one simply nonconformist); three were described as 'papists', and there was one Orthodox and one Lutheran. Perhaps many of these allegiances were more token than the students cared to admit before the Warden, but only two declared themselves as being of 'no religion'. It was not until the mid 1960s that the JCR abandoned its subscription to *The Church Times*, though its replacement by *The Beano* suggests the low esteem into which the Church was falling.

The undergraduate body occasionally requested more representation, but such requests were normally stonewalled. In 1948, for example, the fellows rejected a request by the JCR President that he be permitted to attend their meetings to state his grievances. A request to establish a joint SCR/JCR food committee in 1949 was met with the statement that the undergraduates could meet with the Bursar at any time. Keble undergraduates remained fairly conservative, although there were signs of mobilization at the time of the Hungarian uprising of 1956. During the Christmas vacation Michael Austin, an undergraduate, had been involved in helping Hungarian refugees across the border into Austria. The JCR were enthusiastic supporters of the scholarship scheme which brought to Keble Laszlo Antal, who had narrowly escaped arrest for student activism at the University of Pecs during the rising; his medical studies were funded by Keble subscriptions. In 1960, in adumbration of things to come, the JCR demanded a boycott of South African goods, but this was declined by the Governing Body.

The old disciplinary order remained in place, and Douglas Price would regularly lie in wait in the fellows' garden (reputedly with glass of whiskey in hand) to greet those climbing in over the walls, rendered easier during the construction of the Besse building. There was still much rowdiness. David Milne records his unease at sconcing in Hall, the deliberate banging of oaks by the participants in a bottle party, keeping others awake, and his scout's remark about the need to clean up the gentlemen's vomit on the staircase at least once per week. And there was much licensed misrule at the bump suppers, throwing of buns, smashing of glasses, burning the boat, singing and drinking, in some of which the dons joined; of the 1959 bump supper, we are told that Denys Potts and Gordon Smith were 'singing with the boys until 12.30', and Douglas Price collided with Martin Fernald, an old decanal adversary, while bicycling through the smoke. In 1963, when Keble went head of the river, Davidge encouraged the burning (along with the boat) of the superannuated washstands now housed in the Clock Tower; and in 1969 the exuberant ringing of the bell by the revellers was such as to cause it to break. It was also from this period that several of the imaginative pranks date.

There were, however, a number of developments which were corroding the structures of the close-knit and tightly regulated community. The curious demographics of the post war period, with many of the students being older because of national service, meant that some concessions had to be made to them. The University abolished the rules about access to pubs and the wearing or carrying of academic dress in the evenings. In 1949 the Keble authorities agreed that the dean's permission should no longer be required for an undergraduate wishing to have a private lunch in his room. There are increasing indications that the tight disciplinary regime was not intended to be enforced in full. James Stuart is remembered as a largely

ineffectual dean, whose 'embarrassed disciplinary interventions took all the terror from that role'. Douglas Price, his successor, may have been more worldly, but his speeches to freshmen left them with the distinct impression that it was the spirit and not the letter of the regulations that was to be observed. Scouts were collaborators in the erosion of regulation. David Penwarden recalls that his scout, recognizing tell-tale signs of a female visitor, would greet his charge with the address 'Good morning sir; good

Above: *Keble group, 1964*

morning madam', and then would thoughtfully provide an extra cup of tea. Nor did the fellows always help. On receiving a complaint from the resident of 5 Blackhall Road that Keble undergraduates were using his parked Jaguar as a stepping stone over the walls, Davidge wrote to the JCR President, requesting him to 'prevail upon the membership to desist from this practice. There are many other ways of climbing into College and if you do not know them, I will show you myself'. The letter was, to Davidge's embarrassment, leaked to *Cherwell*.

Keble was an undeniably hearty college, its members acquiring their reputation for sporting prowess in the 1950s and 1960s. But although the College sported more than its fair share of what today would be regarded as alpha males, the sexual revolution was still some way off.

Above: *The beer cellar opens, 1959*

Below: *Posters and programmes for sixties balls*

Bottom left: *The yak ('Your Actual Keble'), logo for the 1968 ball*

College folklore has it that Christopher Stead as Chaplain warned the young men against getting aroused by the mannequins to be seen in the windows of the department store, Elliston and Cavells. One old member of the 1950s recalls 'only one man who 'made' it with a Woolworths girl, his bed being strategically arranged in the middle of his room each time'. As for homosexuality, there was a scare in 1954 when an American undergraduate claimed that men were engaging in homosexual practices to which the College authorities were turning a blind eye. The Warden took the JCR President into his confidence, and was assured that there was no problem; it was concluded that the 'complainant either exaggerated or did not understand, having a not untypical American inability to realize the difference between the Englishman's pretences and practices, or to understand the peculiar – and admittedly

An ENTERTAINMENT for
Ladies & Gentlemen of Quality
now known as the

KEBLE BALL

*will take place
within the confines of Keble College on
FRIDAY JUNE 18th 1965
commencing at 9.30 in the evening*

KBALL JUNE 16TH 1967 KEBLE

BUFFET IN HALL

Guests will only be admitted to one sitting.
There are four sittings:

11.00-11.45	Green Tickets only
12.00-12.45	Red tickets only
2.00-2.45	Blue tickets only
3.00-3.45	Yellow tickets only

Guests should choose their sitting and collect the appropriate ticket from the lodge. The number of tickets for each sitting is strictly limited.

Both ball tickets and sittings tickets must be produced to gain entry into Hall.

Pipers from the Leeds City Bagpipe Band will entertain guests during the first three sittings.

THE BALL COMMITTEE
Barry Lester

Chuck Lyons	John Spratt
Christopher Whitmore	Dominick Henry
Hugh Stoddart	David Payne

By kind permission of the Warden and Fellows

KEBLE COLLEGE MIDSUMMER BALL
Friday, June 16th, 1967

LIDDON MARQUEE		PUSEY MARQUEE	
9.30-11.15	The Ricky Derges Dance Band	9.30-10.45	The Caribbean All Steel Band
11.15-11.45	The Alan Price Set	10.45-11.30	The Exception
11.45-12.30	The Ricky Derges Dance Band	11.30-12.00	Cliff Bennett and The Rebel Rousers
12.30-1.00	The Alan Price Set	12.00-12.45	Long John Baldry and Bluesology
1.00-1.30 1.30-2.00	Lynda Baron Lance Percival } CABARET		
2.00-2.30	Cliff Bennett and The Rebel Rousers	2.00-3.00	The Exception
2.30-3.15	Long John Baldry and Bluesology	3.00-4.15	The Idle Race
3.15-4.30	The Caribbean All Steel Band	4.15-5.00	The Howlin Wolves
4.30-5.30	The Exception	5.00-6.30	The Idle Race
5.30-6.30	The Howlin Wolves		

Radio London's Keith Skues will act as compere

Organ Scholars Since the War

The organ scholars of the second half of the century have provided their fair share of distinguished musicians. David Owen Norris (1972), now an honorary fellow, is frequently heard as a radio broadcaster. First and foremost he is a pianist, setting out as an accompanist to such diverse artists as contralto Dame Janet Baker and harmonica player Larry Adler. He is also a fine composer. After his Keble days, Simon Over (1984) also initially made his name as a pianist, accompanying many internationally celebrated singers. From 1992 to 2002 he was Director of Music at St Margaret's, Westminster, and the Chapel of St Mary Undercroft in the Palace of Westminster, and since then his career has focused more on conducting. Another Keble musician drawn to the podium is Charles Hazlewood (1986), currently Principal Guest Conductor of the BBC Concert Orchestra, with whom he made his debut at the BBC Proms in 2006. Known to millions as 'the face of classical music for the BBC' (*Daily Telegraph*), he regularly broadcasts from the Proms and has written several popular classical music television programmes, including *Vivaldi Unmasked* and others on Mozart, Beethoven and Tchaikovsky.

Neil Cockburn (1992) has pursued a more organ-related path. He is Head of Organ Studies at Mount Royal College Organ Academy and Curator of the Carthy Organ at Jack Singer Concert Hall in Calgary, Canada. Another former Keble organ scholar to remain closely in touch with the instrument is Philip Stopford (1996), who has been Director of Music at Belfast Cathedral since 2003, where he has set up the

Above: *Scott Ellaway*

Cathedral Youth Choir and Cathedral Voices, both broadening the appeal of music at the Cathedral and providing a wider repertoire. Of the more recent incumbents, Scott Ellaway (2002) has already made a mark, gaining a wealth of experience working with some of the world's top orchestras and artists; he has recently been appointed Artistic Director of Orchestra Europa, Europe's Orchestral Academy.
Simon Whalley

---

sometimes disagreeable – ideas of humour characteristic of a certain type of public school product'.

Requests from the JCR to extend the hours of entertainment for women (essentially confined to the afternoons) were declined by the fellows in 1952, 1955, 1957, and 1959; the modest petition that women be allowed in the newly opened beer cellar on three Fridays a term in 1958 was also turned down. Only at the end of 1962 did the College relax the rules, so that women guests could remain in College until 10.30 p.m. (11 p.m. from 1964). Only from 1964 was one of the JCR guest nights each term designated as one at which female guests might be permitted. From 1969 undergraduates were allowed to bring female guests to lunch and to dinners other than guest nights. By the 1960s it was being claimed that the 'sporting of the oak' became a sign, not of study, but of the entertainment of women. Sexual mores were now changing quite quickly, and by the early 1970s the JCR enjoyed taunting the Governing Body with regular motions

demanding the installation of contraceptive machines.

Although Oxford was, relatively speaking, less troubled by student unrest than other universities, the undergraduate body was becoming more restless about the disciplinary regime. Undergraduates now chafed against the tight restrictions on their freedom of movement, and their ability to socialize freely with the opposite sex. The most obvious indication of change was sartorial: undergraduates abandoned jackets and ties for jerseys; the old school represented by the likes of Price and Davidge were moved to apoplexy by the new 'vulgarity of dress'. The non-resident deans that followed Price were less able to enforce the old disciplinary code: it was characteristic that nothing was done when the lock of the back gate was repeatedly forced in 1965. Nor were undergraduates happy with the old hierarchies. The scholars agitating for the abolition of the separate scholars' table where they were forced to sit, staged a walk-out from Hall in 1963 as the dons processed in to High Table.

Keble Chapel: Changing Styles

John Keble's legacy has been contested within the Chapel built in his memory as elsewhere. There have been several shifts in the intensity of what Vere Davidge, speaking of the liturgy of the College parishes, called its 'candle power'. The pattern of services is clear enough, the nature of the liturgy used sometimes less so. The routines laid down in 1870 for Sunday services comprised early communion, followed by Matins at 9.30 a.m., still allowing undergraduates to attend the University sermon. The College's own sermon was at evensong at 4.30 p.m. Compline was also incorporated into the College's prayer books. Latin hymns were first sung in the Chapel in 1907 when Vincent Coles, principal of Pusey House, presented 200 copies of *Hymni Latini*. When Kidd took over as Warden in 1920 the pattern of services changed to Holy Communion at 7.15 a.m., Matins at 8.00 a.m. and Choral Eucharist at 8.30 a.m., and we are told that the 'eucharistic vestments' were taken into use. This was all controversial, and Kidd was warned by several correspondents that he should be careful lest he alienate those who considered music a distraction to devotion; moreover, there were critics of the College lying in wait for evidence of any ritual excess. But Kidd's Wardenship does indeed seem to have seen an elaboration of the ritual. Douglas Price, a plain Prayer-book Protestant, as an undergraduate in the mid-1930s, was not entirely comfortable with the Chapel services which he claimed were 'a little too high church for me to enjoy them entirely … everyone bowing, crossing, and so on all the time, with the Warden kissing the book and so on'. Kidd was helped by an assistant chaplain (1922–39), Trotter Blockley, who was noted for the sweet voice with which he sang Holy Communion.

The liturgy was simplified under Christopher Stead, Chaplain from 1949 until 1971, and a succession of Wardens who stood for a more austere version of Anglo-Catholicism. It was observed in the mid 1970s that incense had not been used regularly in Chapel since 1939, significantly the point at which Kidd gave way to Carpenter. For all that Farrer offered brilliant preaching, the quality of services may have deteriorated in the later 1960s. Writing of the 8.30 a.m. communion on 10 November 1968, Douglas Price claimed that 'the Warden has deprived this service of all its former dignity without

giving it the alternative virtue of simplicity. Seats are placed across the chancel, the choir no longer in surplices, Mrs Farrer occupying the Warden's stall; I found myself the only person in a surplice; the music was abominable'.

Dennis Nineham shared with the new Chaplain, Geoffrey Rowell, a desire to increase attendances, though they had differences of opinion over both theology and liturgy. Rowell's tenure of the chaplaincy (1972–94) witnessed another period of liturgical elaboration. He altered the pattern of services, so that the Sunday eucharist was switched from the morning to the evening in 1975, and he was responsible for the form

Above: *Dan Cottee puts the choir through their paces*

Far left: *Geoffrey Rowell and Petroc*

Left: *Trevor Mwamba, Bishop of Botswana, with Dennis Nineham, Allen Shin and Charlotte Methuen, June 2007*

Right and below: *Recent services in the Chapel*

of the highly popular service of Advent lessons and carols which the College still retains, as well as the introduction of practices like the imposition of ashes and, more controversially still, the reserved sacrament introduced in 1979, though initially, at Nineham's insistence, without a sanctuary lamp. Rowell did a great deal to maintain Keble Chapel as a powerful presence on the Oxford ecclesiastical scene, and to foster a Christian community in the broader sense (his summer vacation trips accompanied by students became legendary), and he worked hard to draw the parishes into the College, beginning the clergy conferences every other year. But his high public profile in Anglican politics played into the hands of the more vociferous 'anti-clericals' on the governing body, and Chapel issues were regrettably

an element in the rows of the later 1980s. When he left to become Bishop of Basingstoke in 1994, his successor as chaplain, John Davies (1994–9), though very firmly in the sacramental tradition and a strong supporter of 'Affirming Catholicism', a movement of liberal catholics, sought to pare back some of the ritual accretions of Keble worship. Incense was out again; a woman priest presided for the first time in 1996. This signalled an inclusive approach, and the new 'catholic Anglican' style was sustained under Mark Butchers's chaplaincy (1999–2005). Under Allen Shin, Chaplain since 2005 and a liturgist and singer himself, there has been an increase in 'candle power' and the use of incense, but with a firm commitment to the liberal catholic tradition of recent years.

The disciplinary apparatus, both at college and University level, was under attack, and wholly new demands for representation which would have been unthinkable a generation earlier were now voiced. Keble was not immune from these pressures. A left wing caucus (crystallised by 1970 in the Owen Society) sought to promote the radical agenda, and there were serious protests in College about the disciplinary powers wielded by the deans. On one occasion, in March 1969, the JCR orchestrated a walk-out from Hall in protest against the College's decision to send one man down. How far Keble students participated in the set-piece student

demonstrations of these years is not clear, but one PPE-ist was arrested in clashes with police in the Broad in February 1974, in the wake of the collapse of the student occupation of the registry office in the Indian Institute. A JCR President lost a vote of confidence in 1971 for allegedly being too close to the SCR.

But that latter episode can be read two ways, and radicalism in Keble was always muted. The walk out from Hall did not command universal support; one observer notes that those who stayed jeered those leaving. Price noted in June 1968, at the height of the protests against the proctors, that the meeting with the officers of the MCR and JCR was amicable, showing what he thought was the 'real Oxford' in contradistinction to the 'unintelligent anarchists'. In late 1972, a moderate group led by Michael Perham routed the more radical left (led by Tim Blanch, son of the then Archbishop of York) in the elections to the JCR. In January 1974, Perham, later Bishop of Gloucester, although a member of the Labour Club (then a badge of right-wing tendencies) was sufficiently an establishment figure to be the first undergraduate ever to preach in Keble Chapel. Perham's presidency was rocky: just as he was elected, his predecessors declared themselves 'commissars', a move intended in jest, but perhaps taken more seriously than they had intended; the militants later moved for the abolition of gowns, High Table and grace. This was the occasion on which Spencer Barrett made the oracular pronouncement to one of the radicals that, 'As an unbeliever of rather longer standing than yourself, I think it important to respect the beliefs of others. I am perfectly willing to say grace provided that I mispronounce the quantities'. In the ensuing JCR referendum (turnout 50 per cent), two thirds voted for the retention of gowns and grace. The proprieties continued to be maintained by stalwarts among the members of staff like Frank Giles, the Butler, who presided over Hall, 'benign if you were on the right side of him, but capable of the stern imposition of authority'. By the mid 1970s that arch old-school Tory, Douglas Price was noting how much better behaved the undergraduates were.

The defusing of protest probably owed something to the emollient strategy pursued by Dennis Nineham as Warden. In 1972 the Governing Body established the standing committee, with senior members meeting regularly with three nominees of the JCR and one from the MCR, to discuss a wide range of College business. Other changes were the new disciplinary procedures introduced in 1974 and allowing for students (chosen by lot from nominees of the JCR) to sit as members of disciplinary panels, though when put seriously to the test in 1977, they proved unsatisfactory. The deans were worsted by the lawyer representing a student accused of vandalism; it was in the wake of this sorry episode that the College began to think seriously about the employment of a graduate junior dean. Engagement between the SCR and JCR was often

tense in the 1970s and 1980s over issues relating to prices and charges, but the fellows came to realize that student representation allowed a framework of constructive dialogue. In 1984 representatives of the JCR and MCR were allowed to attend at Governing Body meetings for the first time.

Student politicization was (and is) to some extent subject specific. It is striking that, of the JCR Presidents between 1960 and 2007, there have been 14 PPE-ists, eight historians, eight lawyers, four engineers and a handful of others, but few other scientists. For many students the pressures of work, which were mounting in a college which, academically, was beginning to take itself seriously in the 1970s, blunted the 'radical' potential. For others, Oxford meant what it had always been, an opportunity for high achievers to develop their talents across a whole range of activities, sporting, musical and theatrical, as well as academic.

Music and drama continued to flourish. A highlight was undoubtedly Vincent Gillespie's production of *Richard II* in the Chapel in May 1976, with clever lighting effects, and excellent music by David Owen Norris, the organ scholar.

Below right: Dress rehearsal for the new musical 'Swing' in the O'Reilly Theatre, 2008

Below: Posters for various Keble drama productions

Music at Keble in the 1970s

When I arrived from New York, in 1971, I was one of three music students in my year – a trio that later swelled to a quartet with the defection of a violinist from the mathematics department. All were skilled practitioners, apart from me. I was, and remain, capable only of clumsy, inaccurate and, yes, ugly renditions of even the simplest keyboard exercises. On the other hand, I could (then) have told you more than you needed to know about, say, the genesis of Verdi's *Stiffelio*.

But, like Ralph Rackstraw in *HMS Pinafore*, I could hum a little, and I found myself drawn into the realm of the Chapel, an alien environment for a New York Jew. The choir was at the centre of the College's musical life and exemplified a social peculiarity of the Oxford I knew: sopranos and (plausible countertenors being thin on the ground) altos had to be drawn from women's colleges. Can the bait have been a glass of cheap sherry followed by dinner in Keble Hall? Oddly, I think it was. The links with St Hugh's in particular went beyond *Stanford in C*: the two college music societies were informally conjoined. I remember madrigal singing and a performance of something that might have been *Dido and Aeneas* and that might, though I wouldn't swear to it, have been conducted by Jane Glover, then a postgraduate unearthing operas by Cavalli.

Most Keble music-makers were reading other subjects – English, classics, engineering, theology – which leavened our enterprises with interdisciplinary fizz. Barmy indeed was the short-lived Imperial English Grand Opera Company, which specialized in parlour songs and extracts from justly forgotten lyric dramas. Less zany was the Festival of English Song that classicist John Bridcut thought up and that he and I produced

Above: *A vigorous musical life continues. James Bowman in Keble Chapel, 2008*

two years running, engaging both student singers and pretty eminent professionals, whom we savagely beat up on their fees, convincing them that the promotion of English song from the Elizabethans to the twentieth century was a worthy cause. Which, of course, it was.

To return to the Keble-St Hugh's combined music societies, there were also, periodically, white-tablecloth dinners. While my musical life might not have been enriched by these, and while I certainly recall nothing of gastronomic note, one such dinner, in April of 1972, found me seated next to a member of our sister college called Jackie Mitchell. Most evenings, dinner still finds us seated side by side. Keble music gave me much, but nothing more deeply cherished than that.
Ed Schneider (1971)

Malcolm Parkes and Geoffrey Rowell appeared in cameo roles as the gardeners, improvising with some memorable Nineham phrasing and intonation. Likewise, some Musical Society events, like the Albinoni Ensemble and the In Cantonibus Sacris singers, organized by Roger Wibberley in 1977, could pack the Chapel. Another annual summer event of the mid 1970s were the concerts by Tom's Orchestra (founded by engineer Tom Kingston) in the fellows' garden.

Chapel attendances, as we have seen, may have faltered in the 1950s and 1960s, and the numbers intending ordination had plummeted. Nineham, although in tension with the 'Chapel set' because of what some of them regarded as his 'heretical' views, was concerned about falling attendance, and there were a variety of experiments in forms of service early in his regime, particularly under

Above: *The Mitre Club, 1973*

purple bow ties, and the incoming President was crowned with a bib. The fun and games with charades and forfeits continued in Douglas Price's rooms. Perhaps the most memorable evening of this period was the dinner in May 1976 at which the principal guest was 'His Imperial Highness' Prince Petros Palaeologos, who arrived 'bedecked in a sash, with decorations, an embroidered cloak, and long flowing hair', an impression somewhat belying his residence in straitened circumstances on the Isle of Wight. 'I presume he gets his living by selling decorations in the capacity of a claimant to the Byzantine Empire', noted Price drily. Perhaps in 'democratic' reaction to the Mitre Club, a group which nevertheless overlapped with it established the Butterfield Society, whose members dressed up in black tie, ostentatiously positioned themselves close to High Table on formal guest nights, and developed their own rituals around a brick on a cushion, but ate the ordinary student food before retiring for port. It was typical of the more ephemeral student associations which have always flourished in the College environment.

Top: *Oliver Walker conducts the choir in Liddon quad*

Above: *David Owen Norris, Honorary Fellow, runs a master class in the new Music Room*

Right: *Musicians perform in support of Christian Aid, 1983*

the temporary Chaplain Beaumont ('Bo') Stevenson in 1971–2. One contemporary, himself a member, describes the Chapel set as a 'holy huddle sheltering rather self consciously in that vast Chapel'. With the arrival of Geoffrey Rowell as Chaplain in 1972, there was probably a modest revival in its fortunes. Theological discussion flourished in the lunchtime meetings of the Hursley Group, pioneered by Michael Perham, also from 1972. The Mitre Club remained a focus for Chapel-goers and musicians, many of them English literature students in the mid 1970s; it was right-wing in tone, and moderately left-leaning, but Chapel-going people like Michael Perham think they may have been blackballed. Members were required to wear

The biggest change in the College's social dynamics occurred in October 1979, when 32 women arrived at Keble, six graduates and 26 undergraduates. One of the issues was whether the women should be housed together, or mixed from the start on the same corridors as male students; the latter option prevailed, but some practical problems arose, among them the lack of long mirrors for the female students and the absence of locks on the bathroom cubicle doors. That prejudices still existed is suggested by the continuing debate as to whether women should be included in College and Keble Association dinners; the issue was deferred 'for a year or two'. Ruth Nineham called the incoming women together and did her best to help them face the various challenges, but her husband Dennis admits that the College did the minimum. Spencer Barrett famously drew a diagram of the potential sight lines across the College into the rooms where the women students might be housed, in order to preserve decency, and after a while the quality of the loo paper is said to have improved; 'laundry facilities and consequential changes' were debated by the Building Advisory Panel in 1978, and the possibility of sharing sporting facilities with St Anne's was explored, but as late as 1979 the notices in the Lodge were still addressed to 'Gentlemen'. Most of the first women were excited at the prospect, and subsequently put a brave face on it and claimed to enjoy the very male atmosphere, complete with blinds, sconcing, spooning-in and other such delights; a few admitted that it was a difficult experience. These women were hardy, and ready to demonstrate that they could do as well as the men; indeed, Jane Harrigan, one of their number, was elected President of the JCR in 1980. The fact remains that the first women at Keble were taught exclusively by men who were inexperienced at dealing with young women in this way, and were living in an environment which was otherwise exclusively male. Nevertheless, they were not deterred, and most claim that it was a positive experience. There were also soon Keble engagements and Keble babies.

Keble has eclipsed its earlier reputation for spartan living. The provision of accommodation improved markedly with the completion of the successive phases of the ABK buildings in 1970–7 adding 90 rooms to the overall stock. The Arco building opened in 1995, providing another 93 rooms for finalists on nine-month contracts, while the Sloane Robinson Building added another 20 rooms in 2002. For the graduate community, expanding numbers in the 1990s were catered for by the purchase of various houses around north Oxford of varying quality and popularity, and later, replacing them, in 2005 by the provision of 84 rooms on the Acland site. Whereas in 1975 64 per cent of the undergraduate population could be housed in College accommodation, by 2007 the proportion was 78 per cent (it would have been higher had it not been for the increase in the number of students on four year courses). Among postgraduates, 53 per cent can now be housed. An increasing volume of accommodation has been accompanied by improving amenities within rooms. Arco had been conceived with ensuite facilities in mind, and most of the Liddon rooms were converted in 1993–8; as for the ABK buildings, a bathroom on each floor shared between two people was provided as part of the restoration in 2001–3. Keble was among the first colleges to ethernet all its student rooms and by 1998 they were all connected both to the internet and to the University telephone system.

Women's Rowing

Keble women fielded two boats in their first year, 1980, and has had many more Varsity rowers in its first 28 years than the men's club did in its first 80 years, averaging approximately one rower with University colours in College per year (including lightweight rowers) from its founding to today. Participation of Keble women in Eights has been very high, with 25 to 30 per cent of Keble women participating in peak years. As the proportion of women in College has grown in recent years, around ten per cent of women in College have been participating in Eights each year. Though the highest the women have been on the river was 9th in Torpids in 1991, their position in Eights and Torpids has generally been improving since 2000, now holding consistently near the top of division two or bottom of division one, up from their historic low finish in division three in 1999.
Jewell Thomas (2007)

Sport Since the Second World War

Although it is generally thought that sport lost its attraction in the post war years, as colleges began to stress academic achievement, over a third of Keble undergraduates still played first-team sports in the early 1950s. The College sports ground was recovered from Morris Radiators, who had occupied it during wartime, and developed to accommodate cricket, football, hockey and tennis. In the 1950s, the leading club in Keble was athletics with 50 members, described as one of the strongest and most active in the University. Alan Dick (1950) ran the 400m for Great Britain at the 1952 Helsinki Olympics. Added to the long-established clubs, there were teams for swimming, yachting, badminton, water polo, squash and table tennis by this time. Keble's sportsmen were active, but only sporadically successful in inter-collegiate competitions: the footballers won cuppers in 1956 and 1958; rugby, in the doldrums in the 1950s, recovered in the early 1960s when Keble were divisional champions, but they were relegated at the end of the decade. The yachtsmen won cuppers in 1961 and again in 1968 and 1969. These mixed successes explain why *The Record* describes 1971–2 as an 'annus mirabilis' in the annals of College sport; the cricketers won cuppers for the first time and hockey were divisional champions for the third year running. Keble cricket received added attention with the arrival of Imran Khan in the 1970s. Already capped for Pakistan, Kahn captained the University side and became one of the game's greatest all-rounders.

Although the 1890s can lay claim to being the era of the most successful sporting individuals at Keble, the combination of individual and team glory in the 1980s and 1990s makes it the College's golden era of sport. The arrival of female undergraduates brought an added dimension. The mixed hockey team was soon emulating the success of men's hockey (which won its division 17 times between 1970 and 1993), while new sports such as netball and dancesport appeared. When numbers allowed, separate women's teams in football, rugby, tennis and cricket were organized. The burgeoning number of postgraduates enabled MCR teams to compete successfully in cricket, with the help of Paul Hayes and Tim Burt from the SCR. An influx of overseas sportsmen and women on postgraduate courses raised the College's sporting profile in rowing, hockey, rugby and cricket, but also fencing and karate. By the early 1990s there were 33 blues and half blues at the College, and at one point five Keble graduates were playing English county cricket. The success of both JCR and MCR in college and University sports reached its peak in 1992–3. In addition to 33 blues (including seven each in rugby and cricket), there were cuppers victories for rugby, squash, football, hockey, netball, cricket, ice hockey and graduate cricket. Keble athletes were drawn from across the globe, with rugby players from Australia and Ireland, rowers from South Africa and Canada, cricketers from Australia, and hockey players from South Africa.

The sporting glories of the mid 1990s proved hard to sustain, not least because University players were not permitted to play for college sides in league matches; although there were nine rugby blues in Keble in 1993–4, the first XV was relegated. The recruitment of overseas graduate sporting stars tailed off after the death of Paul Hayes in 1995. Success in the 2000s can be more readily gauged by the breadth of participation. Although there are no longer clubs for fives, shooting or billiards for example, there are currently clubs for athletics, badminton, basketball, cricket, croquet, dancesport, darts, fencing, football, gymnastics, hockey, lacrosse, netball, pool, rounders, rowing, rugby, skiing, squash, table football, tennis, ultimate frisbee and wind-surfing, though some are more transient then others. The College supports separate men's and women's teams in hockey, football, cricket, rugby, and tennis, and mixed teams in many other sports. Teams continue to enjoy success: the women won football cuppers in 2007 and topped the 1st Division in 2007; the men's rugby team won cuppers in 2007, and, though deprived of the title in 2008, nevertheless topped the league for the second year in a row; and the dancesport team has been notably successful, winning cuppers in 2007 and 2008.

Alisdair Rogers

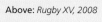

Above: *Rugby XV, 2008*

Left: *Dancesport Cuppers, 2007*

Keble Rowing: the Golden Years

In 1952 Graham Buckley, Captain of Boats, complained about the lack of cachet possessed by Keble when it came to attracting experienced rowers from England's top rowing schools: 'the truth is that Eton, Radley, Shrewsbury, and Bedford are not used to sending their rowing sons to Keble… How we would like to hear that the Eton First VIII stroke was coming up to Keble next Term.' Within five years, Buckley would see his wish for schoolboy rowers granted in abundance, this onrush of rowing talent ushering in the age of Keble dominance on the river.

Keble's rowing fortunes began to turn around in the late 1950s. This change is directly attributable to the influence of Vere Davidge, a Bursar with a noted (and notorious) passion for rowing. Davidge had been involved with Keble rowing in at least some capacity, either coaching or offering general support and guidance to the club when it sought to raise funds for special projects, from the first year he was associated

Above: *Blades, 1932, 1963*

Below: *Keble go head, 1977*

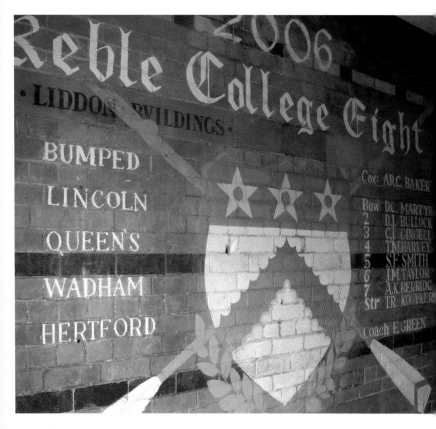

with the College in 1927. In the mid 1950s, however, he began to push for the admission of candidates from rowing schools. In the summer of 1958, four Keble men won the Visitors' Cup at the prestigious Henley Regatta. Three of these, along with a fourth Keble man, would head to Rome to form the nucleus of the Great Britain Olympic VIII in 1960, to become Keble's first rowing Olympians. For the next twenty years, Keble would average seven Varsity rowers (those having earned either Blues or Isis colours) in College per year. As testament to the impact Keble made on University rowing in this period, in 1961 Ian Elliot (one of Keble's 1960 Olympians) became the first Keble man to hold the position of President of the OUBC. Keble men held this position in seven of the next 15 years.

The first VIII in Summer Eights, after spending more than half a century bouncing around near the bottom of the second division or top of the third (each division consisting of twelve boats), stormed up 24 positions in just six years to gain the headship, for the first time, in 1963. The boat comprised entirely Varsity rowers save one, and all had rowed at Eton, Shrewsbury, or another of the noted rowing schools. In 1964, six of the nine men in the Oxford boat against Cambridge were Kebleites. In 1967, Keble either won or was represented in the winning crew of every single competition organized by the OUBC.

While the influx of top-quality rowers certainly had a clear impact on Keble's position on the river in Eights, the demands of Varsity rowing could also weaken the KCBC. Though there were several years where there were more than eight men in College with colours, only in one year (1969) was the first VIII in Summer Eights composed entirely of men with Varsity colours. After gaining the headship in 1963, Keble lost it in 1964, falling to fourth in 1966, because Varsity training pulled away many or all of the College's top rowers. It is a testament to the strength of KCBC across the board in this period that, when rowed by non-Varsity men against the stiff competition at the top of the first division, Keble only lost three places in these years. Regaining the headship in 1967, Keble won it in six of the next ten years.

For all the emphasis on the headship, a notable feature of this period was the growing democratization of rowing. Having fielded three or four crews for Eights for most of the College's history, Keble had six crews on the river in 1962 and averaged seven crews per year over the next ten years, with 20 per cent of the College participating in some capacity in peak years. The wider College community had caught the rowing bug, and it was about having fun. The motto of Keble's sixth VIII in 1970 was 'we must keep a sharp watch, and try not to paddle swiftly'. Behind them rowed 'The John Keble and Vladimir Illyich Ulianov Memorial VIII', named in playful commemoration of the 1970 centennial of both the founding of Keble College and Vladimir Lenin's birth.

Jewell Thomas (2007)

Top: *Torpids victors, 2006*

Above: *Students at Eights Week, 2008*

There have been some shifts in the last 25 years in the pattern of student sociability. One has to acknowledge that alcohol provides an element of continuity for a significant number of students. The Vagabonds, 12 men who each invited ten guests to their parties with lethal cocktails in the 1970s, were probably the antecedents of the Steamers, founded in 1995 by Nick West and his friends, and maybe both groups owe something to the ethos of the XIII Club, though the choice of rugby shirts with initial letters spelling out STEAMERS over waistcoats says a great deal about changing sartorial conventions. The Steamers were answered by the women in the form of the Octavias. The repeated efforts of the College authorities to ban 'blinds' (such bans are recorded in 1972 and 1994), the welcome drinks organized by second years for freshers, have been only partially successful: they survive in many subjects, with deliberate irony redesignated as 'tea-parties'. Sconcing, revived after the war with the dons' support, died out soon after the College went mixed, though the ambiguity in the attitudes of senior members to alcohol is evident in Douglas Price's undertaking to 'explain the traditions of the College in respect of sconcing' to the JCR as late as 1978. The opening hours of the College bar have been progressively liberalized, and a more varied range of events permitted: in 1980 permission was given for up to four bands a term to use the space; in 1981 the first freshers' disco was held; a juke box was installed in 1985.

The traditional clubs which acted as dining societies have shrunk, but a substitute has been found in the black-tie dinners for which Keble is currently renowned. A regular pattern of thrice-weekly slots, catering mainly for subject and sporting groups, had been established by the late 1980s, though the dinners were scaled back to twice weekly in 1993. Inevitably a source of tension with the College authorities (fellows continue to claim that they cater for the same limited social set, that they are too alcohol orientated, even that the young simply do not know how to behave at a black-tie dinner: when has it ever been appropriate in polite society to go out for 'shots' between courses?), there have been some changes. The notorious pre-dinner cocktails prepared in buckets in the former Henry Ley Room (now, perhaps fittingly, the public toilets in Liddon) were phased out as drinks moved to the bar; standards of behaviour improved with some firm decanal action in the Hawcroft regime of the early 1990s, and more recently with the presence of Gerard McHugh (a man not to be crossed) as College Services Manager; in the last few years the issue has been the competition for slots, and the desire among the

fellows to promote more diverse academically orientated evenings. The days when students gloried in inveigling one of the younger fellows to join them in bopping at DTMs or Park End ('Whatever next? Mr Hollis at Park End dancing to Super-Trouper' ran one speculative and satirical *Rear End* story from 1995, after a series of appearances by Drs Archer and Hawcroft) have perhaps passed, but the student evenings still end up at the night clubs with noxious kebabs consumed on the way home.

Many a tutor would suspect that to focus on alcohol and club dinners may well not capture the reality of the 'average' student experience, and the tensions between

Above: *Keble's first cross-dressing dinner, 1995*

Right: *Students relaxing post-finals 2007*

the academics' perceptions and those of the students representatives continue to shape the interactions between the JCR and the SCR over freshers' week, ever a flashpoint for these issues: in 2007 the Governing Body demanded from the JCR an 'impact assessment' of freshers' week to assess the equal opportunities implications. For Keble students have changed over the past decade, and many would probably agree with the SCR's scepticism about the 'inclusiveness' of the JCR's approach. The student body is now much more diverse in terms of gender, ethnicity and sexual orientation. For many years the proportion of women undergraduates was only about one third, but by 2007 it was 42 per cent, although among postgraduates the proportion is a much lower 32 per cent. Eight of the 17 JCR Presidents since 1990 have been women. There have also been two Asian JCR Presidents in recent years,

Prem Ahwulalia in 1997–8 and Mohsin Zaidi in 2003–4. According to the student ethnicity data of 2007, non-white students accounted for 21.6 per cent of all Keble students (unknowns 7.3 per cent), against a University average of 19.4 per cent. Whereas homophobia was still pretty overt in the early 1990s, several students only coming out on leaving College, the intake of 2006 included so many 'out' gays and 'metrosexuals' that some students quipped that Keble should be redesignated 'Queerble'. The availability

of alternative models of masculinity means that the culture of tolerance for drinking societies and the like is shifting. The College is undoubtedly a more comfortable place to be different.

Student life is, of course, far less focused on the diversions provided by the College than it was in the 1950s. TV and the internet have seen to that. But for many students, Keble continues to provide a framework for their sociability, a powerful source of identity. Student sociability has taken advantage of the greater availability of the telephone, text-messaging and social networking sites like Facebook, but these are devices to facilitate traditional activities like College sport, drama and music. Facebook aficionados will be inundated with invitations to various events for which groups have been established. Students might have retreated from the Library as a work place, as the availability of online resources encourages more to work from their rooms, but new social sites for working have emerged. Café Keble occupies the Douglas Price Room in the Sloane Robinson Building in term time, and its wireless environment provides a space in which students can engage in the species of collaborative working that are discouraged by Library regulations.

The Rowing Society

In recent years rowing has been revitalized by the enthusiasm of old members. The costs of equipment and professional coaching needed to be competitive at the highest collegiate levels and continued to rise in the 1980s and 1990s. In the mid 1990s, it became obvious that if Keble rowers were going to maintain any hope of again achieving the heights attained in the 1960s and 70s, the Boat Club was going to need new channels of financial support. In 1995, Robin Geffen (who rowed in the first VIII in 1979, at the tail end of Keble's strongest years on the river) spearheaded the founding of the Keble Rowing Society, to rally and organize the support of old members for the KCBC, and to provide general support for College rowing. As a result of these efforts, along with the corporate support of Geffen's companies, Neptune Investment Management and Orbitex, as well as the independent contributions of individual old members, the KCBC quickly became one of the best-supported rowing clubs in the University, much envied by other college clubs for its increased access to resources.

In 2006 the College took a long lease on the former University yacht club compound at Binsey, and also opened a new fitness centre in the basement of the Clock Tower. Crews can now train on the water at Port Meadow, unaffected by the constrictions characteristic of the Isis, and off the water in the 'best little gym in Oxford'. Orbitex and Neptune Investment Management have also purchased several top-of-the-line racing shells for the College's crews in recent years. Of these, the KCBC chose to name the men's first-VIII shell, donated in 2005, in honour of Keble's long-serving boatman Peter Bowley, who retired in 2006 after 40 years of loyal service caring for Keble's boats. The club has certainly been on an upward trajectory since this significant restructuring of its funding. In 2006, the KCBC reached an important landmark in Summer Eights, when both men's and women's clubs gained places in their respective first divisions concurrently for the first time in Keble's history.

Jewell Thomas (2007)

Left: *The boathouse in Eights Week, 2008*

Tenmentale History Society, 1886, 1954 and 2008

The rhythm of the student day is still punctuated by the rituals of eating together. Keble is now the only college where formal hall, with the SCR procession, compulsory gowns and grace by one of the scholars, is the only meal available in the evening. For many students the early afternoons are still used for sports. College loyalties are signified less through scarves and college ties than through sweatshirts, splash tops, College 'hoodies' and long pants bearing the Keble logo. The immediate post-war rivalry with Wadham, the object of a series of rags which included painting 'Floreat Keble' on their barge (1952), has been displaced by the rivalry with St John's expressed in good

natured roars of 'Keeeble' by groups of revellers on their way to the night clubs. The College ball may have over expanded in the 1990s, but the scaled back affair of 2007, which was less focused on big bands, more on fun and also a lot cheaper, was held on the same evening as graduation and was a much more College-based event. It was so successful that the SCR sceptics were persuaded to repeat it in 2008, whereas recent balls had only been held in alternate years.

College societies falter from time to time, but many are in good health. The Theology Society was revitalized by John Davies as Chaplain in 1994, and the momentum he established has been sustained; the Music Society was revived by Susanna Fitzpatrick in 1995; the Medical (now Biomedical) Society resumed activity in 1999, Tenmantale in 2007, in the latter case after a long interruption; the Jim Harris Law Society is probably the strongest of the subject-based societies, with regular moots and a better quality 'black tie' (the effect of sponsorship by City law firms). The Mitre Club lives on under a more democratic constitution, open to all Chapel goers, all those attending being required to wear a piece of headgear, the mitre being reserved for the President. The Chapel is still a focus of activity for a significant body of students. The choir in recent years has produced six CDs, and has been on tour in Korea and Japan (2006). Music and drama events have proliferated in College with the opening of the O'Reilly Theatre and the Andrew and Christine Hall Music Room. The organ scholars remain at the hub of a vital musical life. Keble Arts Week has flourished since 1999, with generous support from the Jack Lane bequest to the Keble Association. At least four drama productions per term take place in the O'Reilly Theatre. Although today's students are a lot more outward looking than their forbears of 50 years ago, for many their College identification remains very strong.

Above: *Relaxing in the MCR*

Below: *The JCR fun photo, 2004–5*

Student Journalism

Above: *The Clock Tower, June 1921*

There have been a variety of Keble press organs over the years. Leonard Rice-Oxley founded *The Clock Tower* in 1912. A literary magazine, with essays, poetry, and a sprinkling of club news, it maintained a pretty high standard, albeit with wartime interruptions, until 1957. Serious student journalism has tended to be displaced on to University publications, and what has flourished at the college level, taking advantage of the ease of reproduction with the advent of the photocopier, has been a variety of often short-lived organs, sometimes attempting to disseminate JCR news, but usually satirical in nature. Slightly unusual was *The Aurion* (1972–5), the brainchild of John Bridcut and friends, and with a Chapel bias, sufficiently 'sound', with pieces of a literary and theological bent, to be commended in *The Record*. In the late 1970s we had *Fresh Garbage*, written by Pete Rowlands, Brian Gosschalk and friends, beginning as 'an earnest organ of the left but developing a lunatic life of its own', and *Groundsheet*, the product of JCR President Chris Perrin's call for a more balanced organ that did not imperil relations with the SCR by indiscriminate attacks on its members. In 1983–7 came the 'lavatorial publication', *The Spotted Brick* and its lineal successor *Breeze Block* (Steve Brindle and friends), in the early 1990s *Rear End* (Chris Hunt and friends), in the early 2000s, *The Brick* (Ed Cadwallader and friends). Such publications rely on their readers 'being in the know', their messages only comprehensible to those initiated into the gossip networks that underpin them. Cadwallader's mock epic 'Kebliad', reviewing the sexual foibles of his generation, is incomprehensible without a 'decoder', and one wonders how many students ever really 'got it'.

But student journalism has secured some palpable hits. On the eve of Princess Margaret's visit in 1977, and at the height of the condom machine controversy, *Groundsheet* reported that 'an excited Chris Perrinoid yesterday confirmed reports that only people with the best upper class accents had been chosen for the four-man task force which would have tea with Princess Margate. Mr [Douglas] Price and I employed a special firm of investigators to weed out those with immigrant or northern ancestry',

Right: *A regular cartoon strip in The Spotted Brick featured superdean Martin Oldfield, here thwarting freshers' sociability*

he explained, 'and the four people we chose had to be vetted by the Palace. But they are all four of them really super people'. The irony is of course of its time. At the beginning of Hilary Term, 1995, *Rear End* ran a story 'Four Conferences and a Wedding', a latter-day nativity story with 'the virgin interviewees' turned away from their rooms because the lowly innkeeper Rex [Tester, Steward] had ordered that 'none shall be admitted to the house of Keble unless they are here for a conference and can pay sixty quid a night'; they were dispatched to a temporary refuge in the pigsty known locally as the 'Jayseear', but no food was available because 'King [Ken] Lovett is holding a banquet to celebrate his daughter's wedding'. 'To this day it is heard across the lands, "If called to the town of Oxford don't try to get in to Keble"'. The truth was that interviewees had had to wait a few hours for rooms to be vacated by conference guests, and that later in the vacation (once the interviewing season passed) the Bursar did indeed celebrate his daughter's wedding in College. The College is, of course, a rather small pond, and many students seek to win their journalistic spurs through work on the University papers, *Cherwell* and *The Oxford Student*. The College's most recent journalistic 'success' is Patrick Foster, editor of the latter organ, a man who would do anything for a scoop, constantly a thorn in the flesh of the University establishment, and now a journalist on *The Times* newspaper.

8 CONCLUSION

Oxford University in 2008 is quite different from the University in 1870, when the College opened. It is enormously bigger, with nearly 20,000 students, over 7,500 of whom are graduates, and far more complex. Its annual budget, now approaching £700m, would have seemed quite incredible to Keble's founders. Its medical sciences division accounts for a third of the total and research funding for science as a whole is on a huge scale. The pressures on the University and its colleges, including Keble, are also very great. A shift in the College is apparent as a number of long-established fellows have recently retired, and their replacements must manage their own academic aspirations, the rewards of graduate supervision and research and the traditional tutorial system. Increased internationalism in filling academic posts, especially joint appointments like those held by most Keble fellows, which are shared between a department and the College, has also led to increased competition between colleges and to changing personal priorities. Academic mobility is likely to increase as well, in sharp contrast to the days when Douglas Price and others expected to make the College their life.

A difficult balance must therefore be found within colleges today. In a college like Keble, which has always had large numbers of students but little endowment, there is the further problem that fee income is considerably lower than actual costs. This is especially true of the fees paid by UK and EU undergraduates, but even in the case of overseas graduates and others on 'high-fee' courses, only a relatively small amount of their tuition fees goes to their colleges. The rational strategy pursued by Keble in the past, of keeping student numbers high so as to maximize income, is nowadays no longer sufficient; Dennis Nineham's prescient advice that the sheer physical scale of Keble and its buildings required a considerable income to keep it going remains as true as ever, but the demands on the College and the experiences of its academics as part of the 'collegiate University' are far more complex.

The increase in the fellowship and the appointment of research fellows who also do some tutorial teaching is a sign of these changes. Earlier fellows and tutors would be surprised at the limited number of college-based tutorial hours currently laid down in academic contracts, and at the number of deals being done by departments, whereby college fellows do even fewer. When Tim Jenkinson took up a readership in the Saïd Business School and ceased to be a college fellow in economics, the College thought itself fortunate that it was able to appoint two fellows to replace him; both are members of the Governing Body and official fellows, just as he was, but with combined teaching hours for the College (even without allowing for college hours bought out by the department of economics) fewer than Jenkinson's. Keble has been successful in attracting additional professorial fellows who can bring in their own graduate students and add to the intellectual life of the College.

But the University and each individual college has also had to accept a far greater level of external regulation, and this will soon increase further when their former status as exempt charities comes to an end. Finally, there is also a tension between the economics of global academic competition and the moral commitment, reinforced by public expectation, felt by a large number of Oxford academics towards the role of Oxford in higher education in the UK.

In 2007–8 the College had 248 graduate students on its books, of whom 141 were working on doctorates. Subjects particularly represented were archaeology (12), engineering (19), computer science (16), physics (16) and medicine and biochemistry (20), with six working on subjects falling within the scope of the new Oxford Internet Institute. Topics on which graduate students have recently made presentations in the discussion evenings in the Lodgings include safe drug development, quantum computing, the mathematical aspects of music and the theory of decision-making. There were ten MBA students (Keble was one of the first colleges to admit MBAs) and eight who were taking the BCL or MJur. Others are taking masters' courses, some of which lead into the D. Phil. There is a small but steady flow of Rhodes scholars. International students are in the majority, and recent presidents and vice-presidents of the MCR have included a Rhodes scholar from South Africa, an historian from Pakistan and a computer science student from Poland. Arts subjects tend

to have fewer graduate students, a major factor being the disparity in available funding between arts and science. Undergraduate numbers in the College have dropped somewhat in recent years as a result of deliberate academic policies adopted by the Governing Body, and most fellows would agree that the current number of graduates is also

Above: *Three British Academy post-doctoral fellows, 2008: Eleni Kechagia (philosophy), Sophie Ratcliffe (English), Sarah Apetrei (ecclesiastical history).*

A Week in the Life of a Research Fellow at Keble

It can feel as if I'm treading a fine line in time management: in my research I'm dealing with periods 15,000 years ago, whereas in College I need to balance student teaching within 15 minutes; one can't overrun a tutorial by too much and have them all waiting on the stairs outside one's office.

As a research fellow my duties consist of giving tutorials to Keble undergraduates, sharing the pastoral care with the fellow in the subject and being involved in admissions and interviews. One of the joys of having a five-year position is that I can follow students from their interview all the way to graduation. The big transformation that never fails to impress me occurs at the start of their second year: just three summer months have passed but they come back no longer as freshers but as adults.

Although I teach, on average, a couple of days a week, the students can be a major preoccupation over lunch in College. But lunch is much

more than that; it makes true the old adage of Keble being a friendly college and it can be a focal point of my day. When teaching, I mark essays in the morning and have tutorials in the afternoons. When not teaching, lunch in College breaks my research day.

As with most academics, research time during term is not plentiful, and I am writing this at the start of a new academic year, having left behind a summer full of fieldwork trips abroad studying archaeological material, writing papers and attending conferences. With the advent of the internet and electronic information, most of the articles are online. Trips to the library become more sporadic. At least afternoon seminars have not been replaced yet with video conferencing; it is the wealth of ideas and inspiration that come with interacting with colleagues that makes the wheels of our brains go round.

Nellie Phoca-Cosmetatou

too high, in that it places a heavy additional strain on the time and energies of fellows as well as on staff resources and facilities.

Keble has not been known as a particularly political or intellectual college. Typical responses from undergraduates when asked why they chose it as their college are that they did so because it is a big college, has a friendly reputation, is near to the science area and is good for sport. However, it is currently in touch with nearly 9,000 former students, and the changing patterns of their lives after Keble are often revealed very clearly at alumni events and reunions. The clerical predominance of the early years is visible even now in the older generations, and in the middle age group there are a good number of academics and professors at universities including Oxford, Cambridge, LSE, Manchester and elsewhere, many lawyers, of whom a good number have reached high positions in top law firms or become very successful barristers or judges, and many who have been successful in the city in banking or finance. Industry, business, teaching and the diplomatic service are also well represented among older alumni. The College has not produced many politicians, and they have tended in the past to be Conservatives, like Sir Peter Morrison (1963), PPS to Margaret Thatcher in 1990 and important in gaining the funding for the Arco building. Keble men have held bishoprics at Durham, Gloucester and elsewhere, as well as the posts of Secretary of the Corporation of Church

House and First Church Commissioner. The pattern changes somewhat with later generations of alumni, who include the Labour ministers Ed Balls (1985) and (Lord) Andrew Adonis (1981). Fund management, banking, consulting and IT are also prominent, and a substantial number of Keble graduates now go into research positions and academic posts. But Humphrey Carpenter, the jazz musician and biographer, and Ian Hamilton, poet, editor and critic, were both at Keble, and Keble people in the arts world include Frank Cottrell Boyce (1979), Tony Hall (1970), John Bridcut (1971), David Owen Norris (1972), Charles Hazlewood (1986), Simon Over (1984) and Jeremy Filsell (1982); the younger generation are also achieving success in journalism and the media.

The acquisition in 2004 of the Acland site, between the Banbury and Woodstock Roads and directly opposite the Radcliffe Infirmary site, now owned by the University, was a bold move, driven in the first instance by the need to acquire more and better graduate accommodation. However, the size of the site will eventually allow the College to do much more. It will be possible to include other academic facilities, which will enable interaction between academic subjects and between teaching and research. After an architectural competition, the College again selected Rick Mather Architects to develop the site, and their clever design will allow for all of this and more. At long last all Keble students who want college

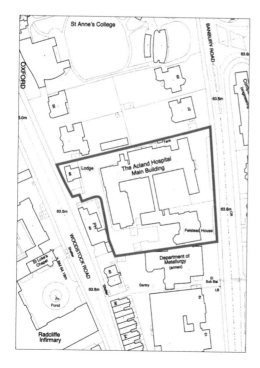

Above and left: *The Acland site*

179

accommodation will be able to be housed. Very importantly, the College has also acquired an extraordinary opportunity to fulfil the very different aspirations of academics who belong to a great university in the 21st century. Keble's location close to so many science departments has always been an advantage. However, with the eventual realization of the University's plans for the much bigger Radcliffe Infirmary site across Woodstock Road, which include the move of many humanities departments and the creation of a new underground humanities library, and the planned development of the science area and the so-called 'Keble Triangle', the centre of gravity of the whole University will undoubtedly shift towards the north, and Keble will then lie at its very heart. Raising the large amount of money needed in order to achieve this vision will be a bigger challenge than the College has ever had. But success will bring Keble to centre stage as it approaches its 150th anniversary in 2020. This will be a remarkable result for a college which, for so much of its history, has thought of itself as being on the edge.

If the story of how Keble has treated its historic buildings has been one of disregard giving way to respect and pride, that of the College as a whole has been one of early determination, even defiance, combined with an abiding sense of being poorer than and inferior to other older and richer colleges (Lavinia Talbot's 'plucky little Keble'). Since the 1970s this has evolved into energy, pride and optimism. The College is one of the largest players in the University, even if it still has one of the lowest endowments. What it has done, it has done through its own ingenuity and from its own resources. It has developed its business side, and in recent years has built up a large number of loyal and regular financial contributions from its old members, in order to improve its endowment and provide the best possible experience for its students. In the later twentieth century it successfully raised the money for a series of architecturally very distinguished new buildings, and was able to attract academics of the highest international calibre. It continues to call forth a fierce sense of pride in its students. Its buildings and its gardens are cared for as never before. How it can still remain true to its traditions is a real question. But with its story of self-help and vigour, its future must be bright.

Left: *Felstead House, 23 Banbury Road*

Above: *Former Acland Hospital frontage*

ACKNOWLEDGEMENTS

Richard Alford
Laszlo Antal
John Backholer
Colin Bailey
Sir Christopher Ball
Hilary Barnes
Penny Bateman
C.H. Baylis
Elizabeth Beattie (Wilkes)
Tim Beattie
†G. Bennett
†M. Bennett
†C. Beresford-Knox
Ted Beresford-Knox
Janet Betts
Caroline Boddington
Roger Boden
Sir Nicholas Bonsor
David Boss
†R.C. Bostrom
A.B. Bosworth
†T.O. Boulton
Howard Bourne
Richard Bowman
Caroline Brett
Tom Brett
John Bridcut
B.P. Brownless
G. Burton
T.S. Byron
N. Caiger
Lucy Camm (Vignes)
†Alec Campbell
W. Franklin G. Cardy
Derek J. Chadwick
Guy Cheeseman
C. Clark
Keith Clark
Ronald J. Clarke
Russell A. Clarke
The Viscount Cobham
Dave Cole
†H.R. Coney

Martin Copus
Philip Corbett
D.W.M. Couper
†O.G.S. Crawford
Simon Cuff
A.E. Currall
A.Cutter
Adrian Darby
†A.L. Davis
John Davies
Lucy Dickens
J. Drysdale
Nigel Edwards
Monica Esslin
J.A.D. Ewart
Tim Faithfull
W.G. Ferguson
R. Fernando
Brian Fieldhouse
Eric Finch
†Sir Edward Ford
N. Fowler
A. Frizell
†Edward Garfitt
John Gedge
James Griffin
Christopher Grimaldi
Eva Gronbech
Peter Groves
Graeme Hall
Ralph Hanna
†F.D. Harris-Evans
†Paul Hayes
†E. Heberden
J. Henig
†J. Hersee
Douglas Henchley
Anthony Hewlett
Russell Hinton
B.G. Hippsley
Basil Hoare
John Holder
Ivor Hooton

Robin Hurley
Julie Hutton (Willcox)
†J.L. Insley
W.J. Iremonger
Peter Iveson
A.W. James
Tim Jobson
†Gareth Jones
D.J. Jordan
Dil Joseph
Steve Kersley
William Key
Maggie Kilbey
A.C. Kirthisingha
B.C. Knight
Richard Lansdown
Mike Lawrence
Brother Lawrence Lew, OP
M. Lerego
Claire Lewis
†E.G. Little
Mr and Mrs H.E.F. Lock
A.F.J. Lofthouse
Trish Long
†R.G. McComas
Henry Maddick
W.D. Madel
Bryan Magee
S.D. Mahony
D.L. Manship
Corinna Marlowe
G.V. Marsh
Rick Mather Associates
H.E. Mr A. Michaelis
Brian Mills
P. Millward
David Milne
Roger Milton
Basil Mitchell
Peter Moonlight
Lady Rosalind Morrison
Roger Nice
Anastasia Nijnik

Dennis Nineham
Michael Orlik
D.J. Pasterfield
David R. Paton
A.B. Pearson
David Penwarden
Michael Perham
Chris Perrin
A. Petty
Robert Petre
Nellie Phoca-Cosmetatou
Colin Podmore
John Poole
†John Pope
†Douglas Price
R.M. Prideaux
Anthony Prince
J. Prosser
C. Pugh
C.T.B. Purvis
Michael Ranson
A.R. Ranzetta
Peter Rawlins
N. Rea
†J.C. Read
R. Reames
Fleur Richards
George Richardson
†E.A.K. Ridley
†M.F. Ring
Sir Ivor Roberts
†Jean Robinson
Alisdair Rogers
Geoffrey Rowell
Marie Ruffle
Roderick Ryman
Roger Sainsbury
Margaret Sarosi
Ed Schneider
Simon Schoenbuchner
B. Sefi
†A.L.H. Sellwood
†C. Shrewsbury

Larry Siedentop
Dennis Shaw
Patrick Shovelton
†A.V. Slater
Brian Smith
Isla Smith
Tessa Stanley-Price
D. Steel
Marjory Szurko
Charles Talbot
Brian Taylor
†S. Taylor
Jewell Thomas
T. Thomson
S. Thorley
†J. Tobin
R.J. Townson
Alistair Tucker
Jeffery Turner
Tony Turner
Geoffrey Tyack
Peter Vernier
David Warwick
J. Wastie
Desmond Watkins
J. Watt-Pringle
Greville Watts
H.J. West
Nick West
†G.S.J. White
†R.N. Whybray
Joy Crispin Wilson
†R.P. Wilson
Alan Winstanley
†G.R. Winter
Clive Wright
John L. Wolfendon
David Yandell
Roger Young
John Zehetmayr

SOURCES AND FURTHER READING

We have drawn on unpublished diaries by Lavinia Talbot, May Talbot, Mildred Lock and Douglas Price, and on a wealth of personal material sent in by old members, all of which is now in the College archives. We have also had many conversations with individuals, including Basil Mitchell, Adrian Darby, James Griffin, Dennis Shaw, Dennis Nineham, Peter North, Larry Siedentop, Geoffrey Rowell, John Davies, Michael Perham and John Bridcut. Documentary materials in the College archives include minute books of the College Council and Governing Body, accounts, collections books, the dean's black book, the Warden's reviews of each past year, the *College Record* and *Brick*, and various examples of student writing and journalism, notably *The Clock Tower*. We are also grateful to Lady Rosalind Morrison for allowing us access to the papers of the sixth Earl Beauchamp, especially the many letters relating to the early years of Keble College.

Ashworth, M., *The Oxford House in Bethnal Green*, Oxford House, 1984.

Avery, D., 'Postal stationery cards of the Oxford colleges', *American Philatelist*, February, 2006, pp. 150–3.

Battiscombe, G., *John Keble. A Study in Limitations*, London, 1963.

Bradley, I., *Oxford House in Bethnal Green 1884-1984*, London, 1984.

Brick Bulletin, Summer 1996.

Campbell, J.W.P. and Price, W., *Brick. A World History*, London, 2003.

Mordaunt Crook, J., *The Architect's Secret. Victorian Critics and the Image of Gravity*, London, 2003.

Curtis, P., *A Hawk among Sparrows. A Biography of Austin Farrer*, London, 1985.

Downes, R., 'Memoirs of a Keble Organ Scholar', *Organ Review*, 1993.

Felus, K., unpublished report on the college gardens, 2003.

Fletcher, S., *Victorian Girls. Lord Lyttelton's Daughters*, London, 2001.

Harrison, B., ed., *The History of the University of Oxford VIII. The Twentieth Century*, Oxford, 1994, especially the chapters by Brian Harrison and Keith Thomas.

Herring, G., *What Was the Oxford Movement?*, London, 2002.

Gray R. and Frankl E., *Oxford Gardens*, Cambridge, 1987, p. 23.

Hill R., *God's Architect. Pugin and the Building of Romantic Britain*, London, 2007.

Jordan, R.F., *Victorian Architecture*, Harmondsworth, 1966.

Keble College Oxford. Conservation Statement, Fielden and Mawson Architects, 2005.

Keble College *Record*.

Keble College Centenary Register, 1970.

Lister, R., *College Stamps of Oxford and Cambridge*, Cambridge, 1966.

Lock, W., *John Keble: A Biography*, London, 1893.

McKenzie, The Reverend H.W., *The First Thirty from Within*, 1930.

Maas, J., *Holman Hunt and The Light of the World*, London, 1984.

Oxford Dictionary of National Biography.

Parkes, M.B., *The Medieval Manuscripts of Keble College, Oxford. A Descriptive Catalogue with Summary Descriptions of the Greek and Oriental Manuscripts*, London, 1979.

Rowell, G., *Hell and the Victorians. A Study of the Nineteenth-Century Theological Controversies Concerning Eternal Punishment and the Future Life*, Oxford, 1974.

Rowell, G., '"Training in simple and religious habits": Keble and its first Warden', in Brock M. G. and Curthoys, M.C., eds., *The History of the University of Oxford VII, Nineteenth-Century Oxford, Part 2*, Oxford, 2000, pp. 171–91

Scotland, N., *Squires in the Slums. Settlements and Missions in Late Victorian London*. London, 2007.

Sherriff, C., *The Oxord College Barges. Their History and Architecture*, London, 2003.

Talbot, E.S., *Memories of Early Life*, London, 1924.

Thompson, P., *William Butterfield*, London, 1971.

Tyack, G., *Oxford. An Architectural Guide*, Oxford, 1998.

Tyack, G. and Szurko, M., *William Butterfield and Keble College*, 2002.

Welsh, J., 'Brick layers', RIBA *Journal*, September, 1995, pp. 42–9.

Wheeler, M., *Death and the Future Life in Victorian Literature and Theology*, Cambridge, 1990.

Wheeler, M., 'Keble, Ruskin and *The Light of the World*', a lecture delivered in Keble College Chapel, 30th January, 1996.

Wilde, O., *Selected Journalism*, edited with an introduction and notes by Anna Clayworth, World's Classics, Oxford, 2004, p. 50.

SUBSCRIBERS

This book has been made possible through the generosity of the following:

Paul Abberley (1978)
Simon Ackroyd (2005)
Michael Adams (1963)
Rachel Ainsworth (1992)
Andy Airey (1985)
Colin Airey (1956)
Bob Alexander (1957)
Richard Alford (1963)
Nuran Aliyev (2005)
Charles Allen (2002)
James Allen (1995)
James Alliston (2004)
Felix Alvarez-Garmon Von
   Gromann (1993)
Ampleforth Abbey
Harry Anderson
Peter Anderson (1979)
John Andrew (1951)
Richard Andrew (1972)
Brian Andrews (1959)
John Andrews (1936)
James Anstead (1993)
Ray Anstis (1957)
Sarah Apetrei (2003)
Andrew Archer (1992)
David Armstrong (1955)
David Asher (1952)
Leonard Atherton (1960)
Jason Atkinson (1997)
Jeremy Attfield (1994)
Steven Aughton (1990)
Richard Avery (1970)
Bryon Bache (1951)
John Backholer (1986)
Alan Backhouse (1958)
John Baggaley (1951)
Colin Bailey
David Bailey (1982)
Lynsey Bailey (1999)
Andy Baker (2004)
Alistair Balderson (1992)
Christopher Ball
Michael Balls (1957)
Ritchie Balmer (2005)
Roger Bamford (1957)
Alex Baneke (2005)
Sam Baneke (2007)
David Barker (1978)
Colin Barnard (1959)
Hannah Barnes (2001)
Scott Barnes (1975)

William Barnett (1958)
Tom Barns (1937)
William Barns (1898)
Paul Barrett (1979)
James Barron (1963)
Luke Bartholomew (2006)
Michael Bartlett (1985)
John Barton (1966)
Nicholas Barton (1966)
Jonathan Battarbee (1992)
Colin Battell (1963)
James Battie (1955)
Jonathan Batty (2004)
Ian Baxter (1976)
Nicholas Bayley
Raymond Bayley (1965)
John Baylis (1961)
David Beard (1981)
Duncan Beardsley (1981)
Stuart Beaton (1981)
Elizabeth Beattie (1979)
Tim Beattie (1978)
Emily Beeton (1994)
Katherine Beevers (1997)
Caron Bell (2006)
David Bell (1957)
Stuart Bell (1979)
Lisa Bendall
Stephen Bennett (1996)
David Bennison (1963)
Stephen Bentham (1966)
Paul Bentley (1983)
Gabi Benton-Stace (2006)
Aline Beresford (1982)
Ted Beresford-Knox (1968)
Julia Bergman (1990)
Martin Best (2004)
Gerald Bettridge (1956)
David Biddle (1964)
Hannah Billson (2005)
Katherine Binner (2005)
John Bint (1973)
Neil Bird (1979)
Ronald Birkett (1947)
Arun Birla (1993)
Douglas Birrell (1988)
Sophie Bishton (2003)
James Blades (1953)
Chris Blake (1978)
Bill Blanchard (1985)
Ross Bland (2003)

Blenheim Girls
Julia Bloxsome (1979)
Nina Bobe (1987)
Roger Boden (1965)
Walter Bodmer
Peter Bolton (2005)
Kate Booth (1994)
Keith Borer (1952)
David Boss (1951)
Nigel Bottomley (1989)
Thomas Boultbee (1943)
David Boulton (1971)
Howard Bourne (1969)
Julia Bowden (1986)
Kate Bowen (1997)
Natalie Bowkett (2005)
Philip Boyd (1943)
Ian Brackley (1966)
Joshua Bradbury (2007)
Valerie Brader (1998)
Kevin Bradley (1984)
Robert Bradshaw (1939)
Keith Brain
Michael Braisher (2003)
Tom Bramley (1990)
Edward Brangwin (2004)
Christopher Bray (1977)
Michael Brearey (1958)
Timothy Brears (1981)
David Brecknell (1950)
Stephen Breukelman (1973)
Philip Briant (1949)
John Bridcut (1971)
Andrew Briggs (1972)
Siân Britton (1982)
John Brocklebank (1964)
Anton Brod (1957)
Marc Brodie
Joel Brookfield (1998)
Kenneth Brooks (1975)
Andrew Brown (1959)
Ian Brown (1996)
Patricia Brown
Richard Brown (2007)
Sylvia Brown
Lesley Browning (1985)
Kit Brownlees (1967)
Nicholas Brownlees (1971)
Graham Bryant (1960)
Jane Bubb (1983)
Martin Buckland (1972)

Anthony Buckley (1981)
Graham Buckley (1949)
Andrew Budd (1980)
Peter Bull (1966)
Graham Bullock (1963)
Tyrrell Burgess (1951)
Charles Burke (1947)
David Burke (1992)
Michael Burns (1976)
Timothy Burt
Chris Burton (1981)
David Burton (1963)
Gregory Burton (1983)
Philip Butler (1961)
David Butts (1945)
Bill Byrne (1968)
Michael Cabell (1946)
Ed Cadwallader (2000)
Jim Cadwallader (1970)
Nick Caiger (1972)
John Cairns (1984)
Lucy Callaghan (2001)
Andrew Calvert (1991)
Stephen Cameron
Charles Cameron-Baker (1962)
Lucy Camm (1979)
Richard Camp (1956)
David Candler (1948)
Christopher Canning (2007)
John Caperon (1981)
Gus Carey (1981)
Benjamin Carlton Jones (1999)
Jesus Carrasco Abad (2004)
Andrew Carter (1979)
Michael Carter (2005)
James Cashmore (1973)
Jonathan Cates (2004)
Nikki Catt (2000)
Peter Cave (1960)
Andrew Chadwick (1971)
Derek Chadwick (1966)
John Chambers (1967)
Yvette Chan (2001)
Terence Charlston (1980)
Mary Charrington (1982)
Gregg Chavaria (1995)
Eric Chen (1998)
Stuart John Cherry
Nicola Chetwynd-Stapylton
   (1985)
John Clark (1952)

Stephen Clark
David Clarke (1973)
John Clarke (1965)
Ronald Clarke (1937)
Russell Clarke (1949)
Nick Cleaver (1954)
Sophie Clements (1996)
Kenneth Clempson (1949)
Jacqueline Clifton-Brown
   (2002)
George Clissold (1948)
Ian Close (1975)
James Cloyne (2001)
Jonathan Coad (1963)
Stephen Coakley (2004)
Amy Coan (2006)
Trevor Cocker (1948)
Sara Cody (1995)
Will Collin (1985)
John Colvin (1974)
Richard Connell (1973)
Charles Conner (1939)
Bruce Connock (1958)
Mark Conway (2007)
Andy Cook (1987)
Jonathan Cook (1994)
Martin Cook (1978)
Anthony Cooke (1949)
Christopher Coombe (1971)
Roger Coombs (1953)
Graham Cooper (1959)
Lynn Cooper (1997)
Martin Copus (1973)
Cathy Corbett (1981)
Philip Corbett (2004)
Juliet Cornford Chapman
   (1988)
Caroline Corry (1995)
Tom Cottrell (1960)
John Coughlan (1995)
Dudley Couper (1954)
Ruth Cowen
David Craigen (1991)
Stuart Craker (1983)
Edward Crocker (2005)
Simon Crutchley (1982)
Maria Cruz Lopez (2004)
Simon Cuff (2006)
David Cummings (1980)
Christopher Cunningham
   (1954)

Colin Cunningham (1960)
Eric Cunningham (1948)
Arnold Currall (1949)
John Curry (1959)
Neville Cusworth (1958)
David Cutter (1951)
Lucy Cuzner (1986)
Robert Dale (1979)
Stephanie Dale
Andrew Dalkin (1974)
John Daly (1991)
Patrick Danby (1958)
Peter Dancer (1951)
Edward Dang (1984)
John Dant (2001)
Andrew Dark (1984)
Andy Darley (1983)
R.H. Darwall-Smith
Cecil Davidge
Alan Davies (1957)
Anthony Davies (1959)
John Davies (1955)
John Davies (1976)
Laura Davies (1998)
Peter Davies (1945)
Peter Davies (1982)
Roger Davies (1962)
Vic Davies (1988)
Walford Davies (1959)
Dai Davis (1976)
Robin Davis (1958)
Peter Dawson (1949)
Michael Day (1975)
Norman Day (1960)
Victoria de Breyne
Quentin De Bruyn (1995)
John De Newtown (1971)
Niels Dechow
Rex Delicate (1958)
Derrick Denner (1956)
Paul Dennis (1969)
Martin Denny (1991)
Anna Denton (1994)
Samir Desai (2001)
Sunil Dhall (1993)
Jasbir Dhillon (1988)
Alastair Dick-Cleland (1980)
Lucy Dickens
Marnie Dickens (2004)
John Diggle (1946)
John Diggle (1963)
Roy Dilley (1979)
Harry Dillon (1957)
Peter Diplock (1949)
Philip Dixon (1981)
Phillip Dobbs (1970)
Christopher Dodd (2003)
Stephen Doerr (1978)
Patrick Doherty (1971)
Christopher Dolan (1963)
Alec Don (1983)
Derek Donaldson (1950)
Tim Donnelly (1980)
Richard Doughty (2003)
Alan Douglas (1952)
Jayne Dowle (1986)
Barry Downing (1956)
Bernard Drake (1951)

Glyn Drew (1951)
Dean Drizin (2003)
Stephen Drummond (1982)
Jane Drysdale (1982)
Rowan Duffin-Jones (1977)
Iain Duncan (2000)
Emma Dunford (1998)
Alan Dunwoodie (1995)
Katherine Dunwoodie (1995)
Martin Dyson (1956)
David Eastwood
Simon Eccles-Williams (1971)
James Edelman
Chris Edge (1985)
Geoffrey Edge (1959)
Nigel Edwards (1970)
Roy Edwards (1947)
Nigel Elliott (1968)
Anthony Ellis (1974)
George Ellis (1955)
James Ellis (2004)
Gerald Ellison (1973)
David Elphinstone (2002)
Kaye England (1984)
Monica Esslin-Peard (1979)
Norman Evans (1950)
John Ewart (1942)
Pierre Faber (1995)
Andrew Fairbairn (1952)
Tim Faithfull (1964)
David Farrant (1978)
Caroline Farrer
Dick Fawcett (1955)
Mike Fawcett (1972)
Michael Fay (1971)
Todd Feldman (1990)
Tony Fells (1945)
Shaun Fenton (1989)
Tristam Fenton-May (1997)
Bill Ferguson (1952)
Jose Fernandez-Calvo (1997)
John Fidler (1958)
Brian Fieldhouse (1950)
David Fill (1953)
Eric Finch (1963)
Stroma Finston (1983)
Graham Fisher (1980)
Denis Fishleigh (1952)
Charles FitzGerald (1959)
Rachel Flanagan (2003)
Katherine Flashman (1987)
Allison Fleetwood (1987)
Susannah Fleming (2005)
Andrew Fletcher (1969)
Cyril Fletcher
Richard Flint (1990)
James Foley (1992)
Ian Ford (1964)
David Forrester (1954)
Patrick Forth (1981)
F.J. Foster
Nick Fowler (1986)
Michael Fox (1960)
Nicholas Fox (1994)
Andrew Francis (1973)
Duncan Fraser (1977)
Dennis Freeborn (1946)
James Fretwell (1953)

Jeremy Freyou (1999)
Janine Fries-Knoblach (1989)
William Frost (1939)
Andrew Fussell (1962)
Jonathan Gal (1989)
Ioannis Galanakis (2001)
Jason Gallian (1991)
Karen Garberg (1998)
Morten Garberg (1998)
Alan Gardiner (1945)
David Gardiner (1973)
Jonathan Garnett (1978)
David Gatliffe (1964)
Helen Gaynor (1990)
Nicholas Gealy (2004)
John Gedge (1980)
Bob Gee (1950)
Robin Geffen (1976)
Tony Gelston (1953)
Nicholas Gent (1960)
Jos Gibbons (2007)
Denis Gibbs (1948)
Ailsa Gibson (2000)
John Gibson (1999)
Emma Giddings (1994)
Roger Gilbert (1950)
Caroline Gilby (1982)
Bernard Gill (1954)
Paul Gillard (2007)
Vincent Gillespie (1972)
Susan Gillingham (1980)
John Gillions (1975)
Charles Gillow (1976)
Joanne Gilvear (1987)
John Gittins
Stephen Glover (1975)
Hugh Goddard (1972)
Marc Goergen (1993)
J.P. Golunski
Shaogang Gong (1986)
Barry Goodchild (1959)
Jon Goodfellow (1983)
Andrew Goodwin (1993)
Estelle Goodwin (1979)
Philip Goodwin (1979)
Christopher Gosden
Frank Gough (1953)
Russell Goulbourne (1992)
Stephen Gower (1979)
Jan Grabowski
Simon Graf (1993)
Mark Graves (1988)
Robin Gray (1945)
Christopher Green (1982)
David Green (1985)
John Green (1930)
P. Green
Barry Greengrass (1958)
Michael Greenhalgh (1967)
Steven Greer (1976)
Helen Gregson (1981)
David Grice (1952)
John Grieves (1955)
Clive Griffin (1970)
Jim Griffin
Geoffrey Grime (1968)
Nicholas Grimshaw (1983)
John Grimwade (1945)

Bill Groves (1961)
Henry Guest (1996)
Michael Gwilliam (1966)
Karl Hack (1984)
Andrew Haig (1964)
Richard Hall (1948)
Tony Hall (1970)
Douglas Halliday (1936)
Ian Halliday (1979)
Michael Halliday (1964)
D. Hamilton
Laura Hamilton (2003)
Ruth Hampton (1998)
Richard Hanford (1957)
Ralph Hanna
Henry Hanning (1962)
Janet Harbison (1994)
Felicity Hardman (1995)
Shaun Harkin (1977)
Kit Harling (1969)
Richard Harrington (1976)
Joshua Harris (2007)
Keith Harris (1961)
William Harris (2001)
Heidi Harrison (1992)
David Hart (1958)
Ian Harvey (1973)
Michael Harvey (1995)
John Haslam (1972)
Jonathan Haw (1963)
Michael Hawcroft
Nigel Hawke (1973)
James Hawkes (2007)
James Hayduk (1998)
Tony Hayes (1989)
James Hayhurst (1996)
Ronald Hayter (1937)
Jack Hazelgrove (1957)
Ben Hearn (1994)
Sholto Hebenton (1957)
Robin Hellier (1975)
Douglas Henchley (1930)
Peter Hendry (1948)
David Henthorn (1964)
Stefan Herr (2007)
George Herring (1974)
Jemma Hetherington (1993)
William Hetherington (1954)
Dyson Heydon
Patrick Hibbin (1972)
Miguel Hidalgo (1990)
David Hill (1959)
Geoffrey Hill (1950)
John Hill (1952)
Philip Hill (1974)
Russell Hinton (1951)
Marc-Olivier Hinzelin
Keiichi Hiramoto (1991)
Julian Hirst (1977)
Simon Hirst (1977)
Basil Hoare (1948)
Geoffrey Hobson (1958)
Jonathan Hobson (1996)
Felix Hofmeir (2001)
Michael Hogan (1973)
Peter Holden (1983)
John Holder (1955)
Ralph Hollinghurst (1955)

Peter Hollingworth (1970)
Cameron Holloway (2007)
Malcolm Holmes (1974)
Tom Hooker (2006)
Ivor Hooton (1947)
Vicky Horrobin (2000)
Iain Horsburgh (1969)
Robin Howard (1946)
Ian Howe (1984)
Kate Hubert (1985)
Geraint Hughes (1955)
Liam Hughes (1970)
Nicola Hughes (1993)
Nigel Hulbert (1972)
Carolina Hummel (1987)
Peter Humphries (1978)
Andrew Hunt (1972)
Christian Hunt (1991)
Simon Hunt
Robin Hurley (1954)
Roy Hurst (1959)
Denis Hutchings (1950)
Jared Hutchings (1990)
Mark Hutchinson (1992)
Julie Hutton (1983)
Peter Hutton (1982)
Derek Hyland (1957)
John Illingworth (1955)
Jane Ingham (1990)
Derek Ingledew (1959)
David Ireland (1980)
Lee Irving (1990)
Peter Iveson (1959)
John James (1962)
Mary James (1983)
Walter James (1930)
Jo Jamieson (1979)
Nick Jefferies
Nathan Jeffery (1995)
Charles Jefford (1949)
Paul Jeffreys
Geoffrey Jenkins (1954)
Philip Jenkinson (1962)
Peter Jennings (1956)
Roger Jermy (1964)
Joe Jewell (2005)
Tim Jobson (1962)
Peter Jocelyn (1945)
David John (1957)
Nicola Johns (2003)
Stephen Johns (1962)
William Johns (1949)
Andrew Johnson (2007)
Hayley Johnson (2007)
Scott Johnson (1999)
Paul Johnson-Ferguson (1985)
Kate Johnston (2002)
Robert Jolliffe (1980)
Alwyn Jones (1995)
Frederick Jones (1946)
Harold Jones (1955)
Jeffrey Jones (1940)
Kevin Jones (1979)
Marc Jones (1983)
Rosanne Jones (1986)
Colin Juneman (1966)
Eleni Kechagia (1998)
David Keegan (1978)

186

Jessica Keen (1992)
Tony Kelham (1961)
Peter Kelly (1977)
Ray Kelly (1960)
Nicholas Kembery (1988)
Michael Kemp (1956)
David Kemshell (1981)
James Kendrick (1949)
David Kerner (1985)
Joseph Kerrigan (1965)
Bill Key (1948)
Leonard Kibble (1963)
Michael Kidd (1959)
Charlotte Kight (1990)
Maggie Kilbey (1979)
Roper Killick (1958)
Anthony King (1970)
Kenneth King (1951)
Malcolm King (1979)
George Kingston (1967)
Tom Kingston (1970)
Kathy Kingstone (1981)
Alex Kirby (1959)
Arthur Kirby (1945)
Zöe Kirby (1995)
Alexander Klein (2005)
Bryan Knight (1955)
Chris Knight (1964)
David Knight (1957)
Helen Knight (2004)
Ian Knowles (1981)
Neil Kurzon (1993)
Elizabeth La Farge (1999)
Martin Lacey (1998)
Fiona Laffan (1993)
Mark Laflin (1998)
Anthony Lam (1992)
Kam Lam (1977)
Mike Lambert (1959)
Richard Lamey (1995)
Philip Lane (1959)
David Lang (1960)
David Langley (1974)
Richard Lansdown (1954)
John Latham (1971)
Jud Laughter (2000)
Matthew Lavin (2002)
David Law (1979)
Aidan Lawes (1977)
Ben Lawrence (1992)
Christopher Lawrence (2005)
David Lawrence (1967)
Mike Lawrence (1966)
Nicholas Lawson (1980)
Raymond Lawton (1947)
David Leaning (1957)
Stanley Lee (1962)
Simon Lees (1982)
Dick Leeson (1953)
Andrew Leighton (1992)
Marie Lemon (2003)
D.B. Lenck
Roderick Leslie (1973)
Frankie Leung (1974)
Claire Lewis (1993)
Graham Lewis (1997)
John Lewis (1999)
Martin Lewis (1973)

Nigel Lindrea (1962)
Wilfried Lingenberg (1993)
Sarah Linnard (1983)
William Linnard (1951)
David Lipman (1958)
Robert Llewelyn (1951)
Charles Lock (1974)
William Lock (1986)
John Lohan (1957)
Massimo Lolli
Stephen Loncar (1996)
Paul Long (1966)
John Lonsbrough (1944)
Randy Love (1971)
Damien Loveland (1985)
Anne-Claire Loverseed (2001)
Susi Lovett
Chris Lowe (1982)
Richard Lowkes (2005)
Robert Lucas
Clare Ludlam (1999)
Roger Lui (1993)
Angus Lund (1990)
Tom Lupton (1975)
Anthony Macaulay (1967)
Robert Macdonald (1990)
Julian Macey-Dare (1985)
Alasdair Mackay (1985)
Cal MacLennan (1986)
Robert MacVicar (1973)
Sebastian Madden (1993)
Henry Maddick (1946)
Ian Maddick (1958)
Derek Maddison (1978)
David Madel (1958)
Bryan Magee (1949)
John Maguire (1964)
Stephen Mahony (1974)
Graeme Maidment (1983)
Izzat Majeed (1969)
James Makepeace (1960)
Frank Mallett (1955)
Jocelyn Manning Fox (1994)
David Mansel Lewis (1950)
Ray Marriott (1965)
David Marshall (1981)
Mary Marshall (2001)
Andrew Martin (1976)
Eric Martin (1961)
Hannah Martin (2007)
James Martin (1952)
Vicky Martyn (1988)
Klaus Marx (1953)
Bianca Massa (2005)
Colin Mather (1987)
Nicholas Mather (1992)
Jannet Mathers (1982)
Camilla Mathews (2003)
Gyan Mathias (2007)
Camilla Matterson
John Matthews (1978)
David Maule (1973)
Jim Maun (1995)
Chad Maybin (2001)
Sonia Mazey
Ross McAdam (2003)
Ben McCann (1994)
Malcolm McCulloch (1956)

Richard McCulloch (1946)
Simon McDermott-Brown (1974)
David McDowell (1993)
Barry McEwan (2001)
Vera McEwan (1985)
Amy McGee (2002)
Austin McGill (1980)
Gavin McGillivray (1977)
Sean McGinley (1988)
Daniel McGowan (2003)
Robert McGown (1939)
Robert McGrail (1945)
Conor McGrenaghan (2007)
Helen McLachlan (1999)
Jonathan McLaughlin (2007)
Gamon McLellan (1968)
Anna McLeod (1998)
Kelly McMullon (2007)
James McWilliam (2003)
Robin Meats (1957)
James Meekings (2001)
Edward Meier (1994)
Volker Menze (1998)
Colin Menzies (1963)
Susan Mepham (1979)
Suzie Merchant (2001)
Tom Merrick (1963)
Charlotte Methuen
Iain Meyer
Toby Miller (2006)
Andrew Millinchip (1976)
Brian Mills (1951)
Robin Mills (1967)
David Milner (1949)
Patrick Milner (2007)
Basil Mitchell
Daniel Mitchell (1991)
Felix Mitchell (1941)
Grant Mitchell (1998)
Michael Mitchell (2007)
Bruce Moffat (1956)
Thomas Monteiro (2002)
Philip Moore (1960)
Tony Moore (1950)
Philip Morgan (1951)
William Morgan (1935)
David Morris (1983)
Stanley Morris (1955)
Terence Morris (1966)
Simon Morrison (1963)
Bernard Moseley (1947)
Denise Mottram
Peter Mountford (1959)
David Movrin (2005)
Alex Msimang (1989)
Tanya Msimang (1990)
Benjamin Mueller (2006)
Benedict Muggridge (1977)
John Muir (1953)
Stephen Mullins (1974)
Timothy Murphy (1969)
Chinmaya Nagaraja (1998)
Ron Naylor (1956)
Philip Neal (1989)
Derek Netherton (1952)
Nicola Newbegin (1996)
David Newbery (1968)

Christopher Newbury (1975)
B.J. Newman
David Newman (1988)
Nigel Newson-Smith (1954)
Matthew Niblett (2002)
Roger Nice (1962)
David Nicholls (1996)
Peter Nichols (1980)
Rosemary Nicklen (1997)
Ross Niland (1996)
Robert Nokes (1958)
Peter Norris (1959)
Peter North (1956)
Trevor Norwitz (1987)
Penny Nugent (1985)
Michael Nuth (1957)
Keith Oborn (1971)
Martin Oldfield (1965)
Michael Oldridge (1989)
Brendan O'Leary (1977)
Niels Olesen (1970)
Greg Olsen (1988)
Richard Orders (1973)
Michael Orlik (1962)
Richard Orton (1953)
Asia Osborne (2006)
Julian Osborne (1970)
Simon O'Sullivan (1970)
Nigel Owen (1995)
Robin Owen (1998)
David Owen Norris (1972)
Robert Owens (1984)
Keith Owers (1954)
John Packer (1964)
Marco Pagni (1981)
George Paling (1948)
Judith Palmer
Philip Palmer (1959)
Timothy Palmer (2005)
Christopher Palmer-Tomkinson (1960)
Margaret Pankhurst (1983)
Keith Panter-Brick (1946)
Bala Paramanathan (1977)
Joanne Pardoe (1995)
Richard Parfitt (1980)
Sean Park (2004)
Alan Parker
Jean Parry (1965)
William Parry (2007)
Brian Parsons (1996)
Dave Parsons (1982)
Derek Pasterfield (1956)
Mukesh Patel (1979)
David Paterson (2000)
David Paton (1955)
Anthony Pattinson (1959)
Ole Paulsen
Maurice Payn (1949)
Stephen Payne (1993)
Tom Peachey (2004)
Allan Pearson (1939)
David Pearson (1975)
Stephen Pearson (1985)
Andrew Peerless (1975)
Owen Pegg (1951)
O.S.M. Pele
Jodie Pennells (2005)

Nicholas Pennington (1958)
David Penwarden (1953)
Michael Perham (1971)
Antonio Periquet (1987)
Chris Perrin (1975)
Trevor Peterson (1998)
Eric Pfaff (1939)
Tony Phelan
Jane Philpott (1982)
Christopher Piachaud (1963)
Keith Pickering (1953)
Graham Pickup (1985)
Blaine Pike (2005)
John Pilgrim (1972)
Lucy Pimm (2007)
Vernon Pinnell (1948)
Martin Platt (1977)
Colin Podmore (1978)
Michael Points (1951)
David Pollock (1960)
Waiming Poo-Cheong (1996)
John Poole (1953)
John Pope (1955)
Andrew Porter (1983)
Simon Porter
Alexandra Potter (2005)
Denys Potts
Dick Povey (1961)
Brian Powell
Ghillean Prance (1957)
Roderick Prescott (1951)
Adam Preston (2007)
Thomas Preston (2007)
Donald Price (1949)
Reg Price (1947)
William Price (1962)
Roy Prideaux (1934)
John Priestland (1987)
Nicholas Prins (1975)
C.J. Proctor
Daniel Proctor (2004)
Richard Pryke (1955)
Christopher Pugh (1975)
Helen Pugh (2002)
Stephen Pugh (1976)
Helena Pullan (1987)
Christopher Purvis (1970)
Nick Putnam (1975)
Geoffrey Quail (1996)
Judith Quest
John Quinby (1968)
Simon Quinn (2005)
George Radford (1958)
Michael Ranson (1948)
Anthony Ranzetta (1955)
Peter Rawlins (1969)
Daniel Rawnsley (2006)
Michael Rayner (1960)
Timothy Rayner (1970)
Caroline Redfern (1983)
Abi Reed (1996)
Allan Reed (1952)
Ben Reed (1993)
Adrian Rees (1974)
Anthony Rees (1968)
Bill Reeve (1954)
Gordon Reid (1964)
Gesine Reinert

Neil Renfrew (1996)
Tim Reynolds (1975)
Kaffy Rice-Oxley (1997)
Richard Rice-Oxley (1962)
Michael Richards (1958)
George Richardson
Fabian Richter (1993)
Anna Ridley (1998)
Peter Ridley (1958)
Petra Riedl (1997)
Mark Rigby-Jones (1994)
Athos Ritsperis (1990)
Kris Robbetts (1996)
Chris Roberts (1993)
Dave Roberts (2001)
David Roberts (1963)
Hannah Roberts (1993)
John Roberts (1969)
Louise Roberts (1988)
M. Robinett
Alan Robinson (1948)
Antony Robinson (1963)
Chris Robinson (1988)
David Robinson (1956)
Frank Robinson (1957)
Gareth Robinson (1979)
Holly Robinson (2006)
Martin Robinson (1981)
Paul Robinson (1953)
Randeep Robinson (1995)
Alun Roderick (2001)
Alisdair Rogers
Chris Rogers (1996)
Kevin Rogers (1976)
Paul Rogers (1997)
Ali Roomi (2004)
Hillel Rosen (1985)
David Rosier (1970)
David Ross (1972)
Malcolm Ross (1928)
Gregg Rowan (1999)
Geoffrey Rowell
Keith Rowland (1976)
Bill Russell (1969)
David Russell (1995)
Hannah Russell (1995)
Peter Rutter (1951)
Roderick Ryman (1973)
Amir Sabeti (1992)
Roger Sainsbury (1959)
Gerard Saldanha (1980)
Christopher Samler (1976)
Jaskiran Sandhu (1997)
Edward Sandoval (2000)
Erik Sansom (1953)
David Saunders (1948)
Michael Saunders (2000)
Philip Sayers (1964)
Steven Schneebaum (1974)
Edward Schneider (1971)
Simon Schoenbuchner (2006)
Chris Schofield (1965)
Mark Schofield (1978)
Catherine Scott (1989)
Heidi Scott (1987)
Paddy Scott (1994)
William Scott-Jackson
Roger Searle (1958)

James Seddon (2004)
Colin Sedgwick (1965)
Kevin Sefton (1990)
Michael Selby (1956)
Paul Selvey-Clinton (2003)
David Senior (1955)
Peter Sergeant (1956)
Erik Serrano Berntsen (2001)
Ian Sewell (1950)
Noor Shabib (2007)
Peter Shackleford (1964)
Kannon Shanmugam (1993)
Vicki Shanmugam (1993)
David Shapiro (2007)
Vivek Sharma (1988)
Phillip Sharp (2006)
William Sharrod (1961)
Dennis Shaw
Geoff Sheard (1985)
Ross Shiels (1964)
Sam Shillcutt (2000)
Andrew Shilston (1974)
Allen Shin (2001)
Maksym Shostak (2003)
Patrick Shovelton (1938)
Charles Shrewsbury (1940)
Harry Shuttleworth (1992)
George Silber (1951)
Peter Simcock (1974)
Mark Simmons (1987)
John Simpson (1950)
John Simpson (1953)
Charles Sinclair (1937)
Diane Sinnett
Andrew Skelton (1995)
Colin Skinner (1980)
Jeremy Skog (2001)
Peter Slade (1989)
Chris Slater (1975)
Timothy Slater (1958)
Caroline Smart (1998)
Alastair Smith (1998)
Andy Smith (1980)
Brian Smith (1951)
Christopher Smith (1984)
Howard Smith
Hugh Smith (1985)
Isla Smith
Joan Smith
Juliet Smith (2001)
Michael Smith (1938)
Peter Smith (1998)
Roland Smith (1961)
Timothy Smith (1997)
Dick Snailham (1950)
Deryck Solomon (1972)
Andrew Soye (1970)
Derek Sparrow (1955)
Katya Speciale (1992)
Dunstan Speight (1991)
Will Spencer (1997)
Dominique Spillett (1986)
Bernd Sprenzel (1997)
Ruth Springer (1996)
Witold Srzednicki (1946)
Elaine Staniforth (1990)
Paul Stanley (1951)
Tessa Stanley Price (2004)

Francis Steele (1972)
Howard Stephens (1946)
Robert Stevens (1952)
Jane Stewart (1983)
Keith Stewart (1983)
Christian Stobbs (2004)
John Stobbs (1973)
Richard Stockdale (1977)
Ian Storr (1965)
Patrick Street (1986)
Ian Streule (1993)
Mike Styles (1959)
Amy Sutherland (2007)
Laura Sutherland (2004)
Ian Sutherland-Smith (1964)
Virginia Swigg (1988)
Phillip Swingler (1964)
Jim Sykes (1961)
Miceala Symington (1987)
Stewart Symons (1952)
Michael Synge (1953)
Michel Syson (1955)
Maen Tabari (2005)
Serge Taborin (1994)
Hajime Takata (1984)
John Talbot (1971)
Katherine Talbot (2003)
Michael Talbot (1993)
Nick Talbot (1988)
Zain Talyarkhan (2007)
David Tan (1996)
Lionel Tarassenko (1975)
Nick Tasker (2006)
Alan Taylor (1945)
Brian Taylor (1949)
Christine Taylor (2007)
Paul Taylor
Paul Taylor (1972)
Paul Taylor (1999)
Roger Taylor (1962)
Matthias Tecza
Patrick Temple (1968)
Justyn Terry (1983)
Nigel Terry (1976)
Ian Thomas (1988)
Michael Thomas (1965)
Ralph Thomas
Ralph Thomas (1965)
Verity Thomas (2006)
Freya Thomas Monk (1992)
Jeremy Thompson (1973)
Phoebe Thompson (2007)
Roger Thornhill (1964)
Rebecca Threlfall (2007)
Jeremy Thurbin (1989)
Peter Tidmarsh (1949)
Joanna Tinworth (1995)
John To (1974)
Hsien Min Toh (1996)
John Tolson (1956)
Hugh Tompsett (1945)
Brian Tooby (1966)
Lucy Tooher
John Towler (1958)
Gillian Traub (1996)
Daniel Travers (2007)
David Trebilcock (1949)
Michael Treplin (1961)

Kalpen Trivedi
Jeremy Trood (1981)
Peter Trueman (1970)
Vanessa Tse (2007)
Sophie Turenne (1994)
Derek Turnbull (1962)
Michael Turnbull (1955)
James Turner (1931)
Jeffery Turner (1956)
Tony Turner (1953)
Brian Underwood (1959)
Tony Vale (1980)
Robert Vanhegan (1960)
Ian Vaughan (1946)
Stephen Vaughan (1979)
Ed Venables (1993)
Salvador Venegas-Andraca (2000)
Peter Verdult (1996)
Tom Vick (1987)
Nicholas Ville (1980)
Alison Vining (1984)
Colin Von Ettinghausen (1998)
Anne Wagstaff (1982)
Mark Wagstaff (1982)
Nicholas Wainwright (1970)
Geoffrey Walford
Georgina Walker (1986)
Jonathan Walker (1982)
Ruth Walker (2006)
Simon Walker (1988)
Mike Wallace (2003)
Steven Waller (1976)
Richard Walters (2003)
Richard Warboys (1988)
Christopher Ward (1985)
Judith Ward (1985)
Tessa Ware (1996)
Timothy Warman (1960)
Michael Warne (1947)
Richard Warren (1991)
Robert Warren (1965)
Tony Warren (1950)
David Waterston (1993)
Alison Waterworth (1991)
Desmond Watkins (1952)
Colin Watson (1994)
Jonathan Watt-Pringle (1981)
Anthony Watts (1956)
Greville Watts (1955)
David Way (1966)
Adam Webber (2006)
Craig Webber (1975)
Andrew Welch (1981)
David Welch (1949)
Derek Welch (1948)
Edward Welch (1991)
Philip Welsh (1966)
Jim West (1945)
Lizzie West (1998)
Nick West (1993)
Olivia West (2007)
Simon Whalley
Dan Wheeler (1988)
Paul Whipp (1979)
Andy White (1971)
Kevin White (1958)
Pamela White (1990)

Michael Whitehouse (1948)
Keith Whitford (1968)
Robin Whittaker (1969)
Andreas Whittam Smith (1957)
Bret Wightman (1977)
Charles Wilby (1973)
Gary Wilkes (1975)
Christopher Willcock (1950)
Andrew Williams (1996)
Anthony Williams (1957)
Eric Williams (1945)
Trevor Williams (1954)
David Williams-Thomas (1959)
Benjamin Wilson (1994)
Dan Wilson (1999)
Daniel Wilson (2005)
David Wilson (1955)
Janet Wilson (1989)
Philip Wilson (1977)
Robin Wilson
Gareth Winrow (1978)
Alan Winstanley (1961)
Peter Wintle (1985)
Jonathan Withey (1996)
John Wolfenden (1957)
Frederick Wong (2006)
Chris Wood (1960)
Eddy Wood (1952)
John Wood (1952)
Natalie Wood (2001)
Sam Wood (2004)
Stephen Wood (1961)
Victor Wood (1962)
Stephen Woodard (1984)
Tom Woolgrove (1990)
Simon Woolhouse (1983)
David Woollett (1971)
Keith Woollgar (1970)
Martin Worley (1964)
Rosie Worrall (2006)
Jeremy Worth (1998)
John Wray (1951)
Alan Wright (1943)
Clive Wright (1954)
Georgina Wright (1994)
Laksh Yadav (2001)
David Yandell
Yasuhiro Yano (1972)
Richard Yeabsley (1992)
Janet Yeh (2000)
Mike Younger (1964)
Mohsin Zaidi (2003)
Debbie Zambardino (1980)
John Zehetmayr (1941)
Alexa Zellentin (2005)
Malte Ziewitz (2006)
Jonathan Zittrain
Ben Zola (1995)
Michael Zola (1965)
Hans Zust (1973)

INDEX

One of these Bookcases is t
be made and placed in its
proper position for Mr Butterfi
approval

wide

do -

wide

do -

do -

wide

do -

$2' 7\frac{1}{4}"$

$6' 9"$

$7' 0"$